The Well Family:
A Developmental Approach to Assessment

THE WELL FAMILY

A Developmental Approach to Assessment

Judith H. Kandzari, B.S.N., M.A.
Assistant Professor, School of Nursing,
West Virginia University, Morgantown

Joan R. Howard, B.S.N., M.S.N.
Associate Professor, School of Nursing,
West Virginia University, Morgantown

with Martha S. Rock, B.S.N., M.S.N.
Assistant Professor, College of Nursing,
University of Delaware, Newark

Little, Brown
and Company
Boston

To Our Families

Contents

Preface

The goal of this book is to provide direction to the nurse in recognizing, promoting, and teaching wellness behaviors to family members at all stages of development throughout the life cycle. Wellness behaviors acquired and refined throughout life provide the structure for a lifetime of wellness in all dimensions of health—physical, emotional, and spiritual—within the family's many environments.

A wellness philosophy is important to the continued well-being of the family, which is the basic social unit in all societies. As the role of the family in contemporary society is examined, and as roles of family members change, wellness of the entire family unit becomes a relevant and viable concept for present and future generations.

The belief in family is predicated on the assumption that families want to be more well, and that the value of wellness assumes some place in the family's value hierarchy. Regardless of a family's position on the wellness-illness continuum, each family has a goal of becoming more well to at least a small degree in one or more aspects of their lives. Whether the family can achieve a higher level of wellness hinges on several requisites.

The family members must first have an awareness of wellness principles. They must desire to become well, to move from where they are to where they want to be. They need the vision to see the benefits of a higher level of wellness, physically, psychologically, and spiritually. As the goal comes nearer, the vision becomes reality. The family needs the will to commit themselves individually and collectively to a goal of high-level wellness. To effect the goal, knowledge is needed to give direction, and skills are needed to translate the knowledge into behavior. These steps in the process of becoming more well need to be considered by the nurse in all phases of her work with the family. Goals can be set and wellness behaviors can be learned.

The teaching and reinforcement of wellness behaviors are the responsibility of the family throughout the life cycle. Acquiring a lifetime repertoire of wellness behaviors is a developmental process of learning skills and behaviors. This process occurs over time. It occurs when the person believes he is responsible for his own actions and is willing to learn about and make lifestyle changes to become more well. The goal of learning and practicing wellness behaviors throughout life incorporates effective development of strengths in promoting wellness in all dimensions of health. Integrating these goals into the daily lives of family members requires hard work and the mutual respect, warmth, and vitality that characterize a psychologically well family. The synergistic qualities of the human organism and the family system promote the enhancement and further growth of wellness in all family members. The modeling effect of family members on each other can make each experience count for persons other than the one experiencing it. This then increases the impact of the nurse who works with the family to develop wellness behaviors. Teaching one teaches many.

The role of the nurse in enhancing family wellness is supportive and complementary to that of the family. The nurse teaches parents so they can teach the children. She teaches and encourages wellness lifestyles in the parents so they can achieve a higher level of wellness for themselves and provide a wellness role model for others. She provides information about resources and about how the family can learn about resources on their own. She encourages self-responsibility in all phases of wellness teaching and supports all efforts of the family to learn and refine wellness behaviors. She recognizes the strengths of the family as the greatest resources for achieving wellness and encourages the love and vitality that are the cornerstones of these strengths. She supports the wellness goals of the family and guides the family in their learning endeavors.

The nurse has the responsibility, too, to look beyond the family unit to the many systems that affect the lives of the family. The community, the school, the workplace and the broader environment of society all have some bearing on the wellness of families. These systems can positively or negatively affect the wellness of one, several, or all members of the family. The nurse in her role as community development agent can affect one or more of these environmental systems and thus the wellness of families and their communities. Further, the nurse as a role model needs to become a living example of wellness, practicing wellness behaviors to the fullest extent possible in her own life.

This principle suggests directions for a family wellness model for nursing, founded on the premise that wellness exists in every person and family to a greater or lesser degree. The person who is experiencing a defined illness can also be experiencing wellness in some aspect of his living. If wellness or the potential for wellness exists in all persons, then all persons have the potential for learning wellness behaviors appropriate to their stage of development. Families as complex interacting systems can experience wellness to a greater or lesser degree. The wellness model explains the relationship of lifestyle concepts to a concept about a desired state of well-being. It allows the nurse to expect certain outcomes for wellness, given a set of circumstances in the family and the environment. The model outlines roles for both the nurse and the family. It recognizes and maximizes the ability of the human organism to adapt to stressors. It moves the family through illness, recovery, and prevention to the active, positive, vital state of being fully alive to one's maximum capacity. The family who has high levels of wellness in all dimensions of health experiences life to the fullest, and stressors are infrequently perceived as distressors because of effective coping behaviors.

The purpose of this book is to identify the body of knowledge and skills relevant to implementing a concept of wellness in nursing practice. Each chapter addresses a major component of wellness in one or more of the dimensions of health. A comprehensive family assessment tool at the end of each chapter is designed to operationalize the wellness concepts into family-oriented behaviors. The behaviors were developed using the evidence and expert opinions of the many researchers and authors who have touched on various concepts related to wellness.

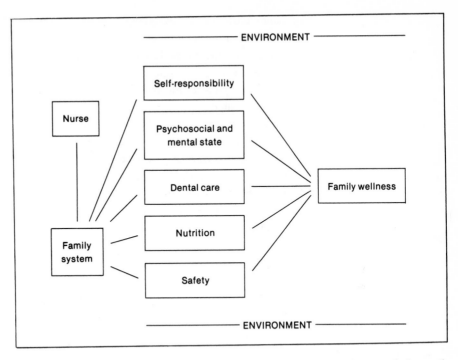

While the validity and reliability of these tools have yet to be determined, the tools have value in providing a place for the nurse and family to begin working together in determining what levels of wellness exist in the various dimensions of the family and what actions remain to be incorporated into a family wellness lifestyle.

The uniqueness of this book is that it addresses wellness components of the whole family in a developmental framework, and it provides tools for systematic assessment of the whole family. Nurses have lacked access to the knowledge to develop comprehensive wellness tools. In this book we have tried to fill in this gap. We hope that the tools will be used by students and practicing nurses in a variety of nursing practice settings and adapted as situations warrant.

Each assessment tool is to be used along with its corresponding chapter. Items are to be interpreted in light of the information provided in the chapter. Because of the developmental framework of this book, some items or sections of each tool may not be applicable because the family does not have a member in that age group. Some assessment tool items are more concrete than others due to the nature of the concepts and content on which they are based. This factor is a limitation of the tools at this point.

Conceptualizing a wellness model of nursing will require a reorientation for many nurses. Many nurses and other health professionals have been educated from an illness philosophy. Those who have worked with persons described as ill have had little training and practice in perceiving the wellness of the client within the context of the family and for using his wellness as a springboard for change. The challenge to each nurse is to expand her horizons and to consider how one might change direction in care-giving by making wellness the philosophical goal instead of only treating an illness. A challenge to nursing and other professions is to subject the concepts and tools described in this book to rigorous research scrutiny in order to develop a scientifically grounded body of wellness knowledge. Bringing about a philosophical reorientation in the practice and teaching of nursing is a major challenge to the future of nursing. Practitioners, educators, administrators, and researchers need to become involved in examining and refining wellness concepts and redirecting their area of nursing to embody this philosophy.

Meeting this challenge will help all care givers change the question from "How can I help this family that is experiencing illness?" to "How can I help this family maximize wellness?" Attempts to answer this question will guide the nurse into new avenues through which she helps families. As she helps families discover their potentials and learn behaviors that will help them reach their goals, she is helping them reach their fullest and richest capacity for living.

Readers will notice that in this book the nurse is referred to using feminine pronouns while the individual is referred to with the masculine. This usage is a literary convenience to avoid the cumbersome "he/she" format. Until a pronoun is invented that covers all persons, readers will have to bear with the authors' preference and should not interpret it as sexist.

We wish to extend our thanks to the following people who have helped us in the production of this book. Special thanks go to Sarah Umble, who diligently typed the manuscript and patiently tolerated our many revisions. We also wish to thank our many colleagues and friends who reviewed our early drafts and made constructive suggestions that helped clarify our thinking and gave valuable direction to future work: Marion Pool, Elizabeth O'Connell, Imogene Foster, Tina Joy, and Francie Sponer. Our families and friends were gracious enough to participate in our photographs. Special thanks go to Gloria Heard and her staff for producing the photographs and figures in this book. The most special thanks of all go to our understanding husbands and children—Stan and Steve, Pam and David, Marc and Melissa. Their support throughout this entire endeavor has been greatly appreciated. And last, but not least, we wish to recognize our parents and siblings who provided us with the strong family background from which we came and gave us the ability to value our present well families, which include our own husbands and children. Our beginnings in wellness started many years ago and continue into our own "new" families. We are grateful for the love, guidance, and support that our parents gave so unselfishly.

J.H.K.

J.R.H.

The Well Family:
A Developmental Approach to Assessment

Notice   The indications and dosages of all drugs in this book have been recommended in the medical literature and conform to the practices of the general medical community. The medications described do not necessarily have specific approval by the Food and Drug Administration for use in the diseases and dosages for which they are recommended. The package insert for each drug should be consulted for use and dosage as approved by the FDA. Because standards for usage change, it is advisable to keep abreast of revised recommendations, particularly those concerning new drugs.

ONE

Learning Wellness: A Challenge for the Family

To ward off disease or recover health, men as a rule find it easier to depend on healers than to attempt the more difficult task of living wisely.

RENÉ DUBOS,
Mirage of Health

Wellness is a concept whose time has come. Health care in fact is illness care, and the vast majority of health professionals are better termed illness professionals. With the high technology, high cost, and high anxiety in which the so-called health care system is rooted today, answers have not been readily forthcoming as to how to improve the system or the quality of life of those who seek its services. As one of the health professions, nursing represents the largest single body of helping persons. Most nurses work with people defined as sick, in institutions designed for treating illness. This illness focus has pervaded health care systems and personnel for a long time and has retarded the achievement of a high quality of life for all. Wellness as a positive force has not been focused on because most behaviors have been learned for the purpose of not becoming ill.

The illness concept is inadequate for now and for the future. Today, people realize that they have an important part to play in their own health. They know that life-style is a guiding force in health status and quality of life, and they further recognize the freedom to make choices. People can choose illness or wellness by behaving in ways that affect health state. Awareness of the dichotomy of concepts leaves people in a quandary. They are keenly aware of what to do for illness because they have been taught by family and health professionals. But what can be done to become well and stay well? How can one gain what is rightfully his—the actualization of his fullest potential for being?

There is little encouragement from health professionals to assume responsibility for health maintenance or to enhance one's total functioning. Because professionals have been taught to respond to the client in a crisis, the client has not been taught how to practice wellness. Health professionals themselves do not always practice wellness behaviors or embrace wellness as a philosophic necessity, and therefore, have been of relatively little help to the individual or family in considering or achieving wellness.

There is, however, a body of knowledge and skills that can be learned and incorporated into daily life. The purpose of this book is to provide the nurse and the family with a framework for assessing and improving their wellness state. Components of this wellness framework addressed include the family system, self-responsibility, psychosocial and developmental state, dental care, nutrition, and environment.

The framework for addressing these questions is most naturally the family. In all cultures the family is the social group designated as the primary transmitter of the values and norms to the children in the society. The family holds great responsibility and though its configuration may be changing, its role in teaching the child all the necessary rules and behaviors is important to the culture maintenance.

The family is the primary source of health care of persons of all ages and is the primary locus for the learning of a wide range of behaviors necessary for living. Within the family are learned the numerous behaviors that contribute to the health of the person. Teaching health behaviors is part of the family's many responsibilities. So to relate the discussion of health and wellness to an appropriate frame of reference, the family is the logical choice. The family is defined as those persons included in the family system by the members themselves. It might not include all biologically related persons, but it could include nonbiologically related individuals. The family is an interactional and not necessarily a biologic framework.

Life is growth, and it follows well-known stages of development that are sequentially dependent on each other. Learning how to become and stay well is also a sequential process and an integral part of each developmental stage. Just as people proceed through physical and psychosocial growth and developmental tasks beginning with infancy, they also learn and practice wellness behaviors beginning with this stage. As each developmental accomplishment becomes part of the integral person, the wellness behaviors become part of the life-style. The person and the family can assess wellness potential at every developmental stage, and identify the wellness behaviors needed.

To understand how family wellness becomes a reality, essential concepts must be considered.

Health

The human organism comprises biologic, psychological, social, and spiritual dimensions and lives in an environment that has physical, cultural, and social characteristics. The state of the person is referred to in relation to each dimension, in either a positive or negative sense—good health or poor health. Health encompasses the wholeness of the person, the gestalt of the human being. Illness and wellness become opposite ends of a continuum, with illness and its complications at one end, and wellness as the positive and sought-after goal. "Health is a multidimensional unity, with body, mind, and spirit all indwelling within each other. It is a dynamic process involving the whole person and his life cycle and life-style in his total environment—physical, biological, and sociocultural" [5]. Humans and all their dimensions, within their environment, comprise the domain of health. It is the qualitative state of being alive (Fig. 1-1).

Wellness

Wellness is the positive pole of a health continuum, with illness identified as the opposite pole (Fig. 1-2).

Figure 1-1. Dimensions of health.

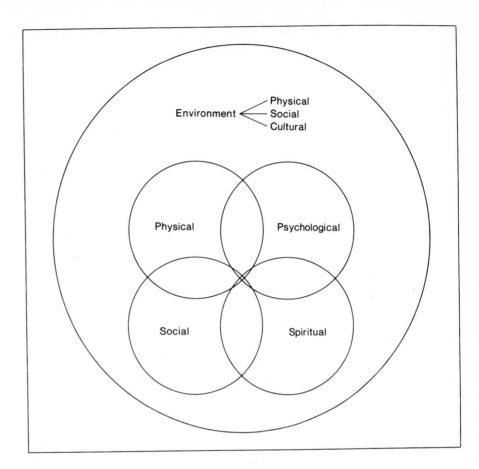

Halbert L. Dunn was an early advocate of the wellness state of health, and he referred to high-level wellness as the ultimate goal for the individual. His definition is still relevant and is the conceptualization used in this book. "High-level wellness for the individual is defined as an integrated method of functioning which is oriented toward maximizing the potential of which the individual is capable, within the environment where he is functioning" [4]. Twelve basic needs of human beings are identified in relation to the integrated self in a changing world. Survival depends on energy sources being available to fulfill such basic needs as food, water, and safety. High-level wellness requires open, facilitative channels of communication, both verbal and nonverbal, which help the individual intersect the inner and outer worlds to have harmony between the two. Dunn also believed

Figure 1-2. Health continuum.

that fellowship and social contacts are important to a fuller understanding of people and their relationship to their environment. Physical, mental, and spiritual growth is important to a high level of functioning. Growth involves the expression of ourselves through the full use of our abilities, and it is affected by such variables as learning abilities, hereditary factors, and maturation responsibilities. Dunn included two other characteristics of high-level wellness: imagination and love. Imagination is the means by which we can project ourselves through creative expression. Love can be directed to persons or institutions—parents, another person, objects, church, or nation. It means being aware of the other person and demonstrating caring. It implies trust and it binds us in fellowship with others [4].

In achieving high-level wellness, Dunn speaks of balance. Stability implies constant change with the individual adapting to internal and external influences. The individual must continually adapt to ever-changing conditions in the environment. The environment must be suitable for meeting the individual's needs. Dunn dealt with spirituality and believed that human beings continue to need to commune with the universe. Even with the magnitude of scientific advances, we are in awe of the larger universe. We still question and search for greater understanding of our world. We continue to need a personal philosophy of living. This philosophy should be in agreement with fundamental societal and scientific beliefs [6, p. 67].

Bruhn and others [1] have further developed Dunn's concept by identifying tasks appropriate for learning about wellness at various points along the developmental continuum as well as those tasks that will enhance an individual's motivation to work toward wellness. They state that a person must complete all of the minimal wellness tasks to achieve maximal wellness at any developmental stage. Failure to complete all of the wellness tasks at any developmental stage would indicate that a person is less well or is falling short of his potential for wellness.

Family Wellness

Families can be said to possess characteristics of wellness that are of prime importance to consider because "you can't really have high-level wellness for either individuals or social groups unless you have well families" [3, pp. 167-168]. The family serves two important functions in society: "It rears the children and it provides an emotional setting for stabilization of the adolescent and the adult personality" [3, pp. 167-168]. The impact of family wellness is that "optimum performance in the family could avert many of the strains and maladjustments that now require pediatric, general medical, and psychiatric service for both children and adults" [3, pp. 167-168]. Dunn defined family wellness [3, pp. 167-168]:

Family wellness has the same elements in it that high-level wellness for the individual has. There must be a direction that the family is taking which is forward and upward. There must be a future for the family, with opportunity for it to develop its full potential. The family must be integrated so that it can operate with wholeness in meeting its problems. It must not be just a collection of individuals held together by convenience.

The urgency of Dunn's statements helps us focus on the pressing need to address the issue of family wellness in the changing and challenging world of today. "Unless man can find ways to encourage family wellness in today's industrial production, there is probably little hope for a high degree of wellness in the human race" [2].

Self-Responsibility

Self-responsibility is a requirement for achieving wellness. Throughout the developmental cycle, each individual in the family has responsibility for learning wellness behaviors appropriate for each stage of development. Self-responsibility begins at birth with the parents' philosophy of encouraging children to grow and develop through wellness childrearing practices. Children learn wellness behaviors as they grow, learning new skills and refining previously learned ones, incorporating them into their life-style. Self-responsibility begins with recognition of potential for wellness, which is closely tied to the completion of developmental tasks. Each of us is responsible for a large portion of our own health. Achieving our wellness potential will not be accomplished by developing new technologies but by developing and maintaining life-styles guided by wellness.

How one accepts responsibility is a lifelong educational process in which values are examined, alternatives identified, and strategies implemented. Self-responsibility begins with parents assisting children and continues with children learning and adding more complex behaviors to their life-style repertoires. Self-responsibility education emphasizes the individual as the decision maker and relies heavily on the skills and knowledge the learner already possesses. Social demand for more self-responsibility in wellness increases with each passing day.

Role of the Nurse in Family Wellness

The 1970 National Commission Study on the nursing role stated that "nursing and other health professions will never begin their essential service until they move in the direction of health maintenance and disease prevention, rather than maintain the almost defensive posture of assisting in care and recuperation" [6, p. 67]. This delineation of the nursing role is highly inadequate. While health maintenance and disease prevention are important, they are defensive in nature and do not project the creative, dynamic evolvement of wellness. The nurse's role encompasses health maintenance but must move forward to embrace wellness.

The nurse assists families by guiding, supporting, and encouraging them in independent and responsible decision making regarding promotion of wellness. Nurses can play a pivotal role in family health care. Their holistic approach prepares them more than any other health worker to deliver wellness care in the home and community. Nurses have the potential for becoming wellness authorities. Their broad background in interpersonal relationships and health knowledge gives them the potential to learn about wellness behaviors that can help the family not only to solve its major health problems, but to promote wellness in its highest sense. Nurses supplement the role of the family in learning wellness behaviors. Even though the family is the primary source of learning experiences for wellness behaviors, many families do not adequately guide and teach children wellness behaviors. In many instances, family members simply do not demonstrate behaviors that promote wellness, or they lack the knowledge to enact such behaviors. Thus the family expects others such as the schools or health professionals to share the responsibility. Nurses, by virtue of their education, knowledge of family dynamics, and liaison with the community, can coordinate activities between the family and the community with the family providing the major impetus for promotion of wellness.

The nurse has skills to promote family adaptation in responding to stimuli that bombard it, regardless of the family's place on the wellness-illness continuum. The nurse in the home, the hospital, or the community setting constantly evaluates the family's ability to respond to the stimuli. The nurse assists the family in manipulating certain stimuli in order to evoke a wellness-enhancing response. If the family is unable to do so, the nurse assumes a more active role. The nurse who does assume the more active role is in fact modeling wellness behaviors for the family.

New roles should be developed for family members, teachers, and others in the helping professions to implement this concept of wellness. Involvement in wellness activities is a natural evolution of the nurse's role and demonstrates the highest level of caring. Nurses involved in wellness-promotion activities will

Express their own concepts of health and wellness to others

Identify areas of primary-care responsibility

Assist clients in identifying health-maintenance needs

Assist clients in assessing and evaluating current health practices

Assist clients in learning behaviors that prevent illness and promote wellness according to growth and developmental levels

Assist clients in identifying values regarding health and wellness

Assist clients in assuming self-care responsibility for their own health behavior

Serve as role models for wellness behavior

Identify family's usual coping patterns

Evaluate the family in regard to stimuli at any given position on the illness-wellness continuum

Participate in the planning and development of health resources and services that include primary care services and quality health services at reasonable cost, allocated in such a way as to be available and accessible to all

Family Wellness Assessment

In order for the nurse and family to work as partners in promoting wellness, they must be familiar with measurable attributes or behaviors that characterize wellness. Such characteristics are behaviors exhibited by the family and its members that assist them in moving toward the wellness pole of the health continuum.

Objectively and subjectively gaining information about their level of wellness is the necessary first step for the family in determining their wellness status and in learning what changes in behavior are necessary to increase levels of wellness. Furthermore, systematic assessment of levels of family wellness will guide assessment of well-being of the overall community.

Family wellness assessment can be accomplished to some degree in any setting. The nurse and family need not be limited by an identified illness in a family member in order to recognize and promote wellness aspects. An assessment tool can be used with one person or with the whole family. Nurses working in community settings will probably find it easier to accomplish a total family wellness assessment because of the nature of the home setting and easier access to family members. However, addressing even one aspect of family wellness with even one family member will have an impact on the whole family's level of wellness.

The chapters in this book address major components of wellness that are encompassed in the several dimensions of health. In each chapter is presented detailed information to explain a particular component and to suggest ways in which a family might work toward achieving it. Information is developed according to developmental stages with appropriate wellness behaviors identified. This structure can help the family and nurse determine what wellness behaviors each person in the family should possess or be working toward as he moves through the life cycle.

WELLNESS ASSESSMENT TOOLS

Chapters 2 through 7 are followed by corresponding assessment tools. Each tool is behaviorally oriented, consisting primarily of specific behaviors that the nurse can observe or the family can identify or report. The behaviors are those that, if acquired and maintained, will help the family member reach his wellness potential.

The nurse using the tool with the family can identify a starting point for discussion about wellness. Items in the tool or its subsections can be used to clarify results of current action and as a basis for setting goals for behavioral change. When used with a family over time, the tools can be a means of seeing whether change has indeed occurred and whether the family has progressed. There may be some behaviors that can be changed, some that cannot, and some improvements that can be achieved only over a long period of time.

The tools are designed to be used in conjunction with every member of the family to assess both individual levels of wellness and areas for further work. When all family members are considered together, the family and nurse gain an appreciation for the progress the family is making in reaching its wellness potential.

In gathering information the nurse should work with all family members, although they need not be considered at the same time. Starting with the area of wellness that is of greatest importance to the family, the nurse should use the tool to uncover strengths and weaknesses in the family, and reinforce the strengths as the starting point for improving the weaknesses. The nurse should validate all observations and perceptions with the family and clarify any information reported by the family. Though data are subjective as well as objective, they should be as accurate as possible.

Learning about wellness behaviors can be a short process or a lengthy one. Certain information may be obtained simply by asking a question formulated from the assessment tool item. Other data involve much more time and require an in-depth interpersonal relationship. For example, assessing wellness of the family system will probably involve the nurse knowing the family on a long-term basis.

Because the tools are organized according to developmental stages, when working with children the nurse will be focusing first on each child's current developmental stage. However, nurses must assess retrospectively to determine whether children have acquired wellness behaviors at earlier developmental stages. If not, nurse and family must work toward helping children incorporate these behaviors into their life-style. Likewise, looking ahead to the next developmental stage, nurses can help the family plan by reviewing the wellness goals and behaviors appropriate to that stage.

The tools have been developed with scores attached to each behavior to indicate how often or to what extent the individual demonstrates the behavior. Using each tool, the nurse should first determine how many points are possible for the family, excluding sections for which there is no family member in that developmental stage and using certain sections more than once if the family has more than one member in a particular stage. The total possible score then allows the nurse and family to compare the score attained with a reference point. A summary section is provided for each assessment tool.

These tools are based on current knowledge as well as projections about what conditions would evoke a wellness-oriented state of health. The numerical scores attained by a family on one or more of the tools are to be used simply as reference points *for that family.* When the family works to acquire or refine wellness behaviors or to perform them more frequently, the score attained on the tool will increase and thereby reinforce the family for their progress toward wellness. These tools represent a modest start toward measuring qualities that are both quantitative and qualitative.

As the nurse and family work together to learn about and to adopt wellness as a life-style, it is our hope that they will find their lives more productive, abundant, and satisfying. Instead of merely adding years to life, we wish to add life to years.

Health professionals must have a commitment to the family as a social system, which is crucial to the continuation of society. When one reads about the "death" of the family as an institution, he is struck with the thought of the lack of any other available resource to fulfill the family tasks. It is suggested that those who study "pathologic" families look at the optimally functioning family first. Their view of the "death" of the family system just might be premature if the well family has not been adequately studied. It is hoped that information about well families will lead to intelligent self-directed change.

References

1. Bruhn, J. G., Cordova, F. D., Williams, J. A., and Fuentes, R. G., Jr. The wellness process. *J. Community Health* 2:214, 1977.
2. Dunn, H. L. High-level wellness in the world of today. *J.A.O.A.* 61:984, 1962.
3. Dunn, H. L. *High-Level Wellness.* Arlington, Va.: Beatty, 1961.
4. Dunn, H. L. What high-level wellness means. *Health Values: Achieving High Level Wellness* 1:12, 1977.
5. Hoyman, H. Rethinking an ecologic system model of man's health, disease, aging, and death. *J. Sch. Health* 45:509, 1975.
6. Lysaught, J. P. *An Abstract for Action.* New York: McGraw-Hill, 1970.

TWO

Wellness of the Family System

The basis for looking at family wellness in all the dimensions of health is psycho-social wellness of the family system itself—how the family relates and interacts as a unit. This chapter describes some concepts necessary for understanding the family and addresses the psychosocial wellness components of the family system.

The family is the basic biologic and social unit that comprises our society. The family as a biologic unit produces human beings, ensuring survival of the human race. The family as a social unit takes on further importance. As the family rears its offspring, and relates to and interacts with other persons and systems in its environment, it takes on many roles and functions that ultimately promote the human-ness and uniqueness of people. How these roles and functions are carried out and the framework within which they occur are of primary concern.

The established nuclear family unit comes with a set of values, norms, and expectations derived from each partner's own family of procreation. The developing family then further develops these values and norms, modifying them to fit its needs within the context of society. Individuals as part of the family unit are then influenced and molded by this value framework. The many institutions, systems, and groups of which the family is a part are ultimately influenced by the value-norm-expectation framework of even a single family. This framework, culturally based and culturally influenced, guides the family as it carries out its functions and is the basis for the many behaviors that the family unit exhibits in its long life as a biologic and social unit.

The biologic and social importance of the family cannot be emphasized enough. According to Rubin, "It is within the family that the child first learns about himself, his relationship to others, and the ways of response and expression that are acceptable or unacceptable" [13]. Children grow, mature, and develop within this framework, which is built, maintained, and remodeled as necessary by their families. The child's physical, psychological, social, and spiritual health and well-being are intimately shaped by his family and by its value-norm-expectation framework.

A family can be described as a system of interacting persons, who are related by blood, marriage, or adoption, and who are interdependent in sharing goals and meeting needs. This definition is obvious and would apply in many instances. It describes a basic biologic unit that is goal directed in meeting the needs of family members. It is limited, however, in that it ignores the broader social role of the family. Duvall's definition implies a broader social meaning by defining the family as a "unity of interacting persons related by ties of marriage, birth, or adoption, whose central purpose is to create and maintain a common culture which promotes the physical, mental, emotional, and social development of each of its members" [4]. This definition highlights the family's role in maintaining the culture from generation to generation and in maintaining a thread of continuity through time; it may be one of the most basic definitions of family available, but it too has limitations. Defining the family as persons related by genetic or legal bonds places a strict limitation on what one may conceptualize as a family. Today with the identified trend toward independence and alternative life-styles, a "family" may be created without the legal bonds of marriage or the biologic bonds of parenthood. The individuals in a commune could function as a system within the larger system of society, filling biologic and social functions, and they would constitute a basic unit while sharing common goals in achieving basic human needs. The family may include biologically related persons or close significant others; who is in one's family is best defined by each person.

Family as a Source of Learning

The family is a basic source of learning about oneself and about wellness for each member. Within the family, one learns the basic set of values, norms, and expectations held by the family, and about the values, norms, and expectations held by society as the family sees them. Societal values are filtered through the perceptual screen of the family. More importantly, the constant feedback provided an individual by his family helps him learn about himself as a person within his environment. The family is a laboratory in which the individual can develop and test his own self-concept, which forms the basis for many of the roles he enacts throughout life. "Basic attitudes, expectations, and beliefs about oneself, and about others are tested and formulated within the microcosmic social world of the family. These basic orientations become the foundation for behavior and interaction as the child moves progressively into the larger social spheres beyond the family" [13]. Social learning occurs and shapes the behavior, attitudes, beliefs, and values of each individual member, and lays the groundwork for psychosocial wellness of each person and future families formed from this family.

The physical, psychological, and social growth process of each member is enriched by the nurturance provided by the family. Nurturance (nourishment) supports each person in striving to grow and develop through all ages and stages of development. A nurturing climate is conducive to full realization of one's potential. From the adult point of view, Satir describes this process as one of *peoplemaking,* with the adults being the peoplemakers, and it becomes the major psychosocial task of the family system. What the adults in the family promote are "feelings of self-worth, positive communication systems, rules which will enhance how they feel and act and finally, a positive link to society rather than being alienated" [14]. But the children in the family are peoplemakers, too, by providing feedback and reinforcement to the adults regarding how their roles are being carried out. The adult who sees the positive fruits of his parenting efforts is further encouraged in a supportive way to nurture and positively promote the development of a growing child. In addition, an adult who feels positively about his childrearing efforts will experience an enhanced self-image and sense of self-esteem, contributing to his growth toward full potential as a person.

Family as a System   To understand the interactional dynamics of the family, the systems concept is a useful framework. The systems concept explains many of the phenomena of human behavior. In essence, systems theory states that the whole is made up of the sum of its parts, which are *interrelated* and *interdependent*. Change in any part of the system causes change in the other parts of the system as the system attempts to regain balance [1]. This concept implies that the whole is *more* than the sum of its parts. It includes the way the parts operate in relation to each other [7]. People systems exist within an environment and constantly exchange energy with it. When the system receives input from the environment, a process of change is set up within the system that then generates output back into the environment. So the system and its environment are interrelated, with each undergoing change based on what occurs in either the system or its environment.

The systems concept can be applied to all combinations of human entities. A single person is a system comprised of the many biologic and psychological processes present in the human being as an organism. These processes in themselves are systems. A family is a system comprised of the individuals who are members of the family. One can also say that a classroom of children is a system, a philanthropic organization is a system, or that persons in a geographic area with its many institutions and systems comprise a community system. The key to deciding whether any given collection of persons is a system is determining whether they are *interrelated* and *interdependent*.

For example, the human body is comprised of many biologic and psychological processes that interrelate to form a whole, living person. The normal phenomenon of pregnancy affects not only the many aspects of the woman's body, but her feelings about herself as a person. She may experience changes in her body image as the biologic processes operate to promote growth and development of the fetus. The changes she experiences will affect her family and how they feel about themselves as persons belonging to a family about to welcome another member. The child who feels threatened by the impending arrival of a sibling may show his feelings through his behavior at home, with peers, and in the classroom setting. Other classmates as well as the teacher will be affected by his behavior. The family system is altered forever on arrival of the new member. The change in configuration of the family system requires change and adaptation by every member as roles and functions take on new meanings. The community system is also affected by the pregnancy. Health systems and educational systems are called on to provide services to the new member of the community. On the other hand, the community has gained a new member who has many potential contributions to make.

The concept of system when applied to the family affords a dynamic and stimulating frame of reference for studying and working with families. It emphasizes profoundly the interrelatedness of family members with each other and the environment. It points out the dynamics of change, that if even one person in the family changes, all others are affected in some way (Fig. 2-1). Systems, while

Figure 2-1. The family system.

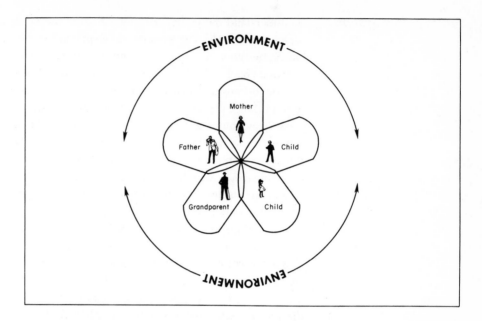

dynamic and changing, strive for stability so that integrity of the system is maintained while growth continues. The potential for growth in a family system is like compounding interest in a savings account. There are many points of interaction with the environment, and each new input adds and compounds to the input received from all other family members.

While the concept of systems is quite simple, systems themselves are extremely complex. Attempting to effect change in all parts of a system at the same time can be an overwhelming prospect for the nurse. In fact, it is quite unrealistic. The nurse can focus attention on one aspect of a system and still effect change. By providing care to even one part of the family system, change can be encouraged that will affect the whole family. Gradually, as more components of the family system are added to her care, the nurse can work with the family as a total interacting, interdependent system, and promote growth and realization of the full potential of the family as a system of unique persons.

The Family and Wellness

The family, with its numerous roles and functions and with its characteristics as a system, holds the key for the wellness of its members and for itself as a total functioning unit. Within the family unit are sown the seeds of wellness behavior for each individual and ultimately for the whole family. By teaching its members the myriad behaviors of everyday living that affect health, the family becomes the primary provider of health care. What one does each day in terms of specific health practices and habits is far more influential to one's state of health than how frequently one seeks care from health professionals. The traditional responsibility placed on health-care professionals for one's level of health is fallacious. Each person is the most important provider of personal health care, and the many behaviors that promote wellness and illness are learned within the circle of the family.

Adults bring to a family unit all the characteristics of their upbringing that affect health. The values each holds in relation to the broad area of health can be traced back in turn to the family. Whether these values predominantly favor behaviors that promote wellness or illness can be traced back to values, norms, and expectations held by one's family. Likewise, the behaviors learned by children that affect wellness are learned primarily within the family unit. Parents are the most influential teachers that children have on the subject of wellness, teaching by words and by example. Dental health may be taught in the public schools, but the child's dental health will be more significantly influenced by the dental habits of his family and by the reinforcement provided to the child for positive dental practices than by whatever is taught in the formal classroom setting. These role models for wellness behavior provided by parents will serve to shape the child and his development throughout life.

WELLNESS AND THE FAMILY SYSTEM

Physical care of members of the family is but one aspect of wellness that is the responsibility of the family. Mental and spiritual wellness of each member falls within the domain of family responsibility. The family's environment also contributes to wellness of the total family. But the wellness of the *family system itself* is a dimension of family wellness not often dealt with or considered. The fabric of wellness of the family as a system is woven daily, with many strands and threads that give meaning and richness to family life. Wellness of the family as a system involves process over time. The ever-changing family system grows and evolves as a unit and as a system. Family systems, young or mature in their levels of development, possess certain characteristics of internal function that affect levels of wellness of the entire range of dimensions encompassed in the concept of family wellness. As inputs add to the family system daily, so the subtleties of wellness of the family system change constantly.

Families that understand how they function and how their system fits into the whole scheme of wellness have the knowledge necessary to develop toward a maximum level of wellness. Knowledge and self-understanding are requisites for positive growth and change. Family members, all of whom contribute daily in innumerable ways to the dynamics of the family system, need to know how the family unit works so they can determine answers to these questions: How well are we as a family unit? Is this how we want our family to work? How can we make it better to achieve the highest level of wellness possible? Well families can become more well. We do not know the upper reaches of wellness; a family's full potential is never completely known. Each family must define and determine its own wellness potential and set goals for attaining it.

A nurse working with a family in any setting who is knowledgeable about wellness components of the family system is in a position to assess the family system. She can use data gathered while working with the family to identify areas for continued growth. This knowledge can then be used as part of the total plan of care with the family to promote wellness in all dimensions. Wellness of the family system is the foundation of wellness in all other areas. The unique contributions of the nurse in the health-care system afford her the important opportunity of promoting wellness of the family system as she works with the family in many different ways.

Nurses can use available opportunities to assess the family's desire and need to learn more about wellness of their family system. Teaching family-system components of wellness and how the individual family fits within these components gives direction to the family regarding how to change, how to increase wellness, how to grow, and how to reach its potential. The nurse whose philosophic base for nursing practice includes promotion of wellness will make use of every opportunity to assess wellness of the family system and to act as a catalyst for improvement in all dimensions of wellness.

Wellness Criteria of the Family System

The framework for studying wellness of the family system revolves around three categories of criteria: (1) how the family members relate to one another, (2) how the family members function together, and (3) how the family relates to the world outside the family. All variables encompassed in the concept of wellness of the family system fall into these categories and form the items in the assessment tool. Complexity of this concept is astonishing, but the skills and attributes that are characteristic of wellness of the family system can be learned. Wellness of all family systems can be improved. There are many perspectives on the internal organization and internal relationships within the family, each of which yields different views of relevant criteria. Various studies and authors have looked at the family in light of some criterion or criteria related to some aspect of wellness, such as family system competence [8], emotional health of children [17], sound personal health practices [11], family strengths [10, pp. 87-94], optimal functioning [8], psychological health of the family [8], or being energized [11]. Because of their focus on "non-ill" families, findings and insights from these authors and studies give direction for determining wellness criteria of the family system.

Family Members Relating to One Another

INDIVIDUALITY AND AUTONOMY

Autonomy and individuality are two interrelated components of wellness of the family system. Individuality refers to the uniqueness of each person in the family and to the respect of each family member for the individuality of himself and every other family member. Recognizing and respecting one another as individual persons, rather than as beings who merely fill roles such as mother or father, is a component of wellness of the family system [10, pp. 87–94]. Individuality also includes a tolerance for and responsiveness to each individual in the family [11] which is in contrast to conformity, when each person is expected to be like all the others. In a family system that is well, individuality encompasses a freedom of each family member to grow and develop into a self-actualized person. A family that tends to the individuality of its members encourages each member to experience life uniquely, to reach out, seek, and take initiative in growing and learning about life. Unconditional and lasting respect for the person is also characteristic of individuality. Differences are tolerated and conflicts are approached through negotiation that respects the right of others to feel, perceive, and respond differently. There is no pull or push toward a family oneness that obliterates or even negates individual distinctions. Individuality encourages autonomy, self-development, and self-responsibility in children, so that skills necessary for adult roles are learned throughout the entire period of childhood.

Autonomy has been identified with Lewis's healthy, competent families [8] and with Pratt's energized families [11]. Autonomy is closely related to individuality and involves development of each family member as a person who is separate from the other family members, yet part of the well-knit family group. Autonomy and dependency achieve a balance. Several factors promote development of autonomy: clear communication within the family, sharing of thoughts and feelings among family members, and a sense of responsibility within the family for individual thoughts, feelings, and actions [8]. Emotions are accepted and shared, and each person knows he is responsible for his own feelings and actions. Development of autonomy begins early in the developmental life of a family and affords opportunities for personal growth and fulfillment throughout life. Autonomy is a necessary component of wellness of the family system because it encourages and supports the development of self-responsibility necessary for ongoing assumption of adult roles and functioning at a high level of wellness.

Total acceptance of each person in the family underlies both individuality and autonomy. Well families accept without question each person in the family, and through a system of mutual respect for one another, as well as support for uniqueness, individuality, and personal autonomy, self-responsibility and self-growth flourish. The supportive nature of such a family encourages continued development of wellness of the family system.

COMMUNICATION

Communication patterns provide another component of wellness of the family system. All human interactions take place through verbal and nonverbal messages communicated from one person to the other. From the moment of birth, the infant receives communication from care givers, and primarily from family members. The growing child learns the meaning of life through the messages communicated to him from those around him. The persons around him most of his early life are his family members so the significance of the kind and quality of messages communicated within the family unit becomes very important. During the first 5 years—the years of most rapid growth and development—the child interacts primarily with his family members, which is why the communication within and among family members is so significant to development of children and to the well-being of the entire family thoughout its life cycle as a family.

Varied and regular interaction among family members is characteristic of the well family [11]. This interaction occurs through shared participation in tasks in the home as well as in leisure activities, in events that are structured as well as those that are unstructured and spontaneous, and in activities that are physical as well as those that are primarily communicative. All family members, adults and children, are involved with each other. No family member is excluded or left out. Well families interact regularly with each other, giving a sense of dynamism to the family's interrelationships.

Interaction in a well family is characterized by communication that is free, open, and spontaneous, with each family member contributing his share to the free-flowing spontaneity. Humor and wit are common in families where communication is spontaneous and open [8]. While serious subjects may be discussed, apparently well families do not make dreary, dull conversation.

In a well family, communication deals with any and all matters of concern. Communication occurs in depth rather than superficially. Family members feel free to talk about ideas, beliefs, values, concepts, or any subject of interest. Emotions and feelings are shared, not hidden [10, pp. 87-94].

The emotional tone of well families is one of affection, friendliness, warmth, and caring, as determined by the communication patterns observed in the family [8]. Family members regularly express caring for one another, which encourages caring feelings for others outside the family unit. A feeling of warmth pervades the family system communication network. Parents express warmth and affection for one another. Family members express feelings about each other as well as about family issues. A range of emotions is permitted in the well family. If one family member is angry at another, he expresses it, and expresses it to that person [17]. All feelings are human and to express them is normal. Communication is straightforward with no evasiveness or mind reading. Hidden meanings are absent [8].

Communications are clear but not obsessively clear, with every statement clearly spoken and verbally punctuated. Well families communicate with such openness and spontaneity that interruptions are tolerated and accepted [8]. Information is requested and given. Family members do not put each other on the spot. No one feels threatened by disagreeing with another, and there are no scapegoats. Family members are able to cooperate without being intimidated by differences [12].

A family system that has a high degree of wellness with regard to communication also has a high degree of empathy. Empathy means the quality of "putting yourself in another person's shoes" or "getting under the other person's skin." It is the capacity to understand what another person is feeling and to communicate it

[8], which leads to a depth of genuine understanding among family members. In well families this understanding is experienced consistently by all family members. Each family member feels he is understood. When he communicates feelings, he feels as though other family members understand and respect these feelings. When he communicates ideas and opinions, he feels that other family members respect and understand his views, even though they may not agree with him. Each family member communicates his own uniqueness, and he in turn respects the uniqueness of the other family members.

Communication as the vehicle for socialization shapes the everyday life of each family member. Conceptions of oneself and of other family members are formed, modified, and reinforced through the continuous processes of communication and interaction [16]. In a family system that has achieved a high level of wellness, concepts of self and others in the family are positive, as developed through the clear, open, and spontaneous communication patterns, and the warmth, respect, caring, and empathy that result. Each interaction and each message communicated adds new input for wellness into the communication system.

BONDING

Bonding is that quality or characteristic that brings people together, holds them together, and causes them to interact within the group [16]. Bonding is the psychological rationale, the "why" for all other aspects of wellness of the family system. When studying communication, we need to ask why these persons communicate at all. When studying individuality and autonomy, we need to ask why these individuals are here together in the first place. When looking at patterns of decision making, we need to ask why they get together to make decisions at all. Bonding is the psychological glue that holds people, in this case family members, together over time. Bonding keeps family members together as each grows into a self-actualized person. It keeps family members together when they are faced with physical distances as children grow up and start brand-new nuclear families of their own. Bonding keeps families together through times of stress. It keeps them interacting as a whole family unit. Lack of bonding is indifference. Bonding cannot be observed in the way that communications or interactions can be observed. It is an important component of wellness of the family system but can only be inferred from observation of family dynamics as a whole.

Bonding occurs within families between subunits of persons such as husband and wife, as well as among all individuals in the family [16]. As children are born, the process of bonding occurs first between mother and child, and then between the child and the father and other members of the family. Bonds change. They allow acceptance of new members into the family and prevent breakup of the family when threatened from the outside. Bonds allow the openness of the family system to continue and allow new input into the family to result in a new level of equilibrium rather than disintegration. Bonding implies interdependence. Persons who do not need each other in some way have no need to come together and stay together. Interdependence and psychological sharing of oneself with other family members is characteristic of bonding.

The parental bond is perhaps of primary importance, for the parents are the first unit of the nuclear family. Lewis [8] found that the parental coalition played a crucial role in the determination of family competence. The bonds between the parents result in a marriage that is effective in meeting the needs of both partners. Partners express affection for each other and function with a high degree of complementarity. The marital partners demonstrate a fit between their individual skills, pride in each other's assets and strengths, and therefore experience no competitive pulls. This fit sets the stage for family network bonds that encourage positive relationships between parents and children and between siblings, so that undesirable emotionally charged alliances with opposite-sexed persons within and outside of the family are avoided [8].

Bonds help provide the sense of security we need to grow and to be able to risk engaging in new experiences. If the sense of bondedness is secure, then each family member feels the security he needs to face challenges, and the support he needs if he fails. But bonds change over time. Indeed they must change for wellness of the family system to continue over the life span of the family. The bonds that brought a couple together as young adults must change as the family unit expands to accommodate children and then contracts as they grow up and leave home. Bonds that cause very close relationships between parents and infants must change to allow growth and development of children into mature and responsible adults. The family system that is characterized by a high level of wellness in bondedness changes the nature and quality of bonds as abilities and needs of its members change, allowing for the growth, individuality, and autonomy of each member. Bonding that promotes wellness must be examined from time to time by family members, so that more glue may be applied in times of extreme stress, or lessened or dissolved when the time comes for a child-becoming-adult to strike out on his own. Thus the nature and quality of bonding changes as the family grows and develops and as physical and social maturation occur. The bonds that attract and hold siblings to one another change as they grow to form relationships with peers and others outside the family. The existence of bonds appropriate to the wellness needs of each member and the ability of these bonds to change as the family changes characterizes wellness of the family as a system.

Family Members Functioning Together

ROLES AND ROLE RELATIONSHIPS

The family can be viewed as a system of roles. Role expectations are learned primarily through interactions with others in a group [3], and thus the family maintains the primary group for modeling some role relationships and teaching expectations of others. Interaction, learning, and socialization continue throughout the lives of all family members. Patterns of behavior are developed on the basis of what others expect or demand. Ideas of what behaviors and attitudes are appropriate for a given role are developed within the family through communication of expectations by various family members [3]. The family defines the role behaviors expected of each person within its own unique cultural framework. Parenting behaviors that are considered normal in one family system may not be acceptable in another.

The various tasks and identities are divided and grouped into roles, and this unique system of roles determines the way the essential business of family life is carried out. Each family member is cast in a particular set of roles, thus depending on the other family members playing their roles to make it possible for him to play his roles. If this does not occur, he must persuade others to change their roles so that he can change his [16].

Roles occur in pairs or larger role systems, and not as single units. In order for a woman to assume a mothering role, someone else must assume the role of the child. One cannot assume the role of husband unless someone else assumes the role of wife. A role is always a way of coping with some other role. The role of the relevant other must be learned in order to learn and master the role one is playing. Working out the details of family roles is a process of continual changes and bargaining [16]. Changing features and demands of society make other demands on role relationships of the family. The well family is able to change and adapt its role relationships to meet its and society's needs.

As each family works out its unique pattern of roles and role relationships, the acceptance of the roles themselves is important and not the content of the roles [17]. Each family unit will show differences in how specific roles are carried out, but all family units must show a high degree of acceptance of roles. A very important role relationship in terms of acceptance consists of those roles assumed by the parents in the family. Three roles are played by the parents: work roles, which include earning a living and doing housework; parental roles, which include childrearing; and the marital roles, which include the parents' relationship with each other. It is crucial to the wellness of the family that parents accept and perform successfully these three roles [17]. All three roles are necessary to meeting the needs of the family members, and a well family will meet these needs to a high degree in each role relationship. When a role is either not accepted by the one who is expected to fill it or not filled in the manner expected by the family, family need fulfillment will suffer.

In enacting the marital roles, husband and wife must feel enrichment and fulfillment, and that his or her physical and emotional needs are met. A direct relationship has been found between the degree of emotional health in children and the degree to which the relationship between the parents was positive [17]. Both husband and wife in a well family have high regard for each other and seem to have had their expectations of the partner met or surpassed [8]. Although marital styles differ, husband and wife in a well family share profound affection for one another, have significant opportunities for intimacy, and rely on truly respectful negotiation as hallmarks of their relationship [8].

The parental roles in a well family are characterized by a total acceptance by the parents. Both parents enjoy their children, being with them and looking after them [17]. Childrearing, though challenging, is a pleasant and enjoyable experience, and one that is satisfying to both parents. One who is dissatisfied with his role as a parent makes an effort to avoid the children and spends a minimal amount of time with them. Obviously, children do not feel the warmth and personal respect for themselves as persons when a parent accepts his role only to a minimal degree.

In the well family, work roles are accepted and seen as a means for growth. Well families see work, whether earning a living or maintaining the house, as an opportunity for creativity and expression of one's individuality and worth. With inflationary forces in society resulting in more and more wives and mothers joining the ranks of gainfully employed, challenges to the family unit arise in the area of work roles. Role relationships are changing, as changes occur in who works outside the home and who does what work inside the home. In the well family, the process of respectful negotiation that characterizes role development prevails in this area. The bonding that helps the family weather crises and other changes holds the family together here also. Out of change comes a new level of stability, as durability of the family system is maintained.

Roles are accepted but are also flexible [10, pp. 87-94, 11]. As events occur that stimulate change in the family system, family members must assume different functions and role behaviors. In a well family, when necessary, a father will fill some aspects of the mother's role and vice versa, as well as children assuming some parenting functions [10, pp. 87-94]. Not only does this reversal meet the immediate need of the family for a role function to be exercised, but it gives the family member the opportunity to sample the flavor of the other person's role. The capacity for empathy is enhanced, and the potential for a higher level of wellness is maximized through greater mutual respect and understanding.

Exercise of parental roles in childrearing is an important aspect of role relationships. Children create new demands by creating the need for new interaction patterns [15] and consequently for new roles and role relationships. The development and raising of children place special demands on the parents in a society that has many stresses. Nevertheless, in well families parents develop and maintain spontaneous, warm relationships with their children and welcome the opportunities and challenges of parenthood. They enjoy their children and interact with them frequently and consistently.

Parents in well families spend time with their children, not just discussing activities but doing them. As children grow through the preschool years, develop peer relationships, and become involved in activities outside the home, outside activities may easily usurp parental responsibilities of interacting and playing with their children. Parents are generally not doing as many things with their children as the children would like [11]. With the number of varied extracurricular activities available in some communities for social and cultural enrichment, the amount of time away from the family unit can become extensive. Children should take advantage of opportunities for enrichment, but in doing so should not be denied opportunities for activities with the family as a whole. It becomes a challenge, then, for the family who wants to achieve a high level of wellness to make time for meaningful physical and social interaction with their children, and to help achieve a balance between activities that are centered outside the home and those that involve the family.

Discipline of children is another component of wellness of the family system in the area of childrearing. The family with a high level of wellness uses discipline as direction to keep children from doing something that will cause them harm or to guide them in a positive sense [17]. Discipline is used not for the parents' convenience or to meet their needs or to impose their values or interests. Discipline is not constrictive but growth producing. Discipline in a well family helps children learn how to make the right choices. In a well family, discipline is a form of stimulation that is used to guide and encourage, not force or restrain [6, pp. 10-23], so that children can grow and develop to their fullest potential and maintain a positive self-concept. Discipline used by well families encourages self-confidence, self-responsibility, autonomy and individuality, and a sense of justice.

Both parents in the well family assume responsibility for discipline, and respect each other's views and decisions. Acquisition of self-discipline by the child is fostered by this pattern of shared responsibility in the parents. Coalitions between one parent and the child are avoided, and the child learns that he is respected because his parents respect each other.

DIVISION OF TASKS AND ACTIVITIES

Another characteristic concerns the extent to which tasks and activities of family members are sharply differentiated on conventional definitions of age and sex roles, or the extent to which there is interchangeability and flexibility in task performance [11]. The flexible and egalitarian pattern is closely related to and consistent with individual freedom and responsiveness to the individual [11]. In well families, when individuality in task performance is encouraged, persons have the latitude to shape their roles within the family to themselves rather than have rigid role specifications forced on them. Individuals in the family are encouraged to develop their unique qualities. The mutual respect and understanding, individuality and development of autonomy that characterize so many other aspects of wellness of the family system apply here too.

In terms of the family functioning to meet its needs, a flexible organization of family tasks enables the family to mobilize for maximum productive effort [12]. When family members develop role tasks and activities according to interest and ability rather than age and sex stereotypes, they are more likely to show greater dedication to doing the job well, and greater consideration for the needs of the other members of the family. Flexibility allows for greater adaptability when contingencies arise and family members have to perform tasks not usually part of their roles. Families with high levels of wellness demonstrate egalitarian and flexible organization of role tasks and activities.

GOVERNANCE AND POWER

Governance and power are two variables that influence how the family functions together, and three types predominate. In the first type of governance, each person attempts to achieve a desired end without compromise or serious consideration of the opposing view. Threats, coaxing, and negativism are characteristic, with one person winning and the other losing. Raw use of power is common and resistance and resentment are maximized [2, pp. 117-128]. This type of governance is not conducive to the warmth, respect, empathy, and individuality that characterize the well family.

In the second type of governance, rules are developed that are accepted by all family members as more or less fair. Rules govern allocation of resources, allocation of authority, and how contested decisions are negotiated. When rules are the basis of the governance structure, who enforces the rules and who is free to challenge or change the rules becomes extremely important [2, pp. 117-128]. The risk to family wellness is in discerning whether the rules that are enforced are truly agreed on by mutual consent of all family members or whether one or more family members are forcing acceptance of their rules. When rules are decided on in advance and are enforced consistently, little opportunity exists for the creativity and individuality that are common in well families and that are necessary to reach many of the decisions important to the well functioning of the family.

The third form of governance is more compatible with the notion of wellness of the family system. This form of governance is government by principles. The basis of this form is internalized principles of good judgment. Each member of the family is self-governed and no one has the responsibility of governing the others so long as the family operates at this level. Authoritarianism and patterns of dominance and submission are absent. A few controlling principles guide the governance of the family, and when rules do exist they exist by contract among the family members and not by dictum [2, pp. 117-128]. Power is shared, for each family member has power over himself. Self-responsibility is encouraged and rewarded by feelings of mutual respect among family members.

Obviously this form of governance can work only in families where parents value this form of governance and where it is consistent with their system of moral principles. Then it can be taught to the children by guidance and example as they grow up. Teaching children good judgment occurs over time, but when and as it is achieved children are able to contribute in a positive way to this form of family governance. In addition, children learn self-discipline and self-responsibility through another interactional system in the family. This form of governance is a learned style of interaction among relatively mature family members, and its presence in most of the decision-making situations indicates a high level of wellness of the family system.

DECISION MAKING AND PROBLEM SOLVING

In families with a high level of wellness, decision making and problem solving are dynamic, creative processes. Numerous options are explored, and if one alternative does not work the family backs off and tries another, instead of trying to make just one option work [8]. A well family has the capacity to solve many types of problems, including emotional ones, by encouraging self-discovery and by paying attention to all problems, large and small [17]. Perspective in living is gained, so that small problems do not seem exceedingly complex and larger problems do not seem overwhelming. Difficult problems are seen as solvable, and the family is able to direct its creative problem-solving abilities to the task.

Well families tend to attempt actively and energetically to cope with life's problems and issues on a daily basis and not to avoid the challenge of confronting a problem. They show an openness to new ideas, information, techniques, opportunities, and resources [11]. Whatever is available and appropriate to the decision-making or problem-solving effort will be employed. All family members affected by a decision are involved in making the decision. Flexibility in decision making is characteristic. Rigidly applied rules for decision making do not exist.

In well families, less time is spent in making decisions than in less competent families [5]. Skills in decision making are learned and practiced by all family members, and responsibility is shared. Therefore decision making need not consume inordinate amounts of time. Depending on the content and context of the decision, one family member may make the final choice of alternatives. But this is agreed on by all family members, and an impasse or a "no-decision" situation is avoided. The business of the family must be carried out, and the well family makes contingencies for the knotty decision-making situations so that the family's needs can be met.

LEADERSHIP AND INITIATIVE

In well families, leadership is shared, cooperative, and effective [9]. Effective leadership requires that parents have greater influence and that one parent, depending on the context of the situation, takes a more dominant leadership role with the other parent cooperative and supportive of this leadership [9]. This leadership provided by the parents is not exercised in an authoritative way, but is modeled, so that children can learn by experiencing a cooperative, mutually respectful system of leadership, and can see that it is effective in meeting the family's needs.

In the well family, children are encouraged to seek and use opportunities to develop leadership skills in matters directly related to them. As skills are learned, they are used; the family benefits from the ability of another member to develop his potential for leadership at whatever level is appropriate to his level of growth and development. Leadership is learned during childhood and developed throughout life. The well family provides a training ground for leadership development that is warm, supportive, and caring and that tolerates failure as well as success.

Along with leadership of individuals in the family, the well family demonstrates a kind of leadership as a unit: initiative. Well families take the initiative with life itself [8]. They reach out constructively and respond to input from all sources. New sources of input and new challenges are constantly being sought. The well family actively and dynamically seeks. It is seldom passive. Human encounters outside the family are sought and are expected to be warm and caring, as in the family itself [9].

Relating to the World Outside the Family

The last major component of wellness of the family system relates to the family's ties to the outside world, which is a rich source of input to the family, a living open system. No family can meet all its members' needs all of the time. It depends on the outside world for enrichment, stimuli, information—all part of the flow of input into the family system.

INVOLVEMENT IN OUTSIDE COMMUNITY

The well family maintains dynamic ties with the broader community through participation of all family members in external groups and activities related to the family's needs. This participation includes leadership, membership, and participation in clubs, groups, and activities by all family members [11]. The well family provides constructive input into the larger systems in the community, and thus wellness of the community is also promoted.

Society's resources, whether recreational, cultural, or educational, are used extensively to learn about the world from many vantage points. The tremendous variety of stimuli from many different sources are available only to well families, with initiative to seek out and use them for continued growth necessary to achieve the highest level of wellness possible.

In interacting with the world outside the family, each family member is able to use outside groups as reference points for wellness of the family. The family's level of relationships with each other and their functioning as a unit are assessed through the self-concepts of each member. One sees oneself through the eyes of others and receives reinforcement and support for the well functioning of his family through the positive regard received from other groups.

The components of wellness of the family system are many and varied. Wellness of this dimension of the family does not depend on the presence of any one of the variables discussed, nor does the absence of one denote lack of wellness. High levels of wellness are possible and not rare [8]. The skills and characteristics inherent in each component are teachable and learnable, and nurses have an important role to play in learning about wellness and in teaching its components. The challenge is there, and so are the families who are willing and eager to learn more about themselves to achieve a higher level of wellness. With regard to families, Lewis states that the threads of competence can be woven in many and varied patterns [8]. Components of wellness of the family system are developed by each family in its unique way. Each nurse, who enacts her professional role in her unique way, can assist each family she works with to develop further its own highest level of wellness.

Assessment Tool

The nurse's professional background can serve her well in learning about the family because of the value she places on the family system and her communication skills in talking with all family members. To assess a family system requires interaction over time, astute listening, and careful observation of nonverbal behavior. The nurse must listen for nuances in word meanings and what each message means to the sender and receiver. She must observe family members interacting with each other and evaluate the family's reports of other situations and behaviors she could not observe firsthand.

To contrast the family's patterns with the criteria in the assessment tool, the nurse should look for patterns and trends in the family's interactional system. She must ask herself, "What does the family do most of the time?" and then validate her perceptions with the family. When an area of family system functioning is not enhancing family wellness, the nurse can point out this area to the family for consideration. They may also recognize the area and request suggestions for improvement. Based on her knowledge of family dynamics, the nurse can work honestly and openly with the family members to help them meet what they see as their needs. By suggesting how family members can support each other by softening words, taking time to listen, or spending more time with each other, the nurse is helping the family improve the functioning of its system. Nearly all family systems need a little mending now and then, and often only a few suggestions are in order to move to a higher level of family-system wellness.

In using the tool that accompanies this chapter, the nurse will have to pull together data she has gathered over a period of time. She will not be able to ask about communication patterns, but will have to rely on her own observations. Family system assessment is complex and relies more on the skills of the nurse to observe and evaluate her observations than on the family's willingness to "give" information.

Sharing assessment tool items with the family may help the family gain perspective on some possible directions for areas in which the family system can move to higher levels of wellness. Change occurs in small steps slowly, and neither nurse nor family should expect vast changes in a short period of time. The following is a cardinal rule for working with families: change does occur, but it occurs a little at a time over weeks, months, and even years. No matter how long change takes, the family is moving toward reaching its maximum potential for wellness. The direction of change and the family's desire for it are very important keys for the nurse in working with any family that wishes to develop and improve a wellness life-style.

References

1. Brill, N. K. *Working with People: The Helping Process*. Philadelphia: Lippincott, 1978.
2. Broderick, C. Power in the Governance of Families. In R. E. Cromwell and D. H. Olson (Eds.), *Power in Families*. New York: Sage Publications, 1975.
3. Burgess, E. W., Locke, H. J., and Thomas, M. M. *The Family*. New York: Van Nostrand Reinhold, 1971.
4. Duvall, E. *Family Development*. Philadelphia: Lippincott, 1971.
5. Ferreira, A. J., and Winter, W. D. Family interaction and decision-making. *Arch. Gen. Psychiatry* 8:214, 1965.
6. Handel, R. D., and Handel, G. The Family as a Psychosocial Organization. In G. Handel (Ed.), *The Psychosocial Interior of the Family*. Chicago: Aldine, 1967.
7. Lederer, W. J., and Jackson, D. *Mirages of Marriage*. New York: Norton, 1968.
8. Lewis, J. M., Beavers, W. R., Gosett, J. T., and Phillips, V. A. *No Single Thread: Psychological Health in Family Systems*. New York: Brunner/Mazel, 1976.
9. Murrell, S. A., and Stachowiak, J. G. Consistency, Rigidity, and Power in the Interaction of Clinic and Non-Clinic Families. In W. D. Winter and A. J. Ferreira (Eds.), *Research in Family Interaction*. Palo Alto, Calif.: Science and Behavior Books, 1969.
10. Otto, H. A. Framework for Assessing Family Strengths. In A. M. Reinhardt and M. D. Quinn (Eds.), *Family-Centered Community Nursing*. St. Louis: Mosby, 1973.
11. Pratt, L. *Family Structure and Effective Health Behavior: The Energized Family*. Boston: Houghton Mifflin, 1976.
12. Riskin, J., and Faunce, E. Family interaction scales: III. Discussion of methodology and substantive findings. *Arch. Gen. Psychiatry* 22:527, 1970.
13. Rubin, R. The family-child relationship and nursing. *Nurs. Outlook* 12:36, September 1964.
14. Satir, V. *Peoplemaking*. Palo Alto, Calif.: Science and Behavior Books, 1972.
15. Schultz, D. A. *The Changing Family*. Englewood Cliffs, N.J.: Prentice-Hall, 1972.
16. Turner, R. H. *Family Interaction*. New York: Wiley, 1970.
17. Westley, W. A., and Epstein, N. B. *The Silent Majority*. San Francisco: Jossey-Bass, 1969.

Assessment Tool

The nurse should indicate for each item whether the family or family member accomplishes the item according to criteria indicated in the columns. If an item or section does not apply, the points represented by that item or section should be so indicated by marking the "not applicable" column. In scoring at the end of each section, the category "total points possible" means the total number of points that could be attained if every item applied. The "total not applicable" category shows the total items or sections that do not apply to the family at this time; this number should be subtracted from the "total points possible" to obtain the "total applicable" score. When comparing "total applicable" with the "total points attained," the nurse and the family can see the numerical difference in what should or could be achieved and what does exist at the present time. Scores in each section should be transferred to the summary section at the end of the chapter's assessment tool.

I. Family Members Relating to One Another   Points

  A. Individuality and Autonomy

    1. a. Each family member demonstrates respect for self   (2)_____

       b. Some family members demonstrate respect for self   (1)_____

       c. Very few or no family member(s) demonstrate respect for self   (0)_____

    2. a. Each family member demonstrates respect for individuality of every other family member   (2)_____

       b. Some family members demonstrate respect for individuality of other family members   (1)_____

       c. Very few or no family members show respect for individuality of other family members   (0)_____

    3. a. Each family member is tolerant and responsive to other family members   (2)_____

       b. Some family members are tolerant and responsive to other family members   (1)_____

       c. Very few or no family members are tolerant and show responsiveness to other family members   (0)_____

    4. a. Each family member feels a sense of freedom to grow   (2)_____

       b. Some family members feel a sense of freedom to grow   (1)_____

       c. Family members feel constricted in ability to grow   (0)_____

    5. When conflicts arise in the family individual views are

       a. Always respected   (2)_____

       b. Sometimes respected   (1)_____

       c. Scarcely ever or never respected   (0)_____

    6. Individuals in the family are unique and

       a. Clearly distinct from one another   (2)_____

       b. Fairly distinct from one another   (1)_____

       c. Very similar in thoughts, feelings, and actions   (0)_____

              Total points possible *12*

              Total not applicable _____

              Total applicable _____

              Total points attained _____

  B. Communication

    1. Family members communicate with each other

       a. Regularly   (2)_____

       b. Sometimes   (1)_____

       c. Hardly ever   (0)_____

    2. Communication among family members shows

       a. Much variety   (2)_____

       b. Some variety   (1)_____

       c. Very little variety   (0)_____

    3. Communications are

       a. Always open and spontaneous   (2)_____

       b. Sometimes open and spontaneous   (1)_____

       c. Constricted and rigid   (0)_____

    4. Communications show humor and wit

       a. Frequently   (2)_____

       b. Sometimes   (1)_____

       c. Infrequently or hardly ever   (0)_____

Points

5. Family members discuss
   a. Any matter of interest to the family — (2) _____
   b. Only what certain family members wish to discuss — (1) _____
   c. Very few interests of anyone in the family — (0) _____
6. Communications occur
   a. Usually in depth — (2) _____
   b. Sometimes in depth — (1) _____
   c. Usually superficially — (0) _____
7. The emotional tone of the family is one of
   a. Warmth — (2) _____
   b. Coolness — (1) _____
   c. Neutrality—no emotional tone detected — (0) _____
8. Family members
   a. Frequently express feelings about each other — (2) _____
   b. Sometimes express feelings about each other — (1) _____
   c. Hardly ever or never express feelings about each other — (0) _____
9. The family permits
   a. Expression of a range of emotions — (2) _____
   b. Expression of only certain emotions — (1) _____
   c. Little to no expression of any emotions — (0) _____
10. Communications are
    a. Straightforward most of the time — (2) _____
    b. Straightforward some of the time — (1) _____
    c. Usually filled with hidden meanings — (0) _____
11. Communications are
    a. Clear, spontaneous, with interruptions tolerated — (2) _____
    b. Clear, well-punctuated, with interruptions not tolerated — (1) _____
    c. Unintelligible and frequently misinterpreted — (0) _____
12. When disagreements arise when communicating, family members
    a. Seldom feel threatened — (2) _____
    b. Sometimes feel threatened — (1) _____
    c. Usually feel threatened — (0) _____
13. Family communications show
    a. A high degree of empathy — (2) _____
    b. A moderate degree of empathy — (1) _____
    c. Very little or no empathy — (0) _____
14. Family members
    a. Usually feel understood — (2) _____
    b. Sometimes feel understood — (1) _____
    c. Seldom or never feel understood — (0) _____

Total points possible __28__

Total not applicable _____

Total applicable _____

Total points attained _____

C. Bonding
   1. Bonds are evident through relationships among/between
      a. All family members — (2) _____
      b. Some family members — (1) _____
      c. No family members — (0) _____

Points

2. Family demonstrates
   a. Much capacity for changing bonds over time   (2)_____
   b. Little capacity to change bonds   (1)_____
   c. No capacity for changing bonds   (0)_____
3. Interdependence among family members is demonstrated among
   a. All family members   (2)_____
   b. Some family members   (1)_____
   c. Few family members   (0)_____
4. Each marital partner feels his/her needs are met
   a. Nearly all of the time   (2)_____
   b. Some of the time   (1)_____
   c. Hardly ever or never   (0)_____
5. Marital partners function with
   a. A high degree of complementarity   (2)_____
   b. Some complementarity   (1)_____
   c. Very little complementarity but much separateness (0)_____
6. Marital partners express affection for each other
   a. Frequently   (2)_____
   b. Sometimes   (1)_____
   c. Seldom or never   (0)_____
7. Marital partners demonstrate
   a. Pride in each other's assets and strengths   (2)_____
   b. Some pride but some indifference in each other's assets and strengths (1)_____
   c. Hostility, anger, resentment, or jealousy in each other's assets and strengths (0)_____
8. Marital partners demonstrate
   a. Much cooperation with each other   (2)_____
   b. Some cooperation but some competition with each other (1)_____
   c. Much competition with each other   (0)_____
9. A feeling of security within the family is experienced by
   a. All family members   (2)_____
   b. Some family members   (1)_____
   c. Few or no family member(s)   (0)_____

Total points possible *18*
Total not applicable _____
Total applicable _____
Total points attained _____

II. Family Members Functioning Together
   A. Roles and Role Relationships
      1. Roles within the family are accepted by
         a. All family members   (2)_____
         b. Some family members   (1)_____
         c. Few or no family member(s)   (0)_____
      2. Parents show acceptance of work roles
         a. Most of the time   (2)_____
         b. Some of the time   (1)_____
         c. Hardly ever or never   (0)_____

Points

3. Parents show acceptance of parental roles
   a. Most of the time (2) _____
   b. Some of the time (1) _____
   c. Hardly ever or never (0) _____
4. Parents show acceptance of marital roles
   a. Most of the time (2) _____
   b. Some of the time (1) _____
   c. Hardly ever or never (0) _____
5. Mutual expectations of marital partners are met
   a. Or surpassed (2) _____
   b. To some degree (1) _____
   c. To a minimal degree or not at all (0) _____
6. Marital partners consider that their physical and emotional needs are met
   a. Consistently and to a high degree (2) _____
   b. Irregularly or to a moderate degree (1) _____
   c. Seldom or never or to a minimal degree (0) _____
7. Parents enjoy their children
   a. Most of the time (2) _____
   b. Some but not much of the time (1) _____
   c. Seldom or not any of the time (0) _____
8. Parents feel satisfaction in childrearing
   a. Most of the time (2) _____
   b. Some of the time (1) _____
   c. Seldom or never (0) _____
9. Parents use discipline
   a. Usually to guide children (2) _____
   b. Sometimes to guide but often to force or punish children (1) _____
   c. Usually to force, punish, or constrict children (0) _____
10. Roles within the family are
    a. Highly flexible as the situation changes (2) _____
    b. Sometimes flexible (1) _____
    c. Rigidly followed all the time (0) _____
11. Responsibility for discipline of the children is
    a. Shared by both parents (2) _____
    b. Assumed by only one parent (1) _____
    c. Assumed by neither parent (0) _____

Total points possible __22__
Total not applicable _____
Total applicable _____
Total points attained _____

B. Division of Tasks and Activities
   1. Performance of tasks is
      a. Highly interchangeable and flexible (2) _____
      b. Somewhat interchangeable and flexible (1) _____
      c. Always closely adhered to (0) _____
   2. Task roles in the family are determined
      a. Mostly by each individual (2) _____

Points

b. Sometimes by each individual but also by the leader in the
family (1) _____
c. Mostly by the leader in the family (0) _____
3. Task performance roles are developed according to
a. Interest and ability of the person (2) _____
b. Sometimes according to interest and ability but also by age
and sex (1) _____
c. Age and sex stereotypes only (0) _____
4. The organization of family tasks is
a. Usually flexible (2) _____
b. Sometimes flexible (1) _____
c. Usually rigid (0) _____

Total points possible ___8___
Total not applicable _____
Total applicable _____
Total points attained _____

C. Governance and Power
1. Governance in the family is characterized by
a. Each person being guided by principles of good judgment (2) _____
b. Mutual agreement of family members to a set of rules (1) _____
c. Each person attempting to achieve his or her ends through
threats, coaxing, and negativism (0) _____
2. Rules in the family are
a. Agreed on by all members by mutual consent (2) _____
b. Agreed on by some members and forced on others (1) _____
c. Forced on all members by the leader (0) _____
3. Governance is characterized by patterns of
a. Egalitarianism (2) _____
b. Some egalitarianism but also some authoritarianism (1) _____
c. Authoritarianism and dominance/submission (0) _____
4. Each member of the family is
a. Usually self-governed (2) _____
b. Sometimes self-governed but sometimes governed by an
authority figure (1) _____
c. Governed by some authority figure (0) _____
5. Power in the family is
a. Shared among family members (2) _____
b. Sometimes shared but sometimes assumed by one person (1) _____
c. Usually controlled by one person (0) _____
6. Children are given opportunities for self-determination and
self-governance
a. Frequently, according to growth and developmental stages (2) _____
b. Sometimes but not often, according to growth and
developmental stages (1) _____
c. Hardly ever, or never, at any stage of growth and
development (0) _____
7. Governance by principles is used in
a. Most decision-making situations (2) _____

	Points
b. Some decision-making situations	(1) _____
c. Few or no decision-making situations	(0) _____

Total points possible _14_

Total not applicable _____

Total applicable _____

Total points attained _____

D. Decision Making and Problem Solving
   1. Decision making and problem solving are characterized by
      a. Much creativity   (2) _____
      b. Some creativity   (1) _____
      c. Little to no creativity   (0) _____
   2. When an alternative does not work, the family
      a. Usually tries another alternative   (2) _____
      b. Sometimes tries another alternative but tries to make the first
         one work   (1) _____
      c. Keeps trying to make the first option work   (0) _____
   3. The family is willing and able to deal with a
      a. Wide range of problems, including emotional ones   (2) _____
      b. Narrow range of problems, but sometimes including
         emotional ones   (1) _____
      c. Narrow range of problems, not including emotional ones   (0) _____
   4. The family
      a. Tends to all problems in some way   (2) _____
      b. Tends to some problems, but also avoids dealing with other
         problems   (1) _____
      c. Avoids dealing with any problems as much as possible   (0) _____
   5. Difficult problems are seen as
      a. Solvable, and therefore are dealt with   (2) _____
      b. Not usually solvable but attempts are made to try to solve
         them   (1) _____
      c. Not solvable and therefore are avoided   (0) _____
   6. The family views small problems as
      a. Small problems and not as threatening   (2) _____
      b. Sometimes small problems but sometimes as very complex   (1) _____
      c. Very complex and threatening   (0) _____
   7. The family attempts to cope with life's problems
      a. On a daily basis   (2) _____
      b. Only when the problem becomes a large one   (1) _____
      c. Seldom or infrequently   (0) _____
   8. In handling problems and decisions, the family is
      a. Open to new ideas, information, and resources   (2) _____
      b. Not always willing to try new ideas, information, or resources   (1) _____
      c. Resistant to any new ideas, information, or resources   (0) _____
   9. When making decisions, the family involves in the
      decision-making process
      a. All those who are affected by the decision   (2) _____
      b. Some but not all persons who are affected by the decision   (1) _____
      c. Only the leader in the family   (0) _____

Points

10. Rules for making decisions are
    a. Highly flexible (2) _____
    b. Somewhat flexible (1) _____
    c. Rigid (0) _____
11. Decision making involves
    a. Little of the family's time (2) _____
    b. A moderate amount of the family's time (1) _____
    c. Much of the family's time (0) _____
12. Skills in decision making are learned by
    a. All family members (2) _____
    b. Some family members (1) _____
    c. Few family members (0) _____
13. When the family is unable to reach a decision
    a. All family members agree on who will make the final
       selection of alternatives (2) _____
    b. Some or one family member(s) decide(s) on who will
       make the final selection of alternatives (1) _____
    c. The impasse prevails and no decision is reached (0) _____

Total points possible __26__
Total not applicable _____
Total applicable _____
Total points attained _____

E. Leadership and Initiative
    1. Leadership is
       a. Usually shared, depending on the situation (2) _____
       b. Sometimes shared, depending on the situation (1) _____
       c. Always assumed by one person (0) _____
    2. Leadership is
       a. Usually effective (2) _____
       b. Sometimes but not always effective (1) _____
       c. Usually ineffective (0) _____
    3. With regard to leadership in the total family, parents have
       a. Greater influence than children (2) _____
       b. About the same influence as children (1) _____
       c. Less influence than children or no influence at all (0) _____
    4. When one parent assumes a more dominant leadership role,
       the other parent is
       a. Always cooperative and supportive (2) _____
       b. Sometimes cooperative and supportive (1) _____
       c. Contradictory and divisive (0) _____
    5. The family's system of leadership is
       a. Mutually respectful of all family members (2) _____
       b. Sometimes respectful but sometimes authoritarian (1) _____
       c. Highly authoritarian most of the time (0) _____
    6. In meeting the family's needs, leadership in the family is
       a. Highly effective (2) _____
       b. Sometimes effective (1) _____
       c. Usually ineffective (0) _____

Points

7. Children are encouraged to seek and use opportunities to develop leadership skills
    a. Often (2) _____
    b. Sometimes (1) _____
    c. Seldom or never (0) _____
8. The climate in the family for leadership development in the children is
    a. Always warm and supportive, and tolerant of failure (2) _____
    b. Sometimes warm and supportive, and tolerant of failure (1) _____
    c. Apathetic and nonsupportive, and intolerant of failure (0) _____
9. The family unit as a whole
    a. Frequently shows initiative and actively seeks new experiences (2) _____
    b. Sometimes shows initiative and sometimes seeks new experiences (1) _____
    c. Is passive and seldom seeks new experiences (0) _____

Total points possible __18__
Total not applicable _____
Total applicable _____
Total points attained _____

III. Involvement in Outside Community
    A. Groups and activities external to the family are participated in by
        1. All family members (2) _____
        2. Some family members (1) _____
        3. No family members (0) _____
    B. The family provides input into the larger community
        1. Frequently (2) _____
        2. Sometimes (1) _____
        3. Seldom or never (0) _____
    C. Use of the community's recreational, cultural, or educational resources is
        1. Extensive (2) _____
        2. Limited (1) _____
        3. Nonexistent (0) _____
    D. The family seeks out community resources
        1. Frequently (2) _____
        2. Sometimes (1) _____
        3. Seldom or never (0) _____

Total points possible __8__
Total not applicable _____
Total applicable _____
Total points attained _____

Assessment Tool Summary

	Subtotal points possible	Subtotal not appli- cable	Subtotal appli- cable	Subtotal points attained
I. Family Members Relating to One Another				
A. Individuality and Autonomy	12	_____	_____	_____
B. Communication	28	_____	_____	_____
C. Bonding	18	_____	_____	_____
II. Family Members Functioning Together				
A. Roles and Role Relation- ships	22	_____	_____	_____
B. Division of Tasks and Ac- tivities	8	_____	_____	_____
C. Governance and Power	14	_____	_____	_____
D. Decision Making and Problem Solving	26	_____	_____	_____
E. Leadership and Initiative	18	_____	_____	_____
III. Involvement in Outside Com- munity	8	_____	_____	_____

Total points possible   154

Total not applicable   _____

Total applicable   _____

Total points attained   _____

THREE

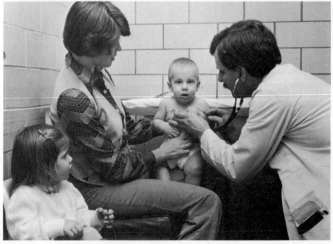

Self-Responsibility: Knowledge and Action for Wellness

Over the past several years, consumers have been inundated with statistics about the enormous rise in health-care costs, little to no change in life expectancy, pollution of the environment, and from both public and private sectors general insults to the pursuit of wellness. How can our lives, life-styles, and general sense of domestic tranquility be so threatened from so many fronts when so much effort and money are spent in our society purportedly for health and the "good life"? Who is responsible for the undesirable aspects of our lives; more important, who can do something about it?

In the past, many people believed that one's personal health was the responsibility of someone else. The someone else often turned out to be the doctor or some other professional health-care provider. But this person was usually an illness-care provider, that is, one who could help us when we were sick, when our state of health had moved from wellness to the illness end of the health continuum. The health professionals could, and frequently did, give us advice, treatments, medicine, and reappointments. If we were lucky, the illness would improve and we would return once again to our previous state of wellness. We were not very concerned about our state of wellness because if we ever departed from it someone or some institution could always patch things up. Wellness was an absence of illness, and when illness occurred a wide variety of well-educated persons were available to treat the illness.

Enter the age of the consumer. We have warranties on appliances, cars, and houses. We hear of protection plans for the buyer. Various consumer groups spearhead efforts to make cars safer, to monitor toy safety, and to watch over many aspects of our lives in the marketplace. We begin to get the feeling that if we want to improve the quality and safety of our products and our environment, we must demand it and work diligently to let manufacturers and other producers know exactly what we—the hundreds, thousands, and millions of members of the consuming public—want in our products and goods, and at what costs and benefits to ourselves and to our environment. The consumer philosophy seems to be establishing a firm foothold in our society. People seem to be saying, "We know what's morally right. We know what we want. It is our responsibility to see that the producers of goods and the providers of services give us what is wholesome, safe, and good for us." This philosophic stand has led to the formation of consumer and other activist groups, working to influence governmental and private enterprises in the expeditious implementation of the consumer philosophy. We have clearly recognized the need to be advocates for wellness in the consuming marketplace.

In matters of health care, we see only a few seedlings of the consumer philosophy applied to personal health and the health-care system. We seldom hear people say, "If I want to be well, I have to do these things to achieve it. It is my responsibility to change my life-style so that it promotes and maintains wellness. I know what services I need to help me achieve wellness and how they should be made available. I must work to see that services are developed and offered in a way that enhances wellness."

We have said earlier in this book that it is from the family that health values and life-style practices are learned. In addition, in the family one learns, develops, and tests a personal philosophy of health, wellness, and self-responsibility for health. Parents teaching children wellness practices can plant, fertilize, and encourage the growth of a philosophy of wellness that encompasses self-care and self-responsibility for wellness. Children who grow up believing that they are the most important health-care providers for themselves and that they are responsible for their level of wellness through health habits and life-style practices, will reach adulthood with the requisite mind set of attitudes and values that will guide them toward wellness. They will prize wellness as the key to that vital and dynamic state of living that is characterized by high-level wellness. Children will thus grow into adulthood saying, "Being well is my responsibility. I am the best advocate for my personal wellness."

That posture of advocacy moves in two directions, each one important and complementary. The first encompasses personal and family wellness practices, and the second deals with health-care services. Both approaches together yield the knowledge and action necessary for wellness, and nurses can help people to examine their personal philosophies of wellness and to acquire the knowledge and skills necessary to implement this dual philosophy.

Responsibility for Wellness

FAMILY ROLE IN EDUCATION FOR WELLNESS

It is important for each member of the family to learn wellness practices for each major dimension of the human organism: physical, mental-emotional, social, and environmental. Chapters 1 and 2 have comprehensively emphasized one or more components of each of these dimensions of wellness of the individual as a family member as well as of the family unit itself.

The family is responsible for educating its members in all matters related to health. Eating a nutritious diet, following sound dental wellness practices, teaching and practicing a life-style that promotes emotional and mental wellness, and promoting and maintaining a well environment are all responsibilities of the family. The family must encourage its members to adopt wellness behaviors or must see that they are carried out if the member is not capable of doing so independently, as in the case of young children or the elderly. The family must tend to its psychosocial dimension—that is, maintain its level of wellness as a system—thereby teaching the children by word and example the how-to's of family wellness for use in establishing new family units. The family should be knowledgeable about resources available for helping to promote and maintain wellness and must teach the children how to gain this knowledge in any community in which they may later reside. They may not know all the resources, but they need to know how to find out about them. Individuals need health to educate themselves; conversely, they also need education to maintain health and to reach a higher level of wellness. As the degree of education about health and wellness increases, the individual and family alike have greater opportunities to reach a higher level of wellness.

How can the members of a family fulfill their functions as wellness educators and wellness practitioners? One way is through self-study. Most general-interest magazines are valuable sources of information, with regularly appearing articles on health that are related in some way to wellness. Newspapers also frequently publish articles that discuss healthful nutrition, wellness practices, and ways to assess and promote more satisfying family life or other interpersonal relationships. Other articles deal with stress management. Several magazines, such as *Today's Health* and *Family Health,* deal solely with matters related to health. Some articles deal with promotion of wellness and not just with prevention of illness, so they are additional sources of information for the family interested in maintaining a high level of wellness.

Bookstores are replete with books, manuals, and other publications geared to the general public that touch on health and wellness. The author of a best-seller will often appear on popular talk shows to promote ideas and themes in the book. Commercial as well as public television networks broadcast informative shows that deal with different aspects of health. Ideally, television programming will continue to evolve from the illness or illness prevention approach to an approach that emphasizes and informs about wellness.

The federal government maintains a center for information on numerous consumer-oriented topics, including health. This center offers hundreds of free or low-priced publications to the consumer. Persons on the mailing list receive a catalog of these publications periodically. A copy of the catalog is available from the Consumer Information Center (Pueblo, CO 81009). Receiving the catalog results in regular mailings.

Community groups are gradually taking a more active role in promoting and providing information about wellness. It is not unusual to encounter health fairs, often sponsored by several groups working together and often held in a shopping center, that emphasize how to stay well as well as how to detect certain illnesses. Often literature is available for the taking. This type of communitywide emphasis allows many persons to be exposed to worthwhile information to assist them in decision making about health. Information is frequently provided about community agencies as resources that focus on wellness education in addition to providing illness-related services. Indeed, many community resources are expanding an illness-oriented service into one that includes wellness considerations. Prevention of illness and promotion of wellness are concepts that are coming into their own, so families are finding more and greater opportunities to learn about health and wellness.

Health programs are available in some communities through health departments, health-education centers, and other health organizations. A variety of topics are covered, pertaining to the wellness of the family and providing knowledge with which to make personal and family decisions about wellness. Topics include parenting, weight control, managing diabetes, and smoking cessation. Local media furnish health information and should be monitored regularly for topics of interest to family members. Parents who are informed about local health events and who participate in those appropriate to their interests and needs provide an important and lasting model for the lifelong well-being of themselves and their children. Health professionals should encourage and commend families who are actively involved in information-seeking activities and who make appropriate decisions for learning about themselves and wellness.

These sources of information should be critiqued and evaluated in terms of their applicability to one's own family life-style. Information should be shared with children in ways they are capable of understanding so that they can learn not only the wellness behaviors but the responsibility for seeking information and making decisions about matters that affect one's level of wellness.

Information Guidelines. In evaluating an item of health information the following guidelines can be used by the family to determine whether the information is worthwhile.

1. What is the purpose of the information item? Is its purpose to shed light on a controversial subject, to present new information, or to sell a product?
2. What information is contained in the item? Is it unfamiliar to the family or does it supplement current knowledge?
3. How is the information presented? Is the approach a rational one, or is the appeal primarily emotional? Does the item attempt to change a value on a blind-faith basis, or are arguments presented logically and sequentially?
4. Does the health item have relevance to wellness? Does the item promote wellness, and will following its advice or using its information enhance the wellness of the family?
5. Does the item stimulate interest in seeking further knowledge about wellness?
6. Can the information in the item be incorporated readily into the life-styles of family members without unnecessary or unreasonable financial investment?

Once these information sources have been evaluated, a home wellness reference library can be started, which could include newspaper clippings, magazine articles, health and wellness books, and magazines for future information and use. These information sources can be shared with extended family members and friends. Knowledge is to share, and it gives the recipient both the power and responsibility for personal decision making.

FAMILY ROLE IN PERSONAL WELLNESS

Families teach their members about many aspects of life. Values are acquired through living with others over the years, and these values in some way guide virtually all our actions. Therefore, each person needs to probe his personal philosophy of living, first to identify his philosophy of health, and second to determine how it affects wellness. Is one's philosophy of health and wellness consistent with life goals? Are health and wellness behaviors consistent with expressed personal philosophy? In working with individual family members, the nurse can offer a forum and sounding board. The nurse is a resource and is available to assist the family in evaluating the sources described. Goal clarification and goal direction are aspects of the nurse's role that form the basis for helping people learn behaviors that will help them reach their personal wellness goals.

Responsibility for wellness clearly belongs to the family and the individuals within it. The bottom line is what each person does in day-to-day life and the effect each behavior has on wellness. No amount of screening or physical examination procedures will make a person well, nor will any amount of teaching about wellness. What the person does with information gained from physical examinations or educational programs will affect his wellness. Our daily behaviors all affect our physical, mental-emotional, or environmental health in some way. Some behaviors promote wellness, while other behaviors promote illness.

Breslow and Belloc [1] have completed studies on the relationship between physical health status and individual health practices. Their findings provide direction for individual wellness and for family responsibility in adopting and teaching wellness behaviors. They found that life expectancy and better health are significantly related to a small number of simple basic health habits.

1. Eating three meals a day at regular times instead of snacking
2. Eating breakfast every day
3. Exercising moderately two or three times a week
4. Sleeping 7 or 8 hours each night
5. Refraining from smoking
6. Keeping weight moderate
7. Drinking no alcohol or in moderation

They found that a 45-year-old man who practices none to three of these habits can expect to live 21.6 more years to age 67, while a man of the same age with six to seven of these practices can expect to live 33.1 years longer to age 78 [1]. Longer life does not necessarily mean a well life, but a life shortened because of illnesses that could have been prevented completely or at least reduced in severity certainly is not a well life. Physical and emotional well-being are both necessary within an environment that promotes wellness. To promote length of life by adopting as part of one's life-style these seven simple habits will enhance mental as well as physical well-being. They evolve from the old axioms of good health: good nutrition, proper rest and exercise, and avoidance of substances known to be harmful to health. These seven health practices are a sound foundation for wellness of the individual. When they are practiced by parents, taught to children, and incorporated into the life-styles of all family members, the groundwork is laid for a family with a high level of wellness in its physical health dimension.

Promotion of Wellness in Family Members

Physical wellness involves more than incorporating the seven basic health practices into one's life. A system of wellness monitoring and illness detection should be developed for each member of the family. Because wellness characteristics and risk factors vary somewhat according to age and developmental stage, each monitoring program will be different. Some guidelines and criteria are presented here for each age category, including appropriate goals. The work of Breslow and Somers has been helpful in the development of these guidelines [3].

INFANCY (BIRTH TO 1 YEAR)
GOALS
1. To establish immunity against specific infectious diseases
2. To detect and prevent certain other diseases and problems before irreparable damage occurs
3. To promote optimal growth and development

Methods. Before discharge from the hospital after delivery, the infant should be screened for inherited metabolic disorders such as phenylketonuria (PKU). Parents should receive counseling in the areas of basic infant care, detection of signs of illness such as skin rashes and gastrointestinal disorders, accident prevention, and immunizations. Continuing supervision by a health professional should be arranged to provide immunizations and to assist with ongoing assessment of growth and development.

PRESCHOOL PERIOD (1-5 YEARS)
GOALS
1. To promote optimal physical, emotional, and social growth and development
2. To encourage development of self-care skills

Methods. Parents should be taught to be alert for accident hazards and common physical illnesses such as sore throats and ear infections, and to provide for and encourage good nutrition, adequate sleep and exercise, and dental practices. Visits to a health professional should be encouraged to complete primary and booster immunizations prior to school entry, and to screen for hearing and vision problems that may hinder the school experience.

With the proliferation of preschool educational and day-care programs, parents should be cognizant of any environment in which their child may be spending significant amounts of time. Light, heat, and the entire physical facility should be conducive to wellness, and the environment free from hazards that might cause accidents. Parents should be knowledgeable about the health philosophy of the care giver or teacher. Does this person require up-to-date immunizations for entry into the program? Does this person encourage parents to keep the child away from school when signs of illness appear? Does the nursery school teach and practice sound principles of health such as good nutrition, care of teeth, and exercise? If these components are not present in a preschool program, parents can work as catalysts and agents of change for an environment and an educational program that encourage and incorporate wellness practices to the fullest extent possible.

SCHOOL-AGE PERIOD (6–11 YEARS)

GOALS

1. To promote optimal growth and development
2. To continue development and refinement of self-care skills
3. To establish patterns of wellness behaviors for nutrition, exercise, sleep and rest, recreation, dental care, and learning

Methods. The leading cause of health problems in the school-age group is accidents; therefore, safety and accident prevention should be of prime concern. Parental expectations of children in this age group should include greater assumption of self-responsibility for health care in all areas as well as expression of a health philosophy that maximizes wellness. Parents can help to promote this climate by praising and rewarding positive health behaviors and by providing role models for their children.

To assist families in teaching wellness to children, a comprehensive mandatory school health-education program should be part of the school experience. Through involvement in parent-teacher groups, parents have the opportunity to influence the school health-education curriculum, which will benefit not only their child but the entire community. Influence can take the form of promoting, supporting, and contributing to the development of the school health program.

The school environment should concern parents of children in this age group. Assessment of the school environment requires periodic tours of the school facility and a continuing dialogue with other parents and school administrators to develop the school environment to promote physical and emotional wellness.

Children of school age begin to participate in organized sports. Although team and individual competition can provide both the means and motivation for physical and mental growth and development, risks for emotional and physical injury are present that can threaten the child's well-being. Parents should determine both the philosophy and the practices of personnel supervising these activities and assess their contributions to wellness of the child. If a sport encourages winning at all costs, with insufficient attention paid to prevention of injuries, the child should not be allowed to participate. Wellness in its holistic sense incorporates physical and mental well-being. Sports activities in school and community settings should encourage and practice this philosophy. If the sports activities do not characterize a wellness approach, parents and other interested citizens must assume an advocacy role to change the practices in sports for children.

ADOLESCENCE (12-17 YEARS)
GOALS
1. To continue optimal growth and development
2. To promote development of identity as an adult, with adult behavior patterns in work, study, nutrition, physical fitness and exercise, sexual relationships, rational decision making about use of drug substances, and preparation for marriage and parenthood
3. To reinforce systematic problem solving

Methods. Young people in this age category should be expected to assume nearly total responsibility for self-care of their bodies. Schools and families must continue to emphasize behaviors that promote wellness to counteract the many peer pressures to the contrary. At this age, children can assume some responsibility for food selection and meal preparation for the family. They should have a developing plan for physical fitness and development, and should have balanced patterns of sleep, study, and work. Youth should be knowledgeable about the sexually transmitted diseases—symptoms, treatment, and resources for care. They should be knowledgeable about contraceptives and where and how they are obtained. Through the school health-education curriculum and the home, they should have opportunities to discuss the physical and psychosocial aspects of sexuality in relation to their current stage of growth and development. They need information and decision-making skills with regard to caffeine, cigarettes, alcohol, and illicit drugs. Because of the high rate of automobile accidents in this age group, each adolescent driver should receive a comprehensive driver-education course, focusing on the physical and mental skills necessary for safe driving. A first-aid component should be part of an adolescent health program in either a driver-education course or the general health curriculum.

The nurse who is part of a school health program can help develop these areas of the curriculum. The nurse working with individual families can discuss all these areas with the family and the adolescent and guide the family members in the use of the many educational resources available. The nurse should encourage the parents of the adolescent to be actively involved in supporting, promoting, or developing the school health program.

YOUNG ADULTHOOD (18-30 YEARS)
GOALS

1. To promote the transition into adulthood
2. To promote optimal growth and development
3. To continue development of skills for career, marriage, and parenthood
4. To update immunizations
5. To screen for selected illness conditions

Methods. Wellness behaviors in earlier stages should be further developed and refined as an integral part of the adult life-style. Nutrition, rest, exercise, and recreation are continuing areas of importance in physical health. Tetanus boosters should be received if they haven't been obtained within the previous 10 years. Women should begin the practice of having annual cervical Pap smears if not already initiated due to sexual activity or childbearing. Monthly breast examination should be done by each woman, preferably at the same time each month, such as the week after her menstrual period or, if postmenopausal, then at a regular time such as the first of each month. A baseline blood pressure should also be obtained.

Career development, marriage, and parenthood are significant life tasks in this age group. Through health education and counseling, the nurse can guide the family member in the development of decision-making skills needed to accomplish these tasks in a well manner. By being involved in community activities, the nurse can promote development of health programs in the workplace as well as the establishment of community-based courses for marriage and parenting.

MIDDLE AGE (31-45 YEARS)
GOALS
1. To promote optimal growth and development
2. To anticipate and monitor development of chronic diseases
3. To prevent chronic diseases through a well-integrated, well life-style
4. To screen for selected illness conditions

Methods. Adults in this age group should practice a daily routine of wellness behaviors: good nutrition with calorie modifications as necessary to prevent obesity, regular exercise, moderate or no alcohol, adequate rest, and no smoking. Smokers in this age category should consider very carefully the long-term effects of this habit, with the damage it can cause to many organs. Adults should be screened regularly for diabetes and hypertension. Each adult in this age group should examine the entire body visually every month for lumps and changes in moles or warts. Women should examine breasts monthly, and men should manually examine their testes for the presence of lumps or other abnormalities. Early detection of cancerous lesions can in some cases improve treatment outcomes.

The nurse can counsel with regard to physical changes in aging persons and help them recognize the wellness aspects of this process, both in relation to their future lives and to the current lives of other family members such as parents.

OLDER MIDDLE AGE (46-60 YEARS)
GOALS
1. To promote optimal growth and development
2. To promote the well life-style of physical, mental, and social activity
3. To detect chronic diseases in the early stages

Methods. Older middle-age persons should continue their well life-style, incorporating nutrition and physical fitness as prime components. Adults of this age group can continue many of the physical and sports activities of their younger years and should be encouraged to do so. Again, some dietary modifications may be necessary to prevent excess weight gain. Physical screening checkups should be obtained for cancer, diabetes, heart disease, hypertension, and vision, as well as self-assessment measures such as breast examination. Some community groups as well as physicians provide these screening services, and adults should be encouraged to use what is available. Visual and tactile checks for lumps should continue on a monthly basis at home. The nurse should encourage periodic complete physical examinations.

OLD AGE (61-75 YEARS)
GOALS
1. To promote optimal growth and development
2. To adapt to physical changes of aging
3. To minimize physical effects of aging
4. To continue to develop goals for meaningful life

   Methods. In the old-age group, some of the chronic diseases are likely to appear. Nurses should encourage and assist these people as necessary in the maintenance of their maximal physical functioning. Screening for diabetes, hypertension, and cancer should continue. A well life-style may need to be modified to accommodate certain changes in physical ability or nutritional requirements. Use of alcohol, cigarettes, and caffeine should cease, and use of drugs for treatment of chronic conditions should be monitored carefully. Physical examinations should be performed as necessary to monitor any illness conditions. Older family members should be encouraged to work with their pharmacists to learn actions and side effects of any drugs being taken, as well as the possible synergistic or antagonistic drug interactions. The older person should be encouraged in the pursuit of wellness behaviors at this time of life, as well as in the younger years, to maximize the period of freedom from child care, employment, and the hustle-bustle and stresses associated with younger families.

ADVANCED OLD AGE (76 AND OLDER)
GOALS
1. To promote maximal growth and development
2. To encourage the continuing practice of a wellness life-style, incorporating physical limitations to the fullest extent possible

   Methods. Many physical infirmities and inconveniences become apparent at this time of life. With the counsel and help of the nurse and other health professionals, the person can stay as well as possible in all arenas of the physical dimension of health given the various adaptations that may be necessary and the various wellness behaviors that have been part of one's life. The nurse may need to assist the family in locating community resources to help maintain wellness, such as Meals-on-Wheels, sheltered care, group exercise classes, and recreational facilities for the elderly. The person should be helped to maintain wellness to the fullest extent possible at home. If and when institutional care becomes necessary, the nurse can help the family secure a facility that recognizes and focuses on the well aspects of the person and not just on the limitations.

Even when death becomes inevitable, the nurse and the family together can help the person continue as much self-care as possible, maintaining the physical and emotional dignity of one who has worked for a lifetime to achieve high-level wellness in all dimensions of living.

The Well Family and Consumerism

CONSUMER PROTECTION

Many individuals, as well as government and private agencies, protect families from fraudulent schemes and unfair selling practices by evaluating the effects of these practices. Information presented in order to sell products can be misleading. A "scientific halo" surrounds many sales pitches in order to give them an aura of authenticity. The family should be wary of persons other than qualified health professionals who claim they can cure or treat aches or assure wellness with a certain product, machine, or special treatment. There is no shortcut to cure major diseases such as cancer, arthritis, or diabetes. There are no miracle cures for overweight except proper dieting. It is impossible to fit false teeth and eyeglasses properly by mail orders.

If a family believes these "health pitchmen" and tries their gimmicks, the condition may worsen. Consumers who try gimmicks often delay seeing a physician about a particular problem. Because there is such faith in these claims, many individuals lose money and even lives. Americans spend many dollars each year on phony cures and "quack" panaceas. Advertising gimmicks lead to self-medication and self-diagnosis. Home cures and folk medicines can complicate the existing problems and also cause delay in seeking medical help. If pain and discomfort are persistent and if symptoms are unusual, medical help should be sought immediately.

Spontaneous remission of symptoms tends to complicate matters more in that the individual assumes the "cure" was a result of the quack treatment. Arthritis victims are particularly prone to spontaneous remissions and therefore are very susceptible to quack treatment. It is recommended that family members check the credentials and reputation of practitioners with their nurse, family physician, and/or consumer-protection agencies. Qualified medical professionals do not canvas the neighborhood for patients.

The *West Virginia Consumer Handbook for Senior Citizens* has identified six clues to assist the consumer in identifying the quack [6, pp. 127-128].

1. Quacks use other people who claim complete cure by the quack's methods, which are not orthodox methods of treatment such as surgery or x-rays.

2. Quacks insist that such conventional methods will not help.
3. They promise a quick "miracle" cure.
4. They may use a secret medicine or machine that only they have.
5. They say they want their medicine or machine investigated by the medical profession because they are sure it is everything they claim.
6. Finally, they claim that the medical profession is persecuting them because it is afraid it will lose patients to them.

If a family has been a victim of fraud or if the family wishes to prevent this occurrence, a family member should write or call the appropriate protective agency. Many agencies exist for this purpose, such as the Postmaster General, the Food and Drug Administration, and Consumer Product Safety Commission, or the local chapter of the Better Business Bureau.

THE WELL FAMILY AND HEALTH PROFESSIONALS

Promotion and maintenance of wellness often involve various health professionals, including the nurse. Families want to trust their health professionals and to know that their relationship with the professional is a partnership in wellness. For some health professionals, however, an illness philosophy is more familiar than a wellness philosophy. Health professionals can learn from well families that wellness is *the* goal in health care. It is possible, with guidance from a nurse who espouses a wellness and consumer-oriented philosophy, to seek health professionals who are willing to be partners with the family in seeking higher levels of wellness.

The family should engage the services of a health professional only after making a fair judgment of credentials, fees for service, and personal characteristics. Whether the family is seeking services from a physician, dentist, nurse, pharmacist, dietitian, or physical therapist, the nurse should urge the family to develop a mental list of what the family expects from the health professional. Consumers of health care are within their rights to hold any and all health professionals accountable for the quality of services rendered. Families should expect and receive high-quality services that help them maintain or achieve wellness.

Consumer organizations are educating the public on how to select health professionals, particularly physicians and dentists. For example, since the Washington, D.C. directory *Taking the Pain Out of Finding a Good Dentist* was published, many other cities have planned similar surveys. The state of Connecticut issued its own *Consumer's Guide to Dentistry* in 1974 [4, p. 67].

In recognition of consumer rights and in the interest of "more effective patient care and greater satisfaction for the patient, his physician, and the hospital organization," the American Hospital Association has adopted a "Patient's Bill of Rights" as a national policy statement. It declares that the hospital's functions should all be conducted with an overriding concern for patients as well as recognition of their dignity as human beings. This document speaks to patients' rights to continuity of care, information from the physician to give informed consent prior to procedures, explanation of fees, information regarding hospital rules, and the right to respectful care as well as the right to refuse care [2, p. 218]. The family should know these rights as consumers, and the nurse should help family members become familiar with this document.

To become well-informed consumers of health services, the family should become familiar with health care terms and the variety of services provided by the various health professionals. The nurse can recommend sources of printed information that the family can use in a program of self-study. The nurse can further discuss with the family the specifics with which they may be unfamiliar.

A topic of great concern to families as consumers is the cost of health services. The family should be willing to ask for a breakdown of items on the financial statement. Popular magazines such as *Reader's Digest* and *Consumer Reports* publish articles that are helpful to the consumer in evaluating medical and dental care and fees charged for services. The American Dental Association also publishes a fee survey of average fees for common dental procedures and treatments in the United States [4, p. 63]. The family may also choose to join a consumer's group that compiles useful information for other consumers. One such group is a unit of Ralph Nader's Public Citizen, Inc., the Health Research Group. In 1974 this group produced a directory of Washington, D.C. dentists and their fees for common procedures [4, p. 65]. The family should be wary of the attitude that the cheapest dentist, physician, or other health professional is the wisest choice.

Just how is the bill for professional services determined? The health professional has paid large sums of money for education, an office, and equipment, including a high overhead of rent, utilities, personnel and supplies, insurances and taxes. The consumer's awareness can also be a factor in establishing fees. Sometimes the consumer's decisions and knowledge can assist the professional in utilizing common sense in choosing treatment and, therefore, possibly reducing costs. Consumers who feel they have been wronged, however, should be encouraged to speak to the professional about the bill. It could be a simple error in bookkeeping that causes a misunderstanding in the relationship. If the family feels they have been wrongly charged and cannot reach an agreement after discussing the bill with the professional, other avenues exist for retribution. There are various federal laws that must be observed by the professional. A few of these are Guides Against Debt Collection Deception, the Federal Communications Commission's Public Notice on Use of Telephone for Debt Collection Purposes, and Fair Credit Reporting Act. These laws protect the consumer against misrepresentation and invasion of privacy, and provide a fair chance to check unreasonable denials of credit. If, after exhausting other avenues the family continues to be dissatisfied, the professional can be reported to his local accrediting group, which sets standards for his practice. Finally, if other avenues fail, an attorney can be consulted [4, pp. 83-84].

The nurse should advise the family to choose a health professional with personal characteristics and wellness philosophy that are harmonious with their own and with whom a partnership relationship can be developed. These considerations facilitate the interchange of ideas and questions. The professional office also has its own personality. It may be cold and too businesslike, or attractive, pleasing, and relaxing for the family. The family should feel at ease and comfortable in the professional's office; this helps dispel anxiety, which may interfere with optimal use of the professional's services. The consumer is entitled to seek more than one opinion. The health professional may refer the family to another specialist on his own initiative or at the request of the family. This referral does not constitute an admission of incompetence but rather a desire to help the family member make well-informed decisions. It means that he recognizes his own capabilities and is concerned about the total wellness of the family.

THE WELL FAMILY AND THE DENTIST

Each family member is entitled to a thorough examination of the teeth, gums, and mouth. X-rays are generally used as a diagnostic tool. Most consumers know little about the range of fees for dental examinations or dental procedures, particularly when moving into a new community. Therefore, many neglect treatment for fear of paying an enormous bill. The same consumer may know the price range of a gallon of milk in several different brand names. The consumer should, however, understand that there is a natural fluctuation in fees based on the location of the professional—whether rural or urban, and also from city to city. The family should ask the local dental society about the range of services and fees that exist in the community so they may know what to expect from the professional selected.

The family should realize that a dentist should not decide too quickly to extract teeth. The *Pennsylvania Insurance Department Guide* reports that probably 6 million teeth are removed each year that should have been saved through other treatment [4, p. 14]. There are "extraction mills" that make little effort to save natural teeth. They may even promise cures for ailments such as diabetes and arthritis as the "bad" teeth are removed. The dentist who recommends extraction should be questioned carefully by the family member regarding the rationale and any other alternatives. The family member can seek consultation from another dentist.

The family should look for a dental professional who is prevention and wellness oriented, and who seeks continuing education experiences for himself and his associates. The wellness-oriented dentist practices holistic dentistry, viewing the person as a whole, not an isolated problem. The dentist should stress proper diet, rest, and exercise. The dental professional should teach each family member how to brush teeth properly, how to use disclosing tablets, and how to use dental floss. The family should ask the dentist about mouthwashes, appropriate toothbrushes, fluoride treatments, and oral hygiene appliances.

THE WELL FAMILY AND THE PHYSICIAN

Choosing a physician can be a consumer dilemma for the well family. The family needs to consider: Do we want a physician in a group practice or a solo practice?

Group practices have become very popular. Professionals have found that they can save money on expenses and offer more to the client with this type of practice. Another advantage to this system is increased accountability of each professional with peers constantly looking over his shoulder. In this system the client can also receive a variety of specialty services under one roof.

What are the physician's credentials? Is he board certified? Is he a specialist? Does his specialty meet the needs of the family member? Is his license up-to-date? The *American Medical Association Directory* will indicate membership in local medical society, American Medical Association, board specialties, and fellowships such as the American College of Surgeons and the American College of Physicians. The family should not hesitate to check on the physician's credentials.

The family should consider a checklist of questions in selecting a physician. Does the physician attend continuing education programs? Does he have a joint appointment on a medical center staff or a teaching institution staff? With what inpatient facilities is he affiliated? Are these institutions licensed and accredited by the appropriate bodies? Is the physician taking new patients? When a physician has overextended his practice and is no longer able to give adequate care to all clients, he may stop taking new patients for a limited period of time. A family member who so wishes may request that his name be placed on a waiting list to be called when the physician is able to see him.

Of great importance to the well family are the helping qualities of the relationship with the health professional, whether physician, nurse, dentist, or other. Does the professional demonstrate a warm, caring, sincere attitude toward clients? The ability to develop this type of helping relationship with the client and his family is an important quality that will help the family to develop a sense of partnership in their health care. The ability to communicate with and to understand the physician is also important to the well family. Does the physician use direct eye contact when speaking to the family member? Does he consider other family members when caring for one? Does he answer questions in an unhurried and understandable manner? Does he convey in his demeanor the sense that questions are welcome, that the family members have a right to information and therefore it should be freely given?

These qualities in a physician or other health professional promote the full development of a rich and effective helping relationship. This sense of partnership between the family and the health professional encourages the assumption of self-responsibility, which is the sine qua non for the continuing and comprehensive health care of the family. Whenever possible, the family should seek the services of health professionals who, through the helping relationship, demonstrate the belief in self-responsibility of the family.

THE WELL FAMILY AND THE PHARMACIST

Drug products are commonplace in most homes. Many well families frequently use over-the-counter and other drug-related products in the maintenance and promotion of wellness as well as in the treatment of illness. We are avid consumers of health products. At those times when a family member becomes ill, drugs are often prescribed as part of the treatment plan. The pharmacist who dispenses prescription drugs is a valuable source of information that the family can use in becoming well-informed consumers. The family should be encouraged to ask the pharmacist about the actions and potential side effects of each drug and any particulars about taking the medication. The family should be well informed about each drug or health product used by a family member.

The pharmacist can assist the well family with the selection of nonprescription medications and health-related products. With so many products available on the market, it is extremely difficult for any consumer to acquire all the information about each product necessary to make an informed choice. Pharmacists have a great deal of information at their disposal about the merits and disadvantages of many of these products. Their advice and counsel should be sought whenever the family has information only for the trial-and-error approach.

THE WELL FAMILY AND HEALTH-CARE SPECIALISTS

Just what is a specialist? This term usually means that a health professional is limited to one particular area of practice, but it is becoming more and more difficult for physicians and dentists to proclaim themselves specialists. There is a trend toward specializing, and there are more and more stringent requirements such as additional education and national board accreditation. These strict requirements may indicate a tight union to keep competition down, which in turn means increased prices for the consumer. There is no guarantee to the consumer that the board-qualified person is more competent than one who is not board certified; generally, however, the board-certified person has more experience and education.

The well family who want to become wise consumers need to know what type of health worker can be more useful for various needs. Following is a list of commonly recognized dental specialty "-dontias" recognized by the American Dental Association [4].

Orthodontia—straightening teeth
Pedodontia—children's dentistry
Endodontia—root canal therapy (diseases of the pulp)
Periodontia—disease of gums and supporting structures of the teeth
Exodontia—oral surgery
Prosthodontia—construction of special appliances to provide mechanically for
    such deficiencies as a cleft palate; artificial tooth construction [4, p. 126]

Dental specialities include

Dental Public Health—the aspect of public health that deals with dentists and
    dental health

Oral Surgery—surgical treatment and repair of teeth involving cutting into the jawbone

Oral Pathology—treatment of the essential nature of dental disease through the study of structural and functional changes in tissue and organs of the oral cavity

Medical specialists include [7]

Allergist—one who is concerned with sensitivities to allergens

Anesthesiologist—one who administers anesthetics

Cardiologist—heart specialist

Dermatologist—skin specialist

Endocrinologist—one who deals with the endocrines or ductless glands and their functions

Gastroenterologist—one who deals with pathology of the stomach and intestines

Gerontologist—a specialist in the science of old age

Gynecologist—one who deals with the female organs and their functions

Internist—one who treats internal disease, not a surgeon

Neurologist—a specialist in diseases of the nervous system

Neurosurgeon—a specialist who does surgery on the nervous system

Obstetrician—one who treats women during pregnancy

Ophthalmologist—a specialist in the treatment of eye disorders (sometimes referred to as an oculist)

Orthopedic surgeon—a specialist dealing with locomotor structures such as the skeleton, joints, and muscles

Otolaryngologist—a specialist in diseases of the ear, nose, and throat

Otologist—a specialist in ear diseases

Otorhinolaryngologist—a specialist in diseases of the ear, nose, and larynx

Pathologist—a specialist diagnosing morbid changes in tissues removed at operations and postmortem exams

Pediatrician—a specialist who treats children

Plastic surgeon—a specialist who deals with the restoration and repair of external physical defects by use of grafts of bone or tissues

Proctologist—one who specializes in diseases of the rectum and anus

Psychiatrist—one who specializes in the treatment of mental disorders

Radiologist—one who practices diagnosis and treatment by radiant energy

Rhinologist—a specialist in diseases of the nose

Surgeon—a medical practitioner who specializes in surgery

Urologist—one who specializes in disease of the urinary and genitourinary tract

Osteopath—one who is licensed to practice medicine and surgery, including some elements of manipulative therapy; today generally recognized as having training comparable to the medical general practitioner

Other health-care specialists include [7]

Chiropractor—one who manipulates spinal vertebrae to promote healing

Optician—one who is skilled in grinding lenses according to prescription

Optometrist—one who is licensed to measure visual acuity, to prescribe glasses, and to perform other nonmedical procedures (sometimes called an oculist)

Orthoptist—a technician trained to correct defects of ocular muscles through eye exercises and visual training as prescribed by the oculist

Psychologist—one who treats the mind

The Well Family and Financing Health Care

Nurses as part of the health-care system are often the closest persons to whom the client can turn, so it is important for nurses to have background information on methods of payment for health services. Nurses can thus answer the family's questions and help the family choose the appropriate method of payment. Obviously, there is a link between clients' optimal level of functioning and the type of protection and coverage chosen.

Personal payment with fee-for-service has been the major mechanism for financing health care in the United States. As third-party payments become more widespread, it is essential for nurses to understand how health-care financing affects the family. Charity, industry-supported health care, voluntary insurance, and public insurance are other methods of financing health care in America. Usually, all of these are seen in varying degrees in various countries.

Medicare represents our form of public health insurance, which gains its support through general tax revenues. Medicare is a result of a 1966 amendment to the Social Security Act. This form of insurance removed financial barriers to medical care for all persons aged 65 and over and for certain disabled persons under age 65. This federal program is designed to protect these people from catastrophic debts incurred by chronic illness.

It should be noted that nearly all existing financing mechanisms are geared toward medical care for the treatment of illness rather than maintenance of wellness. Now, however, there are more and more health-maintenance, employer-sponsored plans, such as the Health Insurance Plan of Greater New York and the Kaiser-Permanente Health Plan, which provide comprehensive health service through comprehensive group practice. These plans focus on prevention and wellness promotion as well as on treatment of illness. It may be hoped that health care in America will turn toward systems that value and promote wellness.

The health maintenance organization (HMO) movement is one of the leading proposals in the development of a national health insurance system, which encompasses both a system of care and a system for payment. The government seized on this idea as a possible answer to the rising costs of health care. The HMO movement is spreading, involving a variety of sponsors—private organizations, insurance companies, labor unions, consumer groups, and government groups.

The HMO concept is a prepaid insurance program in which the consumer pays a set monthly or yearly fee. This fee remains the same regardless of the type or amount of service rendered. Coverage includes comprehensive health care and emphasizes preventive health care. These organizations believe that it is less expensive to keep people well by prevention and early treatment than to rehabilitate them after disease has stricken them. In many HMOs, educational efforts are part of the system of health care, with the goal of teaching families how to stay well and seek early treatment if illness occurs. Not only can dollars thus be saved, but wellness and self-responsibility for wellness are encouraged.

The Nurse's Role in Family Self-Responsibility

Advocacy and accountability describe the nurse's responsibility to the family. For example, at the community level the nurse can encourage informative labeling and the posting of drug prices so that consumers can buy competitively. In working with individual clients, the nurse can assist the family in recognizing and interpreting side effects of drugs, sharing information with the physician, and questioning the pharmacist about drugs. The nurse can have input into the drafting of health insurance legislation, so that the client can be reimbursed for care and can have a choice in seeking care. Furthermore, the nurse is obligated to teach the family wellness behaviors so the health-care system is utilized for prevention and health maintenance rather than only for illness needs. Finally, the nurse must encourage a healthy environment for all people in the community [5].

The nurse can provide information relative to the client's specific health needs, ascertain the client's understanding of the information, and then support the client's decision. The acceptance of the client's decision may be most difficult, in that the nurse may feel that the client's decision may not be in his best interest. The client should completely understand any treatment plan and what this plan means to his personal life-style. Although the ultimate responsibility for wellness lies with the family, the nurse is an important resource in helping the family develop and refine self-help skills, and in espousing a philosophy of wellness from which these skills, behaviors, and self-responsibility arise.

References

1. Belloc, N. B., and Breslow, L. Relationship of physical health status and health practices. *Prev. Med.* 1:409, 1972.
2. Benson, E. R., and McDevitt, J. O. *Community Health and Nursing Practice.* Englewood Cliffs, N.J.: Prentice-Hall, 1976.
3. Breslow, L., and Somers, A. R. The lifetime health monitoring program. *N. Engl. J. Med.* 296:601, 1977.
4. Denholtz, M., and Denholtz, E. *How to Save Your Teeth and Your Money.* New York: Van Nostrand Reinhold, 1977.
5. Kohnke, M. F. Nurse's responsibility to the consumer. *Am. J. Nurs.* 78:440, 1978.
6. Schaupp, D., and Schaupp, F. *West Virginia Consumer Handbook for Senior Citizens.* Morgantown: West Virginia University, 1975.
7. Taber, C. W. *Taber's Cyclopedic Medical Dictionary* (13th ed.). Philadelphia: Davis, 1977.

Assessment Tool

The nurse should indicate for each item whether the family or family member accomplishes the item according to criteria indicated in the columns. If an item or section does not apply, the points represented by that item or section should be so indicated by marking the "not applicable" column. In scoring at the end of each section, the category "total points possible" means the total number of points that could be attained if every item applied. The "total not applicable" category shows the total points for items or sections that do not apply to the family at this time; this number should be subtracted from the "total points possible" to obtain the "total applicable" score. When comparing "total applicable" with the "total points attained," the nurse and the family can see the numerical difference in what should or could be achieved and what does exist at the present time. Scores in each section should be transferred to the summary section at the end of the chapter's assessment tool.

	Yes (2 pts)	No (0 pt)	Not applicable
I. Family Role in Education for Wellness			
A. Family can state sources of information about wellness			
1. Magazines	_____	_____	_____
2. Books	_____	_____	_____
3. Television, radio	_____	_____	_____
4. Newspapers	_____	_____	_____
5. Federal government publications	_____	_____	_____
6. Community group activities	_____	_____	_____
7. Community-based classes	_____	_____	_____
8. Agency services	_____	_____	_____
B. Family can state criteria for evaluating health information			
1. Purpose of information	_____	_____	_____
2. Content of information	_____	_____	_____
3. Method of presentation	_____	_____	_____
4. Relevance to wellness	_____	_____	_____
5. Promotion of further knowledge	_____	_____	_____
6. Feasibility of incorporation into life-style	_____	_____	_____
C. Family has wellness resource materials readily available in the home	_____	_____	_____
Total points possible			_30_
Total not applicable			_____
Total applicable			_____
Total points attained			_____
II. Family Role in Personal Wellness			
A. Family states philosophy of wellness	_____	_____	_____
B. Family states how philosophy of wellness affects state of wellness	_____	_____	_____

	Yes (2 pts)	No (0 pt)	Not applicable
C. Family's wellness behaviors are consistent with expressed philosophy	——	——	——
D. Each adult family member practices physical wellness behaviors			
1. Eats three meals a day at regular times	——	——	——
2. Eats breakfast every day	——	——	——
3. Exercises a minimum of two to three times a week	——	——	——
4. Sleeps 7 or 8 hours each night	——	——	——
5. Abstains from smoking	——	——	——
6. Maintains moderate weight	——	——	——
7. Abstains from alcohol or drinks in moderation	——	——	——
Total points possible			<u>20</u>
Total not applicable			——
Total applicable			——
Total points attained			——

III. Promotion of Wellness in Family Members

  A. Infancy

	Yes (2 pts)	No (0 pt)	Not applicable
1. Infant screened for inherited metabolic disorders	——	——	——
2. Family counseled in basic infant care, illness detection, accident prevention, and immunizations	——	——	——
3. Ongoing health supervision arranged for immunizations and growth and developmental assessment	——	——	——
Total points possible			<u>6</u>
Total not applicable			——
Total applicable			——
Total points attained			——

  B. Preschool

	Yes (2 pts)	No (0 pt)	Not applicable
1. Parents are aware of accident hazards	——	——	——
2. Parents are aware of common physical illnesses	——	——	——
3. Parents provide for and encourage			
a. Good nutrition	——	——	——
b. Adequate sleep	——	——	——
c. Adequate exercise	——	——	——
d. Dental wellness practice	——	——	——
4. Parents provide for ongoing health supervision	——	——	——
5. Immunizations completed prior to school entry	——	——	——

	Yes (2 pts)	No (0 pt)	Not applicable
6. Vision and hearing screening prior to school entry	_____	_____	_____
7. Preschool facility has wellness characteristics			
a. Proper light	_____	_____	_____
b. Adequate heating and cooling	_____	_____	_____
c. Freedom from accident hazards	_____	_____	_____
8. Preschool care giver has philosophy consistent with wellness	_____	_____	_____
9. Preschool care giver teaches wellness practices	_____	_____	_____

Total points possible	_28_
Total not applicable	_____
Total applicable	_____
Total points attained	_____

C. School Age

	Yes (2 pts)	No (0 pt)	Not applicable
1. Family teaches safety and accident prevention	_____	_____	_____
2. Child demonstrates safe behaviors in play and daily activities	_____	_____	_____
3. Child demonstrates increasing responsibility for self-care	_____	_____	_____
4. School has comprehensive health-education program	_____	_____	_____
5. Parents actively involved in supporting, promoting, or developing school health program	_____	_____	_____
6. Parents assess school health environment for wellness characteristics	_____	_____	_____
7. School sports programs promote mental and physical wellness	_____	_____	_____

Total points possible	_14_
Total not applicable	_____
Total applicable	_____
Total points attained	_____

D. Adolescence

	Yes (2 pts)	No (0 pt)	Not applicable
1. Child assumes nearly total responsibility for self-care	_____	_____	_____
2. Child is actively involved in physical fitness program	_____	_____	_____
3. Child states facts about sexually transmitted diseases	_____	_____	_____
4. Child states facts about contraceptive methods and where to obtain them	_____	_____	_____

	Yes (2 pts)	No (0 pt)	Not applicable
5. Child discusses aspects of personal sexual development	———	———	———
6. Child states facts about alcohol and other drugs	———	———	———
7. Child states personal philosophy about use of drug substances	———	———	———
8. Child completes driver education course	———	———	———
9. Child demonstrates first-aid skills	———	———	———
10. Child demonstrates problem-solving skills	———	———	———
11. Parents are actively involved in supporting, promoting, or developing school health program	———	———	*22*
Total points possible			
Total not applicable			———
Total applicable			———
Total points attained			———

E. Young Adulthood

	Yes (2 pts)	No (0 pt)	Not applicable
1. Assumes total responsibility for self-care	———	———	———
2. Reviews and updates immunization status	———	———	———
3. If woman, obtains annual Pap smear	———	———	———
4. Woman examines breasts monthly	———	———	———
5. Obtains and records baseline blood pressure	———	———	———
6. Develops decision-making skills for career, marriage, and parenthood	———	———	*12*
Total points possible			
Total not applicable			———
Total applicable			———
Total points attained			———

F. Middle Age

	Yes (2 pts)	No (0 pt)	Not applicable
1. Modifies nutrition practices as necessary according to caloric needs	———	———	———
2. Obtains screening for diabetes	———	———	———
3. Obtains screening for hypertension	———	———	———
4. Obtains screening for glaucoma	———	———	———

	Yes (2 pts)	No (0 pt)	Not applicable
5. Performs visual inspection of body monthly for lumps and changes in moles	_____	_____	_____
6. Man manually examines testes monthly	_____	_____	_____
Total points possible			_12_
Total not applicable			_____
Total applicable			_____
Total points attained			_____

G. Older Middle Age

	Yes (2 pts)	No (0 pt)	Not applicable
1. Maintains good nutritional practices	_____	_____	_____
2. Maintains physical exercise program	_____	_____	_____
3. Performs regular visual inspection of body for lumps and changes in moles	_____	_____	_____
4. Obtains screening for diabetes	_____	_____	_____
5. Obtains screening for hypertension	_____	_____	_____
6. Obtains vision screening	_____	_____	_____
7. Obtains complete physical examination periodically	_____	_____	_____
8. Obtains annual Pap smear	_____	_____	_____
9. Identifies normal changes due to aging and adapts accordingly	_____	_____	_____
Total points possible			_18_
Total not applicable			_____
Total applicable			_____
Total points attained			_____

H. Old Age

	Yes (2 pts)	No (0 pt)	Not applicable
1. Maintains good nutritional practice	_____	_____	_____
2. Maintains physical exercise program	_____	_____	_____
3. Monitors drugs according to actions and side effects	_____	_____	_____
4. Obtains screening for diabetes	_____	_____	_____
5. Obtains screening for hypertension	_____	_____	_____
6. Obtains screening for glaucoma	_____	_____	_____
7. Performs self-screening for cancer	_____	_____	_____

	Yes (2 pts)	No (0 pt)	Not applicable
8. Obtains physical exams as necessary	___	___	___
Total points possible			_16_
Total not applicable			___
Total applicable			___
Total points attained			___

I. Advanced Old Age
   1. Maintains wellness behavior as developed through life
   2. Identifies community resources as necessary
   3. If necessary, selects an extended-care facility that promotes wellness to the fullest extent possible

	Yes (2 pts)	No (0 pt)	Not applicable
1. Maintains wellness behavior as developed through life	___	___	___
2. Identifies community resources as necessary	___	___	___
3. If necessary, selects an extended-care facility that promotes wellness to the fullest extent possible	___	___	___
Total points possible			_6_
Total not applicable			___
Total applicable			___
Total points attained			___

IV. Consumer Protection

	Yes (2 pts)	No (0 pt)	Not applicable
A. Family can state purposes of fraudulent advertising/practices	___	___	___
B. Family can state pitfalls of fraudulent advertising/practices	___	___	___
C. Family can state characteristics of fraudulent advertising/practices	___	___	___
D. Family can name and state the purpose of appropriate protective agencies	___	___	___
Total points possible			_8_
Total not applicable			___
Total applicable			___
Total points attained			___

V. The Well Family and Health Professionals

	Yes (2 pts)	No (0 pt)	Not applicable
A. Evaluates credentials of potential health-care providers	___	___	
B States what is expected from a health professional	___	___	_
C. States knowledge of local consumer guides (if available) for selection of health professionals	___	___	
D. States components of "Patient's Bill of Rights"	___	___	___

	Yes (2 pts)	No (0 pt)	Not applicable
E. States knowledge of health-care terms and services provided by various professionals	——	——	——
F. States sources of information about health professionals' fees	——	——	——
G. States avenues of recourse if wrongly charged for services	——	——	——
H. Considers personal characteristics and wellness attitude when choosing health professional	——	——	——
I. States willingness to seek opinion of other health professionals	——	——	——
Total points possible			*18*
Total not applicable			——
Total applicable			——
Total points attained			——

VI. The Well Family and the Dentist

	Yes (2 pts)	No (0 pt)	Not applicable
A. States usual professional fees for dental services	——	——	——
B. States local dental society as information resource for fees and services	——	——	——
C. Questions rationale for any extraction and asks about available alternatives	——	——	——
D. Seeks dentist who is wellness and prevention oriented	——	——	——
E. Seeks dentist who teaches all aspects of proper care of teeth to each family member	——	——	——
F. Seeks information about products and appliances for oral hygiene	——	——	——
Total points possible			*12*
Total not applicable			——
Total applicable			——
Total points attained			——

VII. The Well Family and the Physician

	Yes (2 pts)	No (0 pt)	Not applicable
A. Considers system of practice (group or solo)	——	——	——
B. Seeks physician who is adequately and appropriately credentialed	——	——	——
C. Seeks physician who participates in continuing education activities	——	——	——
D. Selects physician who is associated with accredited hospital	——	——	——

	Yes (2 pts)	No (0 pt)	Not applicable
E. Selects physician with skills in promoting a helping relationship	____	____	____
Total points possible			*10*
Total not applicable			____
Total applicable			____
Total points attained			____

VIII. The Well Family and the Pharmacist
    A. Seeks information on prescription and nonprescription drugs from the pharmacist
    B. States actions and side effects of every prescription or nonprescription drug in the household
    C. Seeks information on health-care products from the pharmacist

	Yes (2 pts)	No (0 pt)	Not applicable
A.	____	____	____
B.	____	____	____
C.	____	____	____
Total points possible			*6*
Total not applicable			____
Total applicable			____
Total points attained			____

IX. The Well Family and Health-Care Specialists
    A. States knowledge of roles of various dental specialists
    B. States knowledge of roles of various medical specialists
    C. States knowledge of roles of other health-care providers

	Yes (2 pts)	No (0 pt)	Not applicable
A.	____	____	____
B.	____	____	____
C.	____	____	____
Total points possible			*6*
Total not applicable			____
Total applicable			____
Total points attained			____

X. The Well Family and Financing Health Care
    A. States components of various methods of financing health care
        1. Fee-for-service
        2. Third-party payment
        3. Industry-supported
        4. Voluntary insurance
        5. Public insurance (Medicare)
    B. States components of HMOs as alternative system of health care

	Yes (2 pts)	No (0 pt)	Not applicable
1.	____	____	____
2.	____	____	____
3.	____	____	____
4.	____	____	____
5.	____	____	____
B.	____	____	____
Total points possible			*12*
Total not applicable			____
Total applicable			____
Total points attained			____

Assessment Tool Summary

	Subtotal points possible	Subtotal not applicable	Subtotal applicable	Subtotal points attained
I. Family Role in Education for Wellness	30	___	___	___
II. Family Role in Personal Wellness	20	___	___	___
III. Promotion of Wellness in Family Members				
A. Infancy	6	___	___	___
B. Preschool	28	___	___	___
C. School Age	14	___	___	___
D. Adolescence	22	___	___	___
E. Young Adulthood	12	___	___	___
F. Middle Age	12	___	___	___
G. Older Middle Age	18	___	___	___
H. Old Age	16	___	___	___
I. Advanced Old Age	6	___	___	___
IV. Consumer Protection	8	___	___	___
V. The Well Family and Health Professionals	18	___	___	___
VI. The Well Family and the Dentist	12	___	___	___
VII. The Well Family and the Physician	10	___	___	___
VIII. The Well Family and the Pharmacist	6	___	___	___
IX. The Well Family and Health-Care Specialists	6	___	___	___
X. The Well Family and Financing Health Care	12	___	___	

Total points possible   256

Total not applicable   ___

Total applicable   ___

Total points attained   ___

FOUR

Psychosocial Development and Mental Wellness Throughout the Life Cycle

A comprehensive approach to health and wellness requires attention to the concept of mental wellness and what it means to the full development of each family member. Holism requires examination of those facets of family life that promote and nurture the lifelong development of mental wellness. As family members grow and develop within the family unit, so does the capacity for high-level mental wellness. The intrapersonal and interpersonal psychosocial skills learned throughout the life cycle serve as salient points of reference for seeing *how* the family can promote mental wellness.

The family occupies an important role in promoting mental wellness. Westley and Epstein [29] assert that the personality of the individual is to an important extent a reflection of the organization and relationships of the family in which he grows. A family system that is characterized by wellness tends to be composed of and to produce persons who are mentally well. The specific family factors were addressed in Chapter 2.

The cyclic nature of mental wellness is both characteristic and important. Westley and Epstein found that the root of mental wellness in children was a good emotional relationship between the parents. In families in which the father and mother have a warm, constructive relationship in which each partner feels loved and admired and is able to encourage a positive self-image in the other, children tend to be happy and emotionally healthy. Emotionally well children then have the potential to become mentally well adults who will begin another generation of mentally well persons. How this mental wellness develops is in large part related to the psychosocial development of each person.

The family's critical role in the development of competent adults who exhibit qualities of the highest levels of mental wellness cannot be emphasized enough. Infants do not grow through childhood into adulthood simply by unfolding their genetic endowment. As Lidz has pointed out [16], children require prolonged nurturing care, direction, and delimitation of their vast potential to develop into mentally well, integrated individuals capable of living in society. Early stages of the life cycle that all later development depends on transpire within the family network. Whether the developmental stages evolve favorably or unfavorably depends on how the parents guide the child through them.

How does one come to define positive mental wellness? The possibility of confusion exists with terms such as mental health, mental illness, and emotional health, which are commonly used. Mental wellness is the affective correlate of physical wellness and is characterized by the family member accomplishing the psychosocial tasks for his age and stage of development with a pervasive feeling state of happiness and contentment with his life. Maslow [17] referred to actualization of "inner inherent nature and potentials." Jahoda [11,12] described emotional health as an "active adjustment or attempt at mastery of his environment as distinct both from his inability to adjust and from his indiscriminate acceptance of environmental conditions." Freud said that a person should be able to love and work well in order to be healthy. Many years ago, Menninger [18] defined mental health as the adjustment of human beings to the world and each other with a maximum of effectiveness and happiness.

These descriptions of mental, emotional, or psychosocial health are part of what it means for family members to achieve mental wellness. Consistent with age and developmental stage, mentally well persons successfully achieve the appropriate psychosocial development tasks. They have a trust of themselves and their world and a clear sense of identity. They develop enriching relationships with family and peers. Physical development and physiologic status can promote mental wellness, but they need not hinder it. Mentally well people feel comfortable about themselves, feel right about other people, and are able to meet the demands of their lives at any point in time [19]. They experience a range of emotions and feel enriched and not overwhelmed by them.

Mentally well people have a sense of high morale and spirit that assists them in being active, expressive, and effective in their behavior. Jourard [13] asserts that high-level wellness ensues from having one's individuality respected and acknowledged, being heard and touched by others who care, and being the recipient of love from another. Actualization of potentialities for "inspired" performance of life's activities becomes possible for those who have a high level of spirit.

Achievement of a high level of mental wellness implies that an individual's basic needs are met consistently, that he has a positive self-concept and is able to assume responsibility for his actions to the extent permitted by his age and stage of development. It implies that he is able to cope effectively with stress—that is, the life events that give purpose and meaning to daily living and that are necessary for both survival and lifelong growth.

Stress is a concept with which most health-care practitioners and lay persons are familiar. The contemporary concept of stress has been proposed by the world-famous Hans Selye, through his many years of research in studying physiologic responses to stressors. He describes stress as "the nonspecific response of the body to any demand made upon it" [22]. Stressors arise from events within the body, such as chemical changes, or from those external to it. It does not matter in terms of the body's response whether the agent or situation faced by the person is pleasant or unpleasant. Experiences of life are stress producing and are absolutely essential for growth and the continuation of life itself. Without stress the organism ceases to exist. The presence of too little stress, such as in sensory deprivation, is just as harmful to the human organism as too much stress.

Of interest to this discussion of mental health is the distinction between distress and eustress. Selye describes unpleasant or damaging stress (physical or psychological) as distress, whereas eustress denotes pleasant or helpful stress. The intensity of the distress or eustress dictates the intensity of the body's response. In terms of each family member, the goal is to learn how to adapt successfully to all stress and to try to convert a potential distress to a eustress [22].

Figure 4-1. Components of family mental wellness.

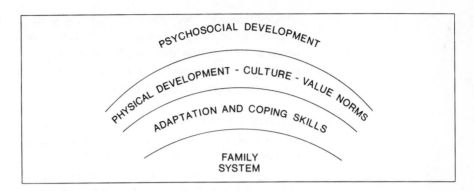

The psychosocial developmental tasks faced by family members throughout life are indeed stressors. They occur naturally and almost inevitably throughout the life cycle. They are necessary to the continued and successful growth of the organism and are necessarily accomplished in an orderly fashion as preparation for the next stage of development. To achieve lifelong and lasting mental wellness, the psychosocial developmental tasks should be accomplished in a eustressful fashion. The loving and supportive network of the family system provides for the possibilities that the developmental tasks will be achieved in a positive way and will provide some protection against the potentially distressful aspects of these life experiences. Whether these life experiences in fact turn out to be positive or negative stresses depends heavily on our perceptions of the event and our abilities to cope with or adapt to these normal changes.

Nurses are in an opportune position to help the family achieve a high level of mental wellness. Their approach that includes the whole family and their background as generalist health-care practitioners afford them the opportunity of interpreting psychosocial tasks of each family member in light of the total family system, its goals, values, and health-care practices. Nurses are in the unique position of assisting the family in interpreting life events in light of objective reality, promoting their coping skills, and helping maximize the family's growth to higher levels of total wellness.

All life events are stressors to the family. They require adaptation, however slight, by all family members as each person in the family system is changed by his life experiences. Adaptation involves skills developed from birth, which allow the person to make the transition from a former state to a present one and to anticipate future ones in a healthful way. Successful adaptation through the developmental cycle to life experiences that may be distressors or eustressors fosters the achievement and maintenance of a high level of mental wellness. Figure 4-1 illustrates the relationship of mental wellness factors.

Infancy

The first stage of life and its greatest stressors will be discussed with an emphasis on the infant's ability to learn wellness behaviors even at this young age. Infants who experience a protective environment with caring role models who fulfill physical, social, and psychological needs will become aware of how to fulfill their needs as well as how their needs are valued by others. Infants whose wellness needs are inconsistently satisfied will have the impression that their needs are of low priority in the parents' value system.

MATERNAL BONDING

A major life event at birth is the act of separating the newborn infant from its mother [31]. Therefore, the concept of bonding or attachment is utilized to describe the close interactional need between mother and newborn. Through this process, the infant's feelings of security and trust are fostered. Securely attached infants show greater exploration of a strange setting in the presence of the mother and a richer quality of play than insecurely attached infants [31]. Through this mutual relationship with the mother, the infant develops the sense of being part of a positive and warm relationship and can build an almost unshakable trust in others.

DISTRUST OF STRANGERS

As infants form this close attachment and preference for their mothers, they in turn develop a suspiciousness toward strangers and exhibit less friendliness toward others. Between 6 and 8 months, this fear of strangers becomes most prominent [30]. This period can be trying for parents because it becomes difficult to use unfamiliar baby-sitters and the infant cries frequently in new surroundings with strange people.

Parents should be reassured that this behavior is healthy and necessary for optimal emotional development. Parents can reassure the infant, who will eventually accept being left with others. Infants who cry when the parents leave generally quiet down shortly afterward. Strangers entering the infant's space should be cautioned to make advances to the infant slowly, allowing the infant to adjust to the presence of someone new. Further, this adjustment may take longer than the stranger expects. In some cases, it may take days for an infant to feel comfortable around an unfamiliar person.

DEPENDENCY

The infancy stage is a critical period of development because of the infant's rapid growth rate and dependency needs. The ultimate goal is the improvement of life as it unfolds for the infant. Development of the sense of trust of others in the environment as well as of self is the crucial task during this beginning stage. The development of trust is enhanced in direct correlation to the eagerness with which the infant's needs are met by others. Infants are open and receiving, ready for visual, touch, and verbal stimulation. They have an overriding need to make their wants and needs known to others. They must constantly deal with external stimuli that determine their comfort. Is the room too hot or too cold? Are noise levels high? Are their physiologic needs being met? Is the diaper clean and dry? Have they received adequate nourishment?

Infants have additional needs that even they have not yet identified. Their beginning need for independence leads them to begin crawling and becoming more mobile. They begin identifying meaningful others who can assist them in promoting their wellness state. These meaningful others should allow infants to develop their self-identity by allowing them to explore their bodies and their environment. They are new to themselves, and the whole world is new to them. They may not voice these needs specifically, but they are all of concern.

Infancy has been equated with the oral stage, in which the child's energies focus on taking in nourishment and relating to the mother. This concept should not, however, be taken too literally. Other sensations, such as vision, touch, voice, odor, body position, and warmth are all important sensations to the infant. It is thought, however, that either too much or too little oral gratification can cause fixation and an inability to move on to the next stage of development.

WEANING

Weaning has long been considered a major frustration in the later stages of infancy. Thumb-sucking frequently increases in frequency and intensity during this time. Currently, however, weaning is believed to cause less trauma than was formerly thought because it is gradually phased out while semisolid foods are added to the diet. Parents gradually accustom the child to taking food from a cup or spoon. Usually a bottle is substituted for the breast, and the baby can continue to be held while feeding.

SOCIETAL EXPECTATIONS

Learning social, emotional, and physical responsiveness to others and to the environment is an important wellness task of the infant. Infants quickly learn that they can gain the attention of those around them by smiling or crying. They set up this adaptive response through interaction with those in their environment and learn that certain responses lead to predictable outcomes. Parents can never show too much love. Infants need to feel secure and wanted in order to develop a relaxed, wellness-oriented attitude toward those around them. They develop these secure feelings through behaviors transmitted by adults around them. These behaviors involve all forms of communication, protection against bodily harm, and meeting biologic needs.

Cultures have differed in what they consider to be workable methods of guiding infants toward adulthood. Expectations can become stressors imposed by the society. Furthermore, it is clear that the manner in which children are raised in a society influences their personalities. Mothers in some cultures, for example, indulge their children while they are young and dependent but after weaning tease the children if they seek closeness. Some believe that infants should be rocked or fed whenever they whimper. Others feel infants should cry intently to "make their lungs strong." Some believe babies should be wrapped in a blanket while others believe they should be allowed to kick freely. Still, among these diverse customs a society cannot survive without taking into account the needs of its individuals. It cannot, for example, neglect the total dependency of the infant, and it cannot neglect the natural sequence of developmental maturation. Children will forever be born into divergent environments, but will continue to adapt to the physical, social, and spiritual environment in which they live. With a wellness focus, the family can adapt positively in a variety of cultures.

Parents are sometimes consumed by the need for their child to meet the expectations of others rather than letting natural behaviors progress at their own rate. This need obviously presents the infant with one of his beginning stressors in life—behaving as others expect him to behave. Parents naturally compare their child's developmental progress with that of other children. Furthermore, parents are tempted to rate their child according to the latest developmental task books. But parents need to understand that their infant will develop at his own rate and that some skills may develop much faster than others. The infant has only so much energy to devote to developmental changes. For example, a child may seem to be lagging in his verbal skills, but may be doing so because he is physically developing so rapidly.

Infants who can feel that their situation is trustworthy can relax and devote their energy to growing and moving on to the next stage of development. They can practice wellness behaviors at this early age by beginning to learn how to handle their stress from within.

LEARNING WELLNESS BEHAVIORS

Before wellness behaviors can be learned, infants must develop an awareness of wellness from role models in their environment. When he is rocked by a relaxed person, the infant's tension decreases and he rests. He loves the comfort induced by swaying and rocking movements, the soft, lilting voice speaking to him, and the smiling and attentive face looking at him. Infants may develop wellness behaviors more readily than adults because they *feel* the results of wellness behaviors earlier. They sense well-being through others. Their senses "take in" what feels good.

In developing mental wellness, even infants do not avoid distress. There is always the demand to adapt and respond. Infants can begin learning to meet stressors and to adjust accordingly. They begin to modify their responses and structure their environment so that unnecessary or harmful stressors are decreased through interactions with the world around them. They can suck and cry; they have a "startle" reflex; they can walk and talk and grasp with their hands; they recognize important others and smile and laugh; they possess an omnipotence they may never hold again—that of helplessness. They watch and listen and are alert to cues that signal what will happen next.

HELPING PARENTS ADJUST TO THEIR ROLES

It takes time for parents to adjust to parenthood. Parents do not always perceive themselves as parents from the beginning. Because a woman becomes a mother does not mean that she is maternal. The nurse can encourage contact time between the infant, the mother, and the father. Support, counseling, and guidance can be given based on her initial family assessment. Timing of nursing care is crucial in that the family experiences immediate needs after arrival of the newborn. The arrival of the newborn is a major life-event change within the family system. But with wellness-focused nursing intervention, the family can experience eustress rather than distress while accepting the responsibility of their newborn into the family system.

The precise techniques for caring for babies are less important than are secure and consistent parents who can enjoy the infant and who form a close, mutual relationship with him. However, an increasing number of mothers are working in jobs outside the home. As a result, infants and small children are finding themselves under the care of baby-sitters and day-care centers. In selecting care givers, the family should look for mature, nurturing people to whom they can entrust their children. The care giver should possess knowledge of normal growth and development as well as of safety measures appropriate to the age of the child. The time spent away from home need not compromise the child's achieving optimal psychosocial well-being. As in the home, the emotional climate of the setting should be warm, nurturing, and considerate of the uniqueness of each child; the parent need not feel guilty because most children adapt well in alternative settings possessing these characteristics.

Many physical and emotional stressors that may manifest themselves in later years can be prevented if the infant is involved in a monitoring program throughout childhood. Children should be seen regularly by a nurse and/or a physician. These visits should include a complete physical examination, emotional and social evaluation, and dental examination with an emphasis on oral prophylaxis. Appropriate educational interventions should begin for parents and children regarding nutrition, play, relaxation, accident prevention, exercise, and sexual development. Children should be referred to other social resources as needed. Hopefully, children and their parents in this monitoring program can obtain support throughout childhood so that improved coping skills can be used to master present and future stressors. Table 4-1 summarizes the common stressors and corresponding wellness behaviors for the infant.

The Toddler Period   The toddler period, ages 1 to 3, is characterized by intense activity and discovery. Toddlers experience an increasing ability to control their bodies and their environment. Their greatest task during this time is to develop self-control and

Table 4-1. Stressors and Wellness Behaviors for the Infant

A. *Common stressors*	2. Parents should
1. Needs identification	a. Provide protective, safe environment
2. Needs satisfaction	b. Provide for physiologic needs
a. Dependency state	c. Assure parent-infant bonding
b. Separation from mother	d. Encourage development of psychomotor skills, such as walking and talking
c. Weaning	
d. Societal expectations	
e. Stranger anxiety	e. Understand cultural expectations for developing child
	f. Provide wellness role models
B. *Wellness behaviors*	g. Encourage strangers to advance slowly
1. Infants should	h. Leave child with suitable mother substitutes to allow free time for selves
a. Communicate needs to others	
b. Feel relaxed and content	
c. Learn to walk, talk, take in proper nourishment	i. Obtain anticipatory guidance from health professionals
d. Feel loved and secure	

willpower. In so doing, they fluctuate between continued dependence and the seeking of independence.

THE BEGINNINGS OF SELF-RESPONSIBILITY

The core conflict for the toddler is one of autonomy versus shame and doubt [30]. While seeking self-control, toddlers can be made to feel shame when forced by others to be dependent in areas in which they can achieve independence. Treated with respect for their abilities, these developing children have enormous potential for vitality, creativity, fulfillment, and responsibility in their lives.

Responsibility is valued in this society, and learning it must begin early. Toddlers begin to realize the need to eliminate body wastes at socially acceptable times and places. They begin developing attitudes toward sexual behavior and increase their awareness of sexual differences. They begin to distinguish between feelings of right and wrong, feelings on which moral values are later built. Language must be mastered in order to communicate wants and needs. Food patterns are changing, and they must learn to accept new and different types of foods. The identification of self and their relationship to others are important tasks that will help determine each toddler's personality.

Stress is an integral part of each of these responsibility areas. Whether there will be distress or eustress is unknown. Various psychosocial, physical, spiritual, and environmental factors will determine the outcome for the toddler: autonomy or shame and doubt.

LEARNING WELLNESS BEHAVIOR

The meaningful others in his life will influence his manner of coping with each of the toddlerhood tasks. While adults model wellness behaviors, the toddler watches and learns to choose accordingly. He can develop a good feeling about himself. He can feel warmth from the touching and holding by others, from the smiling faces and soft voices of others. He can learn to cooperate and communicate with others as they communicate with him. He can have choices and options offered to him within a secure family framework. He can be allowed to explore his environment, again within safe and limited boundaries. He can become nutritionally aware by being offered choices of foods within a well-balanced meal plan. The toddler is driven by his impulses to use his new abilities and to explore his surroundings, but verbal and intellectual abilities lag behind motor development. He is torn between his need for his mother and his need to be separate. These many stressors make up the world of the toddler and his family. Working through them is the job of the child, and adapting to the growing child and his tasks is the responsibility and challenge of the parents.

DEVELOPING BOWEL AND BLADDER CONTROL

The anal phase is descriptive of the toddler period because bowel training has been considered a primary developmental task of the second year of life. Further, the anal zone is a primary source of erotic gratification during this period. Fixations at this stage have been related to various character traits such as obsessiveness, stubbornness, and miserliness. This focus seems to be the result of the emphasis on strict bowel training in Freud's cultural setting. Today, parents are more aware of the need for a relaxed attitude toward bowel functioning [16]. Actually, there is no reason that bowel training should be attempted before the age of 30 months. The child will eventually wish to use the toilet, following the example of other family members. Virtually all children are bowel trained by the age of 3 years, the difference being that those who were trained strictly will have experienced a more distressful process than those who experienced relaxed, positive, and natural guidance.

The passing or withholding of bowel movements seems to be an integral part of another conflict the toddler experiences—that of "hanging on" or "letting go." This vacillation tends to cause him to dawdle in his daily routine. The adult can assist him in this dilemma by using a pleasant, firm, but positive approach with simple demands and choices, consistency in expectations, and the ignoring of temper tantrums. The toddler has little understanding of time; therefore, the adult should avoid making the child wait whenever possible, and rewards should be concrete and given immediately. Simple words that are familiar to the child should be used, but "no" should not be overused. Toddlers are highly distractible, and drawing attention to a new and nondestructive activity can often serve better than a "don't." Parents can be bolstered by the reassurance that the phase will pass.

CHANGING NUTRITIONAL HABITS

Feeding problems are a major frustration to parents during the child's second and third years. Some children learn early that they can assert their independence and gain attention by not eating. Feeding can become the arena for a tug-of-war between parent and child. The child needs to understand that food is a means of satisfying hunger, not a way of coping with anxieties and manipulating others. The mealtime should be a social occasion for parent and child when they can relate pleasantly with one another. Further, parents need to realize that the child is not physically growing as fast as he was during infancy and therefore, needs less food during the toddler years. He needs his hunger appeased regularly, but he does not need anxious concern over every bite of food.

LEARNING LANGUAGE AND EFFECTIVE COMMUNICATION

During these years, the child is also acquiring language ability that will enable him to communicate his wants and needs and to gain a greater ability to control his own behavior. Learning language is an adaptive technique that is uniquely human. Family members are primarily the tutors for this new skill. They are teaching not only sounds, but the culture's system of meanings, as well as ways of thinking and reasoning [16]. Even though toddlers are striving for independence, they are very dependent on the parent for verbal comprehension. The consistency and pleasantness of the parent's reaction are extremely important so that children can develop trust in their ability to interact with language. The parent's repetition of sound encourages children to repeat words and sounds. By the age of 3 years, and sometimes by the age of 2½, the child has acquired hundreds of words. Some children know more than a thousand by this age. Some children make sentences of 12 to 15 words by 3 years of age [16]. Question and naming games are common ways for children at this age to increase intellectual and language abilities. These are interacting games that the adult and child can play together. Even at this early age, the names permit a degree of predictability about the world. For example, the child learns to correlate the term *sweet* with a particular taste sensation, which will allow him to know in advance what a food will taste like. Further, these games give him a sense of constancy about objects.

THE NEED FOR LIMITS

To facilitate optimal mental wellness during this period of many stressors, parents need to be reminded that the toddler needs a balance between limits and freedom in order to feel safe, secure, and loved. Parents are no longer concerned only with satisfying their child's needs and wishes, but must now also limit their activities to ensure safety of the child and integrity of the household. Toddlers do not have the ability to make judgments about their limitations, so parents must carefully and consistently set the limits for them. Limits should be imposed with gentleness and kindness. The adult must remember the child's need to say "no" frequently while trying to assert his independence. There will be conflict after conflict while the child "tests his wings." He needs to be himself and find himself, which is what these years are all about.

The toddler is not naturally obedient. Crossing the street is a good example of ever-changing limits as the child's capacities change. A baby is carried by parents, a small child holds the parent's hand, and a 6-year-old crosses the street by himself, but within the rules he has learned. A mother who takes a 2-year-old to the grocery store can expect him to touch and possibly pull down merchandise. She therefore takes him by the hand firmly or sits him in the grocery cart, without thinking of him as naughty.

The patience of parents in establishing controls helps the child meet new experiences successfully, such as learning to play with other children, going to school, and later, dancing and dating. As he grows older he will feel secure and confident and will adopt the controls the parents have established for his own.

IMPORTANCE OF PLAY

Play is a significant mode of work and relaxation for the toddler. However, he often finds himself within another conflict situation. In this developmental stage, the toddler strives for parallelism in his play group when in actuality he is encouraged by adults to play and share with others within the group setting. In many family activities, particularly dinnertime, the child is expected to participate quietly as a group member with adult manners. However, he is actually striving for independence and wishes to eat alongside but not with the others. As with the infant, the expectations of others can cause increased anxiety for the child. He wishes to be with the group but not to participate in the group. His interest is centered in his own activities.

If used correctly, play modalities provide a medium in which children can learn and feel comfortable. For toddlers, play is an integral and vital part of their being for it is through play that they act out important life events and adapt to society's expectations of them. Further, play can provide sensorimotor development, intellectual development, socialization, creativity, self-awareness, and therapeutic and moral value [30].

Parents may note that the child expends much effort in throwing a ball or fingering tiny objects. It may take much practice before an action can be carried out automatically. He may appear to be playing, but he is actually striving for increased control and muscular coordination.

Play can be one of the most effective tools for the child in managing stress. Playing out anxieties and fears is a means by which the child can cope in any setting. Play relieves tension and leads to relaxation and a sense of security. It provides a medium to release anger and hostility. Throwing bean bags at targets and working and molding clay are two forms of physical release that can lead to emotional tension reduction. Drawing and painting are also creative means of self-expression.

Role play is a special form of play. It has been found repeatedly that children who are allowed to role play before an unpleasant experience are then able to tolerate the experience with much less distress [30]. Some examples of alleviation of stress by role play are the preparation of the child for the first day of nursery school, the first dental visit, going on vacation with the family, and having a regular wellness checkup.

DEVELOPING A ROLE IN THE FAMILY

Development of role within the family becomes a major stressor in early childhood. Wherever the family goes, the smallest child has a certain place for himself, as well as his belongings. The American child acquires things of his own at an early age. There is a special place for his crib, for his chair or car seat, and his toys. Because today's child is living in a type of society that his parents never knew, he realizes at a very early age that he may take on different roles within the family and in society. There is a feeling of creativeness as he develops his role as child, grandchild, and sibling. He comes to realize he is a valued member of the family and that his place is important.

As role is developed, toddlers have many opportunities to learn. Learning is both a necessary and creative process that fulfills developmental tasks and contributes to psychosocial as well as physical growth. Toddlers feel proud to be able to do things for themselves and to see directly the results of their actions. They develop pride in their newfound independence and in the confidence placed in them by their parents. Ideas can be presented to the toddler as brand-new, shining and wonderful parts of his being. As the toddler develops his emotional relationships with others and finds himself, he can begin realizing that his role is an important aspect of his wellness-development state.

The home and family are the center of the toddler's life, but he increasingly moves into contact with new places and people. He goes for walks with his parents and accompanies them to the grocery store. The toddler gains new perspectives of himself as he sees himself through others. How the toddler fits into his new world depends a great deal on the trust and security he has developed at home.

Acceptance of the toddler within the realm of his capabilities and limitations requires patience by all family members. It is helpful for family members to let him know they know how he feels, and that he has a right to express his feelings. This acceptance of his feelings keeps the family in touch with him, and he learns his feelings are respected. These wellness behaviors add to the groundwork for mental wellness established during infancy and propel him through later stages. He develops a way of fitting into the family, of viewing family members, and of being viewed by them. How the child is regarded during these early years influences to a great extent development of the esteem he will have for himself as an adult. Table 4-2 shows the stressors and wellness behaviors experienced by the toddler in his passage through the developmental life cycle.

The Preschool Period

Wellness during the preschool period, ages 3 to 5, involves developing competence and the social ability to master oneself. The preschool period is an age of discovery and curiosity and a time to develop sociocultural patterns of behavior.

Table 4-2. Stressors and Wellness Behaviors for the Toddler

A. *Common stressors*
   1. Dual tasks of obtaining gratification of dependency needs while learning independent behaviors appropriate for age
   2. Acquiring bowel and bladder control
   3. Asserting self
   4. Changing nutritional habits
   5. Learning language and effective communication

B. *Wellness behaviors*
   1. Toddlers should
      a. Continue development of psychomotor skills
      b. Develop self-control and willpower
      c. Develop bowel and bladder control
      d. Develop awareness of sexual differences
      e. Reduce stress through self-expression and play activities
      f. Develop emotional relationships with others
      g. Begin developing awareness of feelings of well-being

   2. Parents should
      a. Encourage autonomy within limits
      b. Provide a safe environment
      c. Provide wellness role models
      d. Provide a wellness-monitoring system in conjunction with a medical professional
      e. Wait for psychological and physical readiness for toilet training
      f. Expect signs of regression in times of distress
      g. Express feelings regarding child's negativism and impulsiveness
      h. Allow child time for play activities
      i. Provide firm but gentle discipline

What better time than this to enhance wellness behaviors, while the child holds so much enthusiasm for learning? He can begin learning how to cope with life's changes and thus can begin assuming responsibility for his mental health state and functioning at his maximum capacity for living.

DEVELOPING INITIATIVE

Erikson maintains that the chief psychological task of this period of life is acquiring a sense of initiative. Conflict arises when the child oversteps the limits of his ability and experiences a sense of guilt for not having acted appropriately [30]. The child at this age has thoughts that are not always congruent with expected behavior. For example, the child may be angry at a sibling and wish him dead. The quote, "step on a crack, break your mother's back" is an excellent example of the preschooler's thoughts being verbalized in a game situation. Explaining to the child that wishes do not make events happen is important in helping the child overcome feelings of guilt and anxiety.

DEVELOPING A CONSCIENCE

Another major task for the preschooler is the development of conscience. He begins distinguishing right from wrong by the way others reward or punish him. He develops moral judgments regarding his and others' behaviors and can accept compromise more easily than the toddler. Discovering that parents do not always live up to their own expectations of moral behavior can be disillusioning for this child, who has concrete ideas about what is right and wrong. This disillusionment helps foster suspiciousness of the motives of others. Parents should make every effort to be consistent and honest with children, admitting to their own mistakes and explaining situations that are confusing to children.

LEARNING WELLNESS BEHAVIORS

In order to function at maximum capacity, the preschooler needs role models who practice wellness behaviors. Parents still hold a major responsibility for modeling in the child's life. If the parents practice wellness behaviors, they will most likely reward the child for similar behaviors. If these rewards are consistent, the child will probably repeat the wellness behaviors. If the child has developed trust and autonomy from previous developmental stages, then he will most likely take risks by taking actions with unsure outcomes.

In a group of studies of childrearing practices of parents of preschool children, Baumrind found that the qualities of competence, independence, affiliation, outgoingness, self-control, and self-reliance were fostered by nurturing, warm home environments in which independent actions and decision making were encouraged and rewarded. His data further suggest that young children are more likely to develop maturity, competence, and social responsibility in the nurturing home where parents exert control and express high maturity demands, but not authoritarian discipline [2,3].

Parents and siblings alike are models for mental wellness behaviors. How the family members react to disappointment, reward, joy, anger, and satisfaction indicates their ability to cope with life experiences. The preschooler carefully observes their reactions, learning how to respond and whether the methods are effective. The mother who matter-of-factly accepts and explains menstruation to her teenage daughter, the parents who encourage independence by happily sending the child to his first day of school, and the sibling who visits the dentist willingly all set the stage for the child's positive response to life experiences.

The action chosen is determined by the person's past experiences in dealing with stressors. The nurse can help the family to become aware of these actions and to change negative behaviors to more positive ones.

PLAY AND PURPOSE

To help the child channel developing initiative, the parent must teach the child where play ends and purpose begins. The parent can be a companion in work and play, setting the example for expected behaviors and role identification for the child. The parent can offer the child an ideal to strive toward, and in turn, the parent should be aware of the child's communications through work and play activities. Play mirrors some of the most important tasks of this period, such as development of socially acceptable behavior, realization of separateness as individuals, and identification of sex role. One of the main goals in differentiation of self from others is learning sex differences and sexually appropriate behavior [30].

SEX-ROLE IDENTIFICATION

Freud recognized the preschooler's need for sexual identity by describing the Oedipal stage. This stage represents the small boy's desire to marry his mother and do away with his father. The young boy is in conflict with his father who is much larger and stronger. This fear leads to the castration complex, fear of mutilation or punishment by the father. The female counterpart to this concept is the Electra complex, in which the young girl hopes to marry her father and get rid of her mother. Because she has no penis, she experiences penis envy rather than castration anxiety. Obviously, sexual identity is a major conflict for children regarding their relationship with parents.

The resolution to this conflict is identification with the parent of the same sex. Children learn appropriate behaviors for their sex through observation and imitation. The child who identifies with his sex and meets the expectations of society comfortably adapts to his surroundings. If, however, he has been raised to act like the opposite sex, he may face conflict on entering school and associating with other groups. If this conflict is not resolved, an alternate sexual identification such as homosexuality or transsexualism may evolve [4].

The kinds of sexual behavior learned and the feelings developed in these early years will have an effect on the person's sexuality throughout life. Preschoolers need simple, direct answers to their questions about their bodies and their sexuality. They should feel comfortable asking these questions. Even though sex roles are becoming more blurred, parents can encourage discussion and understanding of feminine and masculine roles as they exist in our society today. Encouraging a flexible attitude toward the changing views of sexuality helps children to adapt more readily to their culture. With appropriate guidance and reinforcement, they can learn socially acceptable behaviors that will result in feelings of security, acceptance, and accomplishment.

DISCIPLINE

There are various types of reinforcement and childrearing methods, all of which affect mental wellness. For example, some parents prefer to remove all hazardous objects from tables within the child's reach. Others prefer to leave the objects on the tables and educate the child as to what he can and cannot touch. There is no completely right or wrong method of discipline. Parents usually mix methods, which probably confuses the child more than would following a less acceptable method. Some parents are authoritarian and dictatorial, some are very permissive, and some are authoritarian-democratic.

The authoritarian-democratic method of childrearing seems to be the most successful [30]. This pattern is also most consistent with the decision-making structure characteristic of psychologically well family systems. This method combines control with respect and allowance for individuality. Freedom of choice is allowed within limits. Parental control is firm and consistent. Children are allowed to accept the natural consequences of their actions. If they behave in an unwell way, they become ill. If they behave in a well way, they remain well and function at an optimal level. Well behaviors are reinforced and unwell behaviors are avoided or discouraged. Parents should set realistic expectations and demonstrate a caring, listening attitude toward children. Effective communication is provided as part of daily experience, therefore allowing the child a buffer for stress and an effective method for coping. All of these behaviors encourage an "inner-directed" feeling of accomplishment, which leads to the child's ability to move on to new developmental challenges.

IMPORTANCE OF PLAY

The preschooler is changing physically. Most body systems are mature and can adapt to stress more readily. He is less awkward and can handle more gross and fine motor developments such as riding a tricycle, standing on one foot for a few seconds, tying shoelaces, and using scissors to cut out an outline successfully. His drawings advance from a shape stage to a pictorial stage. Parents should encourage drawing and scribbling for development of fine motor control and eye-hand coordination as well as for the pleasure of creating something enjoyable.

Drawing and play are both methods of release and expression for the preschooler, revealing thoughts and feelings he may otherwise be unable to verbalize. They reveal knowledge the child has learned from others as well as his relationships with others. The nurse or parent can encourage the use of dramatic play— including role playing—and drawing as effective techniques for reducing anxiety, relieving tension, and understanding experiences. Relaxation-exercise games can be introduced during these early years so that a foundation is laid for the understanding of mind-body self-modification techniques. The earlier the child learns to modify his own behavior in order to decrease distress, the more likely he will enhance his wellness state over a lifetime.

Anticipatory guidance and planning help the child reduce and control anxieties. Planning can help the child begin directing energy into problem solving. For example, alerting a family to expect questions from a child regarding sexuality may lead the family to clarify their own values about the subject before explaining them to the child. The nurse can assist the family in adjusting little by little to changing developmental needs so that they master small events and, as a result, are prepared to cope with major developmental milestones. Understanding the child's growth and development allows the parents to help the child avoid unrealistic goals that could cause distress.

Mastering life events through play is very important in lowering the child's anxieties when a crisis occurs. This type of anticipatory planning is called "immunization" by Kliman. He suggests that children can be immunized to a wide variety of childhood crises such as moving, seeking new friends, or dealing with a sick family member. He suggests that open communication about these crises should be combined with role models that demonstrate wellness coping abilities [15].

Table 4-3. Stressors and Wellness Behaviors for the Preschooler

A. *Common stressors*

   1. Expectations of others

   2. Ambivalent feelings about wishes and fantasies

   3. Oedipal complex or Electra complex

   4. Developing independence and self-care

   5. Entry into nursery school

B. *Wellness behaviors*

   1. Preschoolers should

      a. Develop competence in themselves

      b. Develop socially acceptable behaviors

      c. Develop conscience

      d. Develop sexual identity

      e. Utilize play and techniques of self-expression to reduce stress

      f. Develop emotional relationships with others

      g. Begin developing problem-solving skills

   2. Parents should

      a. Provide wellness role models

      b. Begin encouraging independence in child

      c. Provide a wellness-monitoring system in conjunction with a health professional

      d. Provide discipline in childrearing practices

      e. Be honest and consistent with child

      f. Provide a nurturing, warm home environment in which independent action and decision making are encouraged and rewarded

      g. Assist child with sex-role identification

      h. Be aware of child's need to play and creatively express self

      i. Set realistic expectations

      j. Demonstrate a caring, listening attitude toward the child

      k. Include child in decision making

The end of the preschool period finds the psychosocially well child eager and willing to move on to new challenges. The next period begins the lengthy separation from the family as bonds continue to change to accommodate the child's move toward adulthood. New groups will supplement the importance of the family. Table 4-3 presents the stressors and behaviors that must be mastered in order to pass into the next stage.

The School-Age Period

The child during the school years begins officially to move into the world beyond the home. Entry into school marks the beginning of his efforts to find his niches in the world, thus contributing to the development of the self-concept, value systems, and cognitive capabilities. In school, the child represents not only himself but the family from which he comes. The beliefs and values of the family are often pointed out to the teacher, to whom the child says, "But my mother doesn't do it like that."

LEARNING TO WORK

The major developmental task of the school-age period is the development of a sense of industry [7]. Children learn work habits, a sense of accomplishment, and self-control, which help them along the way to adult competence. Industry is developed in school through good work habits that make it possible to learn. Even though the child may have attended kindergarten or even a preschool program, success in school requires listening, maintaining attention and concentration, following rules and regulations, and sharing the teacher's attention. These major adaptive skills in developing industry make it possible for the child to experience the new environment to the fullest. When this process is carried to extremes, the child develops a compulsive striving to excel in competition, whereas failure to accomplish a sense of industry results in feelings of inferiority and inadequacy. Through school and home activities, the child learns to accept and face meaningful challenges and the success and sometimes failures that follow.

The responsibility of the school and family is to provide opportunities for the child to face challenges in learning and doing—the stimuli for becoming industrious. The challenges must be real and not contrived and must not be too hard or too easy. The child in school who is given work too hard or too easy will develop an attitude of "why try?" or "why bother?" Either situation results in defeatism, in which the child is no longer capable of realizing the rewards of a job well done. The child who has creative opportunities to work and achieve learns skills that will serve him well throughout life.

As Lidz [16] has pointed out, striving to excel competitively is a valued American trait, and its excesses are often overlooked. Some communities have organized competitive sports beginning at very young ages, and it is not uncommon for parents to view these activities as professional sports in miniature. Some parents develop the win-at-all-costs attitude and lose sight of the very valuable opportunity for the child to experience teamwork. When the goal of winning becomes more important than learning skills and the sharing of victories and defeats, the child's mental wellness is compromised. Industry must be guided by parents and teachers to include acceptance of meaningful challenges and pride in one's accomplishments without the appearance of defeatism or ruthlessness. Through regular contacts with school personnel and careful selection of extracurricular activities, parents can monitor the quality of activities the child engages in and work for changes if they do not promote mental wellness.

PEER-GROUP PLAY

As the child moves outside the family for social experiences, the peer group takes on immense importance. It is primarily a play group, but it aids social and emotional development through the interaction and cooperation that are required. It is the vehicle through which another life experience is faced—that is, the development of a sense of belonging [16], which is the assurance the child gains of being an accepted and integral part of the group and of the broader society outside the family. It encompasses not only a feeling of comfort within the group but an identification with the group and a commitment to its values and ethics. Within the group, the child learns a sense of responsibility, that he can be depended on; this is a trait important in leadership.

The Sense of Belonging. An important aspect of these social peer groupings of children is that they are separate and autonomous from the adult world [24]. The childhood gang or clique of childhood has its secrets, rituals, and rules that belong to the children alone and are not shared or usually observed by adults. The special meeting place or clubhouse typifies the separateness from the adult world and the special sense of belonging that is so valued by children at this age. The child who is not a member of one of these peer groups feels isolated and rejected and is filled with self-doubts and fears that he is not "good enough." Mental wellness in this middle childhood period becomes closely tied to identification with the peer group.

Through the group, composed mostly of school or neighborhood peers, the child is able to gain additional opportunities for evaluation of self-worth. Until this point, data have come from family members, but during the school years the extrafamily groups provide valuable input. A positive self-concept is essential to mental wellness, and school-age experiences are extremely important to its development. Parents need to encourage social relationships between the child and his peers. Through regular, frequent communication, parents need to become aware of the development and flourishing of relationships outside the home. Parents can encourage neighborhood groups to play in or near their home, and encourage the mutual sharing on which friendships are based.

Sex-Role Identification. During the school-age years, the peer groups are same-sex groups, and sex-role activities are evident. The same-sex peer group serves to pass on cultural norms of accepted behavior for the sex from one generation to another. Many activities, jokes, and games played by boys and girls today are the same or very similar to ones played years ago. Some activities are typically boys' activities, while others are strictly the domain of girls. Even activities that are the same for each sex are not played in mixed groups. Sexual homogeneity persists into adolescence and helps children learn social skills and values important for their sexual identity.

The Best Friend. Near the end of the middle school years prior to adolescence, the center of the child's life moves from the peer group to the "best friend." This experience is important and intense for the child because this relationship is usually the first major attachment outside the family. The best friend is a person of the same sex because the empathy required to share feelings at this age usually can occur only with one of the same sex. This expansion of the self to another allows the child to learn how another person experiences events and copes with life. It affords the opportunity to develop a sense of "we," a precursor for later intimacy, and to learn or confirm wellness behaviors in coping with stressors.

The child who is part of a group of school or neighborhood playmates faces many frustrations. As he reaches out into new environments and tests his developing independence, he experiences rejection from the group, loss of a friend through moving or rejection, embarrassment for an awkward act, school difficulties, or failure to be chosen for a team or a party. These are all normal and expected experiences of life. Life, the "teacher," begins early to expose children to some of the cruelties of the adolescent and adult worlds. To weather these small and large storms, the child needs the haven of a loving and secure home where he can share his troubles with a listening and caring parent, and where he can be reassured that he was and still is a worthwhile person. The parents in their nurturing roles must be physically present and emotionally ready to help the child adapt to defeats and disappointments. As the parents help the child to accept these experiences for what they are—life experiences and not tragedian crises—the child will learn to cope healthfully and gain an important skill for mental wellness.

LEARNING TO CARE ABOUT OTHERS

The school-age child is not a fully mature social being and may do or say things that hurt others' feelings. He, in turn, may be hurt by the thoughtless acts of others. These kinds of occurrences are a normal part of the childhood experience but can become distressful. Parents need to help children understand these events in light of the reality of childhood immaturity and stimulate a move toward sensitivity and caring for others. Parents need to be reassured also that if their child is the perpetrator, it does not mean he is a "bad" child or will become one. It simply means he hasn't grown up yet and needs to become aware of how his words and acts hurt others. If he is the victim, he needs much understanding and help in realizing that bad words do not make him a bad person.

LEARNING ABOUT SEX AND REPRODUCTION

Before puberty, which does not often occur during the school-age years, sexual development is limited. Sexual curiosity is not, however, and children have many curiosities about "where babies come from." For the child who has not yet asked questions, parents need to take the initiative in beginning the dialogue. Adolescence and puberty will be arriving all too soon, and children need facts and time to adapt to their future sexuality as adults. It is the responsibility of the parents, supplemented by the school, to see that they get both.

In many schools, girls in fifth and sixth grade are typically shown a film about menstruation produced by a sanitary product company. This experience is incomplete at best for it does not deal with the very personal feelings of wonder, fear, or just curiosity at reaching puberty and reaching reproductivity. Boys are often ignored completely in addressing sexual issues. The parents have two responsibilities that have tremendous implications for the future well-being of the child: (1) to see that facts are presented and feelings discussed at home and (2) to work for schools, churches, and other socializing groups to take into account human sexuality for both sexes when planning curricula and programs. Exploring these feelings about sexuality is as important as providing facts because these feelings assume great import in motivating behavior.

DEVELOPING MORALITY

Moral development makes some interesting changes in the school-age child. Lidz [16] notes that Piaget describes a morality of constraint characteristic of schoolchildren, in which children have rigid standards about punishments. They believe that the same punishment should be meted out for the same infraction regardless of the circumstances. They believe that the hungry 3-year-old should await her turn for food just like her 8-year-old brother. This type of morality develops, according to Lidz [16] because of the immature child's acceptance of his position in the family as inferior to the adults. He accepts the adult's value system without understanding it. As the child reaches the age of 10, he begins to attain a morality of cooperation in which motivation and the social implication of acts are appreciated. He moves beyond seeking punishments that "fit the crime" and begins to comprehend punishment by reciprocity, in which the child who refuses to help the parent wash the dishes can expect the parent to refuse to drive him on an errand he requests. Self-accepted ethical principles based on individual conscience or social contract principles do not emerge until adolescence.

The progression from a morality of constraint to a morality of cooperation seems to depend on the total social environment in which the child lives [16]. The parents, teachers, and peers all influence the development of morality in the child. The level of cognitive development seems to be an important factor in the level of moral judgment achieved.

PLAY AND EXERCISE

Many important stressors have to be faced during childhood. As the child strives to accomplish the tasks and cope with the stressors, what specific aids does he have in addition to the support and role modeling of family and peers? Play and exercise are the number one tension relievers for children. As physical energy is exerted, mental tension is relieved. Because play and exercise are so important throughout life in dealing with the stress of living, it is well worth the effort of family and school personnel to foster development of an exercise mind set and to teach the skills necessary for many play and exercise activities. It is a wellness behavioral system that pays off physically and mentally. The vigor and enthusiasm of childhood are precious ingredients from which to make exercise a life-style habit. Stressors and wellness behaviors for the school-age child are presented in Table 4-4.

Adolescence

As Reres has stated, "If Darwin had wanted to create a time period for testing the stress survival potential of the human animal, he could have done no better than to develop adolescence" [21]. Indeed adolescence is a passage from the relatively secure time of grade-school years to the responsibility-filled world of the young adult. A high level of stress is experienced by adolescents because of the massive physical and emotional changes they experience and the great number of adaptation and coping skills they must draw on. While their bodies are making obvious and radical changes, they are faced with many demands from educational systems, peer pressure, their own changing sexual awareness, and the press of decisions

Table 4-4. Stressors and Wellness Behaviors for the School-age Child

A. *Common stressors*
  1. Development of a sense of industry as manifested by good work habits in school
  2. Entry into school
  3. Excessive competitiveness among peers
  4. Development of a sense of belonging
  5. Acceptance by the peer group
  6. Separation from family
  7. Social relationships with peers
  8. Increasing independence
  9. Growth of positive self-concept

B. *Wellness behaviors*
  1. School-age children should
    a. Accept challenges in school and home
    b. Learn new skills
    c. Accept failures as well as successes
    d. Assume responsibility for actions
    e. Develop increased self-control
    f. Accept adult value system
    g. Appreciate social implications of behavior
    h. Belong to an identified peer group
    i. Develop increased independence
  2. Parents should
    a. Provide opportunities for challenges in learning and doing
    b. Carefully select and monitor extracurricular activities
    c. Encourage social relationships
    d. Encourage group activities
    e. Provide caring and listening atmosphere
    f. Include child in decision making
    g. Help child deal with tension through healthy coping skills

about future life roles and vocation that need to be made. The relative constancy and quietude of the school-age child yields to a transitory period where changes occur rapidly, sometimes so rapidly that adaptation has not the chance to be complete before adaptation to another change is demanded.

DEVELOPING A SEPARATE IDENTITY

All the psychosocial and physical changes that occur during adolescence are part of the major task of developing a sense of self-identity. At the beginning of the metamorphosis of adolescence, the person is still a child, dependent on parents and with an unknown and unshaped future. Lidz [16] points out that by the end of adolescence, the person will be responsible for himself, his adult personality patterned, and his future course indicated. The personality gels into a working integration of what it has been in the past and future potentialities. Mental wellness during adolescence and the potential for wellness as an adult rest on achieving a successful integration. Whether this occurs depends on there having been a reasonably successful passage through all prior stages of development and successful accomplishment of several tasks specific to adolescence, leading to a reintegration and reorganization of personality structure to permit the person to function as a reasonably self-sufficient adult [16]. This new identity is truly the person's own, and not achieved by virtue of being someone's daughter or son. New roles require considerable adaptation, and for mental wellness to achieve its maximum considerable adaptation to the oscillating heights and depths of adolescence are a requisite.

THE STRESSES OF PUBERTY

Early adolescence begins with pubescence and the rapid change in body size and contours. Strange feelings and longings develop, adding an impulsivity and irrationality to the adolescent, who has had little if any experience with these feelings. As physical changes occur, the difference between the sexes heightens and also increases the attraction between them. Teenagers often feel unable to seek help from their parents regarding these physical and emotional changes and therefore must cope with them on their own and within the supportive network of friends. A family climate that is warm, accepting, and supportive leaves an emotional open door through which teenagers can seek help. Feelings are often shared between adolescents, but it may be a case of one inexperienced person trying to guide another. However, the sharing of feelings lets each one know he is not alone. This mutual support is very important, and in his uncomfortable feelings, the adolescent realizes he has company.

A common source of distress to the teenager is either early or late onset of puberty. The girl who physically develops long before her peers can be made to feel embarrassingly different. An interest in boys earlier than her peers may disrupt friendships. The boy who matures early may face the same problem with his peers, but a more major upset is the lot of the boy who matures late. The boy who had his heart set on competitive sports but is unable to participate due to his small size finds himself unwillingly redirecting his interests. The nurse in the school should be alert to these common happenings, help teenagers and their teachers realize it is normal, and be supportive of the teenager's feelings whenever possible. Visits or conferences with the teenager's parents with support of their understanding will help the teenager adapt to perceived "differentness" and will provide assurance that maturation will level the situation.

Heightened Sexual Interest. During this period of rapid body development, a great interest in sexual matters increases. Often small groups form within the peer group to share information or misinformation about sexuality and sexual intercourse. Children who have had comprehensive sex education throughout their lives will find this period less traumatic than those for whom sex is a new and perhaps "dirty" word. Children at this age need information, but they also need the opportunity to discuss their feelings with someone who is informed, sensitive, and caring. Often if feelings can be discussed, they do not have to be acted out.

While parents and the schools share the responsibility for educating about sexuality in its broadest sense, too often this responsibility is not assumed. Sexual deficits in the education of children about health are most serious, and they reflect the ignorance and ambivalence of the family, schools, and community. In their role as educators, nurses should work to mobilize community and family systems to integrate education about sexuality into the educational fiber of the family and school. Not to do so is to say that ignorance is bliss and that teenagers are not worth the energy it takes to develop meaningful educational programs in the home, schools, churches, or other social institutions.

Masturbation. Old myths die slowly, and masturbation falls into this category. Lidz [16] reports a 1973 survey of senior medical students conducted by S. M. Woods in which 12 percent of the students believed that masturbation could cause insanity or homosexuality. In fact, Lidz contends that nearly all adolescent boys and between one third and two thirds of adolescent girls have practiced masturbation, and psychiatrists consider absence of masturbation during adolescence a cause for concern because it indicates a need for intense repression of feelings or self-deception. The thought of masturbation often provokes quiet and concern and thus threatens the adolescent's emotional well-being. This concern is a stressor that need not be perceived as a distressor. Alert and caring parents can anticipate this concern in the teenage family member and can lay the ghost to rest. Masturbation should not be left to become a threat to self-concept.

Adolescent Crushes. Adolescent sexuality is often characterized by a crush on some older and deeply admired person, which represents the use of fantasy in coming to terms with sexuality. The admired person may find crushes quite uncomfortable or even embarrassing and should try to maintain as neutral a stance as possible. Parents should understand this admiration as a normal part of the adolescent's passage into adult sexual roles.

TURNING AWAY FROM THE FAMILY

Lidz [16] has identified middle adolescence as a pivotal time of life when teenagers turn away from the family that has formed the center of their existence for 14 or 15 years. Teenagers begin to give up their perception of themselves as children dependent on their parents and begin to feel capable of directing their own lives. Parents should give them opportunities to do so. This change requires a major reorientation as well as a change in teenagers' actual relationships with their parents. Since the tasks of this stage primarily concern gaining independence from parental supervision and the child's emotional attachment to parents, it is natural that the family becomes an arena of conflict. Even though arguments occur more frequently at this stage than earlier ones, if the relationships between child and parents have been good, and there exists mutual love, respect, and caring between parents and child, then conflict may be minimal.

Changing Bonds. The importance of a stable family base is crucial during this adolescent transition. The family unit must be able to withstand the ambivalence of both adolescent and parents. Adolescents feel the need to free themselves from parental control and influence, and yet they long for the security they are leaving behind. Parents are eager to see the child grow into a competent adult, yet may resist their weakening influence in the child's life. This life stage is one in which family bonds must change in order for the family members and the family system to maintain wellness. Adolescents' need to grow and mature must be met, but they still need the base of a loving and secure family to which they can return as they move on toward adult maturity. Teenagers still need guidance and support, despite their protests to the contrary, but they also need both opportunities to make their own decisions on important matters and the respect of their parents for trying. They need the secure and loving family from which they can venture toward the emotional and physical freedom to learn about their own capabilities and limitations in an adult world. Understanding this process aids parents and adolescents in maximizing progress through this developmental stage and the ensuing mental wellness.

Identification with a Peer Group. The process of separation of adolescents from their families usually involves alliances with the peer group. It becomes the reference group for adolescents to try things out in their own way. The peer group can be a social group that guides social and recreational activities, or it can be a working group at school such as a club, where cooperation and leadership skills are developed to meet group goals. The peer group guides likes and dislikes, grooming, and dress. Parents should recognize this influence and encourage creative self-expression within reason. Practices with which the parents do not agree because they were or are not part of their own life-styles need not become a battleground. When these practices are recognized as a normal and necessary part of adolescence, the parent can relax and give support rather than grief.

Self-concept input tends to come more from peers than from family at this time, and depending on the dynamics of the peer group, can result in some faulty self-conceptions. The peer group represents revolt from the parents toward conformity to age-mates and is part of the symbolization of the so-called conflict between generations. The differences between child and parents are usually not as marked as either parents or child may think, and in fact these differences are inherent in social living and necessary to social change [16].

Conformity to the peer group becomes a hallmark of adolescent life because it provides a feeling of security and belonging. It helps the adolescent to be accepted by peers of both sexes and provides a source of stability to the adolescent who still does not have a secure inner identity. Conformity in appearance and behavior is a necessity, even if the norm of conformity is to nonconformity. The customs and clothing vary with the decade and the socioeconomic group, but the rule for the adolescent is the same: follow the group. The family must recognize and accept this conformity as an expected part of development. It is necessary for the breakaway from the family, the establishment of identity, and the move toward adult roles. Following the group is part of this process and should be seen as assertion of independence from the family en route to the next stage of development, rather than as a rebellion motivated by negative feelings. So much of the success in moving through adolescence depends on the parents and family adapting to changes.

MAINTAINING FAMILY WELLNESS

How may parents and adolescents move through this trying period successfully in a well fashion so that both can move on to the next stage of development? Profound changes such as those that occur during adolescence offer tremendous opportunities and challenges for growth. The juxtaposition of adolescence with the parents' own midlife turning points presents some special concerns. Through the process, the goal for parents and child is the same: to proceed through the stage with the highest possible level of mental wellness. The foundation of trust and respect developed within the family should remain as firm as ever. Throughout childhood, parents have imparted the values and norms of the culture, and if this base has been laid well, the teenager will be more likely to fare well during adolescence.

Limits for behavior should be set that are within teenagers' realm of possibility to achieve but that still give them latitude for decision making. Parents must communicate trust to their adolescents by allowing privacy and decision making and in so doing will confirm their trustworthiness and competence. When the parents' values and behaviors are challenged by the adolescent, they should respond openly and honestly, without anger, defensiveness, and vindictiveness. They must realize that "old" ways must be challenged so that the young person can test his newly developing identity. The parents must trust their roles as parents over the years and their continuing love for and faith in the adolescent. They must praise him for his successes and console him for his disappointments.

Although the bonds between parent and child are indeed changing, they are not broken but are instead taking on a new form as the new roles and relationships develop. Throughout this turbulent period, the family's sense of humor is a great asset. Although times may be troubled or uncertain, the ability to laugh at oneself and at each other becomes an important skill in adapting to changes brought on by life's experiences. Taking on the demands of a major transitional period with good humor can lighten the load and take the too-serious edge off happenings that are not so serious after all. The well family that has developed psychosocially through the years—in which family members feel autonomous, respected, and loved—will encounter adolescence with courage and challenge, providing needed support for parents and the adolescent through the process of establishing new roles, new identities, and new responsibilities as family members. Mental wellness can be achieved when common stressors are understood and met through effective adaptation (See Table 4-5).

Young Adulthood

The young adult years can best be described as the decision-making years. Many of the stresses experienced by young adults are related to the decisions they encounter regarding their future directions. These decisions have great impact on the life-style and goals of young adults as they strive to achieve the developmental tasks. Knowledge of the importance and weightiness of these decisions and life experiences is a stressor.

A stressor itself is neutral. The reactions to it, based on personal beliefs and values, are what give it positive or negative power over one's life [26]. Because young adults are testing out and continuing to develop their belief and value

Table 4-5. *Stressors and Wellness Behaviors for the Adolescent*

A. *Common stressors*
1. Physical changes
2. Peer pressure
3. Demands of educational system
4. Changing sexual awareness
5. Choices regarding future life roles
6. Developing sense of identity
7. Integration of childhood into adult-hood
8. Development of self-sufficiency
9. Increasing sexual curiosity and ex-pression
10. Concern about masturbation
11. Changing bonds with family

B. *Wellness behaviors*
1. Adolescents should
   a. Recognize vascillating feelings about body and emotional changes
   b. Cope effectively with changes in self
   c. Move toward reorientation of re-lationships with parents
   d. Experience successes in decision making
   e. Identify with peer group
   f. Maintain sense of humor
2. Families should
   a. Maintain a warm and supportive climate in the home
   b. Provide information and oppor-tunities for discussion about sexu-ality
   c. Promote and support the school's role in sex education
   d. Involve child in decision making
   e. Move toward a reorientation of relationships with adolescent and parents
   f. Provide guidance and limits
   g. Accept adolescent's role in peer group
   h. Maintain trust and respect with adolescent
   i. Maintain sense of humor
   j. Encourage self-expression in grooming habits
   k. Recognize that grooming is one mode of self-expression for the adolescent

systems, many of the decisions are surrounded by feelings of ambivalence, indecision, and increased responsibility.

Some of the early decisions of young adults focus on leaving home, the decreasing influence of the family, committing oneself to a career, establishing an independent life, selecting a mate, and forming one's own family. As the decision is made to leave home, feelings of ambivalence may surface because of the conflict between the desire for the increased independence and the doubts about the resulting increased responsibility.

LEAVING HOME

Although the decision is made to leave home, a sizable number of young people continue to seek support for their economic needs during their 20s. Some of these young people also expect that their emotional and social needs will continue to be met by family. These young people can be viewed as placing a moratorium on their adulthood. It usually means that there is a delay until the young adult must assume responsibility for full-time career and job and/or marriage. These young adults may be making choices in college or graduate schools, and identity-seeking through travel, temporary jobs, volunteer work, or military service. This moratorium on adulthood brings with it stressors and conflicts related to meeting expectations of parents, self, and society. The mental well-being of these young people can best be promoted by exploring and discussing these expectations and supporting them in independent decision making. Perhaps independence is not possible, but the goal of this group of young adults can be increased self-sufficiency. This time can be an exciting one of testing the waters with family and friends continuing to serve as role models. It can be a time when the rather shallow, one-sided relationship of the adolescent and parent can be changed. It can be a time for young people to become interested in their parents, sharing and exploring the interests, feelings, problems, values, concerns, and joys with the people who raised them. By looking at parents in a different light and perhaps giving parents some emotional and social support, young adults indicate an increased feeling of independence.

THE DECREASING INFLUENCE OF THE FAMILY
Young people in their 20s perceive their roles in the family differently. When they are away from home, the parents see the role of young adults (as well as their own roles) differently, but it may be the younger siblings who are having the greatest difficulty with being left behind. The parents are role models for the young adult, and as the young adult becomes a role model for the remaining siblings he will feel less guilty and be developing useful wellness behaviors.

CAREER COMMITMENT AND INDEPENDENCE
One of the most important early tasks of the young adult is commitment to a career. A major part of Erikson's description of the conflict surrounding identity versus role confusion of the adolescent concerned career choices [8]. One recalls that many people are available during adolescence for advice concerning career possibilities. The actual commitment to a career is usually undertaken in one's 20s. It is interesting that advice on career choice usually becomes very scarce at this time, as it is assumed that the decision has already been made. Young adults often reinforce this assumption, since it is often difficult for them to admit their uncertainty. They actively seek less advice because they believe that they should decide for themselves.

The Need for Career Guidance. Nurses who understand this phenomenon can help young adults and their families to see the dynamics of the situation. Family members can continue to be available for advice and support of the young adults as they make this decision. Nurses can also assist young adults in seeking continued resources, including professional career counselors in colleges, employment agencies, and private practice, friends, family and other adult role models.

There are some basic considerations for young adults in making the decision as to a career: (1) What careers are of interest? (2) What careers does the individual have the greatest aptitude for and why? How much difference is there between these two items? If the difference is great, much frustration may be experienced by the young adult, and this discrepancy becomes a distressful life experience. The young adult may need assistance in breaking these considerations into manageable pieces for a decision.

The nurse may assist the individual or the family in listing the top three careers of interest on a piece of paper. Below each of these, the young adult lists specific aptitudes or qualities one should possess for the career. Immediately below this, the individual lists his specific aptitudes and compares the lists. If there are no or few matches, the individual looks at what it would take from him personally to develop these aptitudes and whether he wants to invest that much of himself. Perhaps before being able to answer how much of self can be invested in a particular career, the systematic assessment of career choice should continue. Under each of the careers should be considered such factors as (1) prospective salaries; (2) the amount, availability, and expense in time and money for the education, training, or other preparation needed; (3) the possibility of finding employment in the chosen field after preparing for it; and (4) the growth potential, stability, and security of the career choice. Because the young adult is involved in a systematic assessment, he will usually be less frustrated and will be developing positive coping patterns that may become part of his repertoire for mental well-being.

After the decision is made regarding a career goal and the step-by-step plan for accomplishing it has been developed, there are the nagging but exciting feelings of whether the job will be what the young adult had hoped it would be. It is of great benefit if one can gain some hands-on experience with the job while learning and preparing for the career. Most employment today does involve on-the-job training, no matter how much or how little education the employee has had previously. Most young people require a few months or a few years to enter a field of employment because the process is prolonged by job changes, job training, and education. It is thus recognized that a few years are also needed to stabilize in the job or career to which a commitment is finally made [9].

Job Satisfaction. Whereas some young adults are very satisfied with their career choices, some become disillusioned and frustrated with the job. If the young person has many responsibilities, it can be more difficult to admit to the disillusionment and the need for change. For some the disillusionment occurs because of the stereotyped notion they have of the job instead of a realistic understanding of the work, such as nursing and medicine. One may become bored with a job. The employment may be exciting for a month or a year or two, but then it becomes routine and unstimulating. The person may feel like just another worker and may be unable to develop a sense of importance, accomplishment, uniqueness, or self-direction. These feelings breed self-doubt, depersonalization, and lack of fulfillment. However, tight job markets, family pressures, too little or too much education, and even fear of discrimination can influence young people in such a manner that they hesitate to look for better jobs. On the other hand, too many job changes can lead the young adult to dissatisfaction with the working world, which is understandable since most people have a need for some sense of permanence and belonging.

The adult should be experiencing a sense of importance, accomplishment, uniqueness, and self-direction in the working world to promote mental well-being. Employees, the individual, and family can help to promote these goals. Often, an individual feels dissatisfied without knowing why; without knowing why, it is difficult to deal with this feeling. Thus, the entire job is changed, which may add more stresses. One strategy that can be helpful is to list the desired positive outcomes of sense of importance, accomplishment, uniqueness, self-direction, and any others identified specifically by the individual. The individual must look at how these outcomes are presently being met and if not met, how they might be met. Even in rather large depersonalized settings, employees may find ways of developing uniqueness within themselves and their co-workers. The co-workers can meet in informal groups for coffee breaks, lunch, or committees and give each other individual attention and a sense of uniqueness, which also helps young adults to maintain control of their life experiences.

In addition to upward mobility and job dissatisfaction, job instability may also indicate the need for a change of job. There is always a great amount of tension involved in a job change. Often one's old friends and sources of support are gone, the work may be unfamiliar, and there is a feeling of pressure to learn quickly to prove oneself capable of the job. If the promotion places one on a different rung of the social ladder, old friends are occasionally placed in an awkward position due to the perceived social inequality. Of course if the job change indicates a move to a new location, there are the additional stresses of finding a home, increasing financial strain, moving the family, locating new schools for the children, and perhaps of seeking new employment for the spouse.

Special Problems of Women. In addition to the concerns already discussed, there are additional life experiences for the woman. According to Erikson, the conflict for the woman of being torn between the desires to pursue a career and the concern about wifehood and motherhood continues from adolescence through adulthood. Society has expected that women transfer their dependence on parents to dependence on a husband and acceptance of his life-style as the source of their identity. More women, however, are striving for more independent roles. Inherent in this also is the need to define themselves as competent, self-respecting, intelligent individuals before marriage. At times, this goal is difficult for the woman to meet because of discrimination. Some employers hesitate to hire a woman, especially one of childbearing age, for fear she will marry, become pregnant, and leave. Therefore, long-term jobs are not offered. Of course, some employers believe women are intellectually inferior and emotionally incapable of handling stressful situations.

Women are handling the discrimination issue in regard to their capabilities by proving they are competent, reliable, and creative employees. Many are demonstrating leadership abilities. But the greater conflict for the woman is role related. The questions in need of a systematic answer are: Do I want to be a wife; do I want to be a mother; can I have a career, be a wife, and be a mother? After these questions are answered, the woman must carefully and specifically look at other questions that will need answers, such as those regarding baby-sitters, day-care centers, and adaptation of the children, the husband, and herself. Another common consideration is whether she can take a break from the career to raise children and then return to work. Perhaps the ultimate question is what does the young adult woman really want from life and what will it take to achieve these goals?

Some women begin looking for a husband by pursuing a career and the unexpected happens. They identify with the work role, develop self-confidence, experience feelings of competence, self-respect, and esteem, and find it is difficult to give this up to become a full-time wife and mother. Therefore, to handle this conflict, it is very important that the nurse assist the young adult woman to focus on goals for self and the establishment of an independent life so that decisions can be made to enhance her mental well-being.

SELECTING A MATE

After young adults have achieved independence from their families and have made career choices, they consider the building of their own lives and a new family entity. Therefore, the primary conflict of life for the young adult is intimacy versus isolation. Wellness behaviors are developed that will promote the achievement of intimacy. Erikson describes intimacy as achieving a fusion of identity with that of others, commitment to concrete affiliation(s) and partnership(s), and strength to abide by the commitment to others [7].

To marry or not to marry is an important question for young adults. There are many societal pressures to marry. There are also the pressures from within to seek an intimate partner to share life's experiences and to meet the needs of belonging, love, self-esteem, and self-actualization [17]. It is during these young adult years that the decisions are made and goals are set to take a claim on life and establish self-reliance and competence. For many, marriage is one means to this end. The single adult expresses life-style advantages of more freedom and autonomy. On the other hand, it also carries with it the threat of loneliness. Single persons can achieve intimacy by spending considerable time seeking companions and nurturing relationships.

If the decision is made that two people are committed to sharing life together, then much effort will be required as the life-styles of two are molded together to form a joint workable framework for the relationship. Marriage comprises compromise, sacrifice, and joint decision making. Also, during the early stages of marriage those flaws that were hidden by love and courtship become clear as one sees the other's weaknesses as well as strengths. Couples entering into a partnership are better able to deal with the stresses of marriage when they have strong identities of self as well as couple identities.

The mental well-being of the couple can be enhanced as each is committed to listening to the other and to being perceptive of needs and feelings. One very definite way of expressing this commitment is by keeping the channels of communication open. Major sources of marital disagreements include money, use of leisure time, in-laws, chores, responsibilities, sex roles, and power [9]. Open discussions or disagreements can be constructive in approaching these potential problems. Certainly, it is better if the offensive can be taken, ideas shared, and plans formulated, before real problems develop and defensive game playing becomes the rule. Kieren, Henton, and Marotz [14] have described marital morale as a more accurate determinant of the state of a relationship than happiness or stability. It is a measure of contentment with a marriage based on the number of personal and interpersonal goals that are being achieved [9].

Nurses can assist the couple in evaluating their goals and becoming more cognizant of them. If the expectations of both partners in a marriage are being met, the marriage is likely to continue. But if the expectations are not being met, then separation is usually the result.

FORMING THE FAMILY

One of the major decisions for the young adult couple is parenthood. Should they have children? If yes, when and how many becomes the question. Children can be invigorating, bringing much pride, love, caring, laughter, and tears to a family. Realistically, they also bring extra work and increased financial responsibilities.

Adequate preparation is essential so that both mother and father anticipate and begin to prepare for the changes that the children will bring to their relationship and life. Parenting classes, prenatal classes, and informal discussions with family and friends are resources. By preparing for these changes, they can maintain and often enhance their mental well-being. Husbands may experience a heightening in their sense of masculinity as they witness the growth and movements of the unborn child [9]. At this time they may perceive their increased responsibility as primarily "father protector and provider." The woman may experience more ambivalent feelings as she loses her figure and experiences some of the physical discomforts of pregnancy. On the other hand, she may enjoy the added attention and increased esteem gained from playing such an important role in the development and birth of a new life.

The many facets of childrearing call for loving communicative parents who are generators of alternatives. There are many stressors present when raising children, but the parents who are flexible and have more than one alternative or option in approaching a given situation are usually developing mental wellness behaviors and role modeling life experiences for the children. Chapter 2 explains the dynamics and stresses of family to be considered by the new family unit. If the young adult couple decides not to have children, then prevention becomes the question. The young couple needs concrete answers. They are in need of information and facts in order to make an informed decision about contraception.

Factors for the young couple to consider in choosing a contraceptive method are convenience, sexual response, accessibility, effectiveness rate, danger to health, and cost. When nurses provide couples with information about the various contraceptive methods, they will be most effective if they establish a warm, comfortable, confident atmosphere and anticipate questions couples may have. It may be embarrassing for some couples to ask their questions. A basic point for nurses to stress is that the most effective contraceptive method for any couple is the method with which they are comfortable and will use 100 percent of the time.

WELLNESS TECHNIQUES

Having looked at some of the stressors related to the life experiences of the young adult, we now outline several strategies or techniques the young adult can employ to promote mental wellness and to continue developing psychosocial wellness behaviors. These wellness behaviors can be helpful throughout all the adult years.

As the young adult uses the previously learned wellness behaviors and expands these to include additional interventions for the promotion of psychosocial wellness, the power of the mind and body unite in dealing with stress. One of the nurse's first tasks is to assist the family in determining whether the stress is useful or destructive. Donald Tubesing [26], an educational psychologist and president of the Whole Person Associates in Duluth, Minn., recommends that the following questions be answered.

1. Do little things irritate me?
2. Do I have trouble sleeping and then wake up tired and grouchy?
3. Do I worry a lot? Feel trapped? Complain? Frequently snap at those I love?
4. Do I suffer physical symptoms?

If the answer is yes to even one question, the family member may be experiencing harmful stress and need to initiate wellness behaviors.

Next, the nurse should assist the family member in identifying stressors. The young adult can keep a daily record of activities, daily situations and responses, and reactions, all of which can aid in identifying harmful stress. It is important that at the end of the day the individual list the feelings he is experiencing, as this is often the necessary clue for assisting the young adult in dealing with the stress.

Third, nurses can assist the family in looking at and assessing what the stress reactions have been, which responses have been helpful, and which have not been helpful. Those responses that have been helpful can be maintained, while attainable alternative responses are shared and formulated for the nonhelpful reactions. Some of the nonhelpful reactions are the result of habitual responses to specific circumstances. Nurses can assist people in breaking poor stress-response habits over a period of time by assisting family members to make other choices consciously. Tubesing offers the following four techniques for taking charge of one's reactions to life experiences [26].

1. Reorganize self. Take control of the way time is spent, by learning to avoid using 10 dollars worth of energy and worry on a 10-cent problem. This waste is often the result of having unclear goals and not being able to separate the decisions and problems into manageable pieces. A helpful strategy is to have the young adult separate decisions into manageable pieces and include a timetable or plan. This plan may be hourly, daily, weekly, monthly, or yearly depending on the situation. When not broken down into manageable pieces, the decisions and their outcomes can become overwhelming and all too time-consuming.

2. Gain control of the environment by developing scene-changing skills. This technique can be used to learn to control the environment. The nurse can assist the family member in identifying the stressors in the environment and in deciding how the environment can be altered. Another strategy to consider is, if one environment cannot be altered, then one might supplement it with diversion, reevaluate it for other strengths, and learn how to compromise. This process often entails setting priorities.

3. Take control of your attitude. Use techniques such as relabeling, whispering, and imagination. *Relabeling* is the "ability to see a promise in every problem." For example, suppose that when a teenager responds negatively to a mother's request, instead of the mother seeing it as rebellion against authority, she sees it as a demonstration of the child's independence. The fact is that the mother's response will be different and less stress will be experienced. *Whispering* is "the art of giving oneself positive messages when things are going wrong." "We all talk to ourselves about ourselves," says Tubesing, "so why not talk nicely?" For example, if a father is uptight about his business, wife, and child he would whisper, "I am a good businessman, husband, and father." *Imagination,* "the art of laughter," is the ability to accept and appreciate the incongruities of life. Tubesing states, "If you can laugh at yourself, it sets one apart from the problem and then it can be tackled from a new perspective."

4. Build your strength. Strength building is another important factor in managing stress and promoting wellness; both physical and mental stamina are important here. This stamina can be accomplished as discussed in other chapters through exercise, eating a nutritious diet, and participating in daily relaxation routines.

Everyone has resources for dealing with stress; some are effective and some are not. When one's customary resources or "energizers" are not working, then new ones can be initiated. The essence of choosing an effective energizer is that it must give a new perspective on life. To assist in identifying resources, Tubesing [26] offers his personal list as an example.

Physical resources: jogging, pruning the shrubs. Emotional: hugging my kids, paying my wife a compliment. Social: phoning a friend, having a party. Intellectual: reading, listening to music. Spiritual: admiring the beauty of the world around me, spending ten minutes meditating.

It is recommended that if one usually turns to physical exercise when feeling stressed (and it is ineffective), then one should try a more calming activity such as needlework, crossword puzzles, or reading. On the other hand, if one normally watches television or reads (and these activities are ineffective), then one should jog, work in the garden, play tennis, or do something more physical.

Through effort, one can break poor stress-response habits by reacting differently to daily life experiences. Identifying stressors and how they are affecting the individual will within a period of time result in new and better ways of dealing with stress, replacing the old destructive ways.

Perhaps the most important wellness-behavior techniques with which the nurse can assist the family are methods of relaxation. She should emphasize the importance of performing these techniques 2 to 3 times daily. These techniques reinforce the mind-body relationship and the unity of the two. The nurse can teach these relaxation exercises in 5 to 15 minutes. It is important that she repeat these with the client several times on successive visits. Three types of relaxation techniques follow.

Breathing Exercises. Breathing exercises can be used to increase relaxation and the ability to cope with stressors, and to reduce feelings of tension. The exercises that follow are written in the second person, so that as the nurse is reading to the family member, he is responding to a directive. When he repeats the exercise to himself, the second person continues to be appropriate.

EXERCISE A (Time: 5 minutes)
Slowly close your eyes.
Let your mind wander aimlessly (pause), and now you are thinking of nothing.
Take a deep breath and let it out slowly.
As you take another breath and let it out slowly, you are feeling your body relax.
Concentrate on your next breath.
Breathe in slowly, gently, and with ease; it feels good to fill your lungs.
Slowly let out your breath.
As you let your breath out, the tensions and concerns of the day go with it.
You are enjoying the pleasures of the day with each breath.
Breathe in and count 1, 2, 3, 4.
Hold your breath and count 1, 2, 3, 4. You are relaxing; as you breathe out count
    1, 2, 3, 4, 5, 6, 7, 8. Repeat 6 to 12 times.
You are comfortable and at peace. Your mind is clear, your body is relaxed, and
    you feel refreshed and calmly active and actively calm.
You take a breath, slowly open your eyes, let your breath out, and smile.

The following breathing exercise works well with individuals who respond to colors. Before beginning, ask the family member his favorite color. Substitute his color in the exercise.

EXERCISE B (Time: 5 minutes)
Slowly close your eyes.
Take a deep breath, let it out slowly, and relax.

Begin concentrating on your favorite color of soft relaxing yellow. As you concentrate on yellow, your mind's eye begins to focus on yellow clouds floating in the distance.

Take another slow, deep breath and let it out slowly.

With each breath, the clouds are moving closer; you feel gradually more relaxed and secure as the soft, billowy yellow clouds surround you.

Breathe in slowly and deeply, counting 1, 2, 3, 4, and hold your breath counting 1, 2, 3, 4.

Let your breath out, counting 1, 2, 3, 4, 5, 6, 7, 8.

As you breathe out, the yellow billowy cloud enlarges and floats lazily about until your next breath.

Breathe in counting 1, 2, 3, 4.

Hold counting 1, 2, 3, 4.

Let your breath out and count 1, 2, 3, 4, 5, 6, 7, 8. Repeat 6 to 12 times.

You are very relaxed and comfortable as you watch the yellow, billowy clouds lazily drift about you.

Breathe normally and watch the clouds slowly begin to drift away.

You are comfortable and at peace. Your mind is clear, your body is relaxed, and you feel refreshed, alert, and calm.

You take a breath, slowly open your eyes, let your breath out, and smile.

Guided Imagery Exercises. The guided imagery relaxation technique can be used anytime and is especially useful for falling asleep. The nurse should use images to which the individual can respond and that are natural pleasures for him. The nurse can ask, "What is your favorite season, color, relaxing pastime, and pleasure for which there is no time or money." From this information, she can construct an individualized guided imagery.

GUIDED IMAGERY FOR SLEEP

Close your eyes. Take a slow, deep breath, let it out slowly, and relax. You have just finished eating an elegant, nutritious meal and are now finishing a refreshing glass of wine. You are relaxed, full, and warm. Your eyes are heavy and you want to sleep. You are slowly climbing a special staircase, and you enter a huge room with a large soft bed. You are so tired now and feel so relaxed you have no cares or concerns. You want only to lie down in the warm soft feather bed. You lie down and as you sink deeper into the feather bed, you sink into a deep, deep, sleep. You are dreaming of pleasant things, and you sleep soundly, quietly, peacefully. You are in a comfortable, relaxed, peaceful sleep.

GUIDED IMAGERY FOR RELAXATION

Slowly close your eyes. Take a slow, deep breath and let it out slowly. You feel the tensions leaving your body as you concentrate on the scene. You are the star actor and the spotlight is on you. The air is crisp and cool outside, and you hear the wind blowing. But you are stretched out in front of the fireplace on the floor, on a fluffy soft carpet and pillow. You are warm and toasty from the warmth of the fire in the huge stone fireplace. You hear the soft music in the background, and you snuggle down into the carpet and become more relaxed and secure as you hear the crackle of the fire. The carpet is like a soft cloud cushioning you. You sink deeper into the cloud. The soft smell of burning wood permeates the air, and you feel warm and relaxed and hear only the crackle of the fire as the music drifts off in the distance. All of your concerns have drifted away, and you are relaxed, warm, and drifting into a comfortable restful sleep. You feel safe, comfortable, and warm as you are stretched out in front of the fire, and you feel sleepy, restful, and warm. (If used as sleep technique, stop here; if not, then proceed.)

Allow 2 to 3 minutes of quiet rest. You are feeling rested, relaxed, and very competent in the handling of the activities of the day. In your relaxed state, you will be alert to the decisions you will be making; you will feel calm and relaxed within yourself. Take a deep breath, open your eyes, and smile as you feel alert and refreshed.

ANOTHER GUIDED IMAGERY

Close your eyes, take a deep breath, and let it out slowly. As you take in another breath, you are concentrating your thoughts on a happy, relaxing day at the beach. Let your breath out, and feel yourself relax and become more comfortable. It is warm and the sun is bright as you lie on the warm beach. The sun feels good on your skin, and you feel the pleasant, cool breezes from the ocean. As you lie there peacefully, you hear the rhythmic lapping of the water against the shore, and it quietly echoes the sounds of the beach. With each breath, you are more relaxed, comfortable, and sleepy. Your body relaxes in the sun and you feel well. Pause for 1 to 2 minutes. You are feeling comfortable, and you slowly open your eyes. You are awake, alert, refreshed, and feel calmly active and actively calm.

A SHORT DAYTIME RELAXING RESPITE

Close your eyes, stretch your body, extend your arms and legs, tighten your muscles—tight, tighter—take a deep breath, and as you let it out relax your muscles and relax your body. Think of this as a relaxation shower. Repeat it three times. Stretch your body, extend your arms and legs, tighten your muscles, take a deep breath, and as you let it out relax your muscles and relax your body. Your body feels relaxed and your mind wants to be relaxed too. As you become more relaxed, your mind lazily wanders to vivid thoughts of a warm spring day. (Pause.) As you look up into the cloud-filled sky, you see soft, billowy clouds floating by. You begin concentrating on floating like the clouds. You see a soft, billowy cloud coming your way; it slows and you snuggle into it. It is soft and comforting, and your mind and body are at peace floating, floating quietly and leisurely. (Pause for 1 minute.) The cloud slows, you feel good, and the cloud is gone. As the clouds disappear, you open your eyes, smile and feel alert, refreshed, and comfortable.

Another, perhaps more effective method of teaching the relaxation techniques is to tape-record them and leave the tape with the family. If the techniques are utilized in the morning, then the mental and physical wellness stage is set for the management of the day. It is also recommended that they be practiced in the evening as this helps to assure a good relaxing night's sleep. These exercises can also be used when one feels the need to enhance the mental wellness state. The techniques can be utilized almost anywhere and anytime since they take only 3 to 10 minutes and require only some degree of privacy, comfort, and relative quiet. For best results, these techniques should not be practiced immediately after eating

Table 4-6. Stressors and Wellness Behaviors for the Young Adult

A. *Common stressors*
   1. Increased independence
   2. Leaving home
   3. Decreasing influence of the original family
   4. Career choice
   5. Selecting a mate
   6. Forming own family
   7. Increased responsibility
   8. Choice regarding parenthood
   9. Two-career families

B. *Wellness behaviors*
  Young adults should
   1. Assume responsibility for decision making
   2. Assume responsibility for reorientation with family of origin
   3. Commit themselves to a career
   4. Experience a sense of well-being in the job situation
   5. Be able to fuse own identity with that of an important other person
   6. Commit selves to a relationship with an important other person
   7. Identify feelings regarding parenthood
   8. Prepare for parenthood
   9. Be loving, flexible, communicative, wellness-oriented parents
  10. Creatively manage stress
  11. Encourage spouse to share in socialization of children

as they can slow digestion. A relaxed mind and body is better able to cope with the major and minor events of the life experiences. Table 4-6 summarizes the stressors and wellness behaviors of this young adult period.

Middle Adult Years

The life-style of adults in their middle to late 30s and 40s is based on the earlier decisions made in their 20s, but these decisions are implemented in more conservative and conventional ways. Havighurst proposed that the primary social concerns of early adulthood are rearing children, managing a home, taking on civic responsibilities, and finding a congenial social group [10]. The social concerns and stressors involving family and community relationships will be discussed first, as these are most common for the adults in their 30s.

As discussed in the young adulthood section, the majority have already made the decision concerning parenthood. Those who chose not to have children are still experiencing the questions and doubts of others and perhaps self-doubt about the decision. The self-doubt is present because they know it is not too late to reverse the decision. Therefore, some couples will reexamine the decision and evaluate any shift of priorities, readiness, or desire to have children.

Adulthood is characterized by the individual's ability to set goals to continue growing, then maintaining, then progressing, and then stabilizing. Adults in their 30s and 40s are so busy making efforts to prevent being caught up in the humdrum of the demands of daily activities that they lose sight of the goals and may find themselves in a rut.

GENERATIVITY VERSUS STAGNATION

Erikson [7] identifies the major conflict of the adult years as generativity versus stagnation. He describes the adult who is striving for generativity as someone who has (1) concern for establishing and guiding the next generation; (2) concern for others, which includes "belief in the species"; and (3) concern for productivity as well as for progeny. This conflict does not mean one must have his own children; generativity has a much broader meaning than producing children. The crux of generativity relates to the benefit of others. Therefore, adults can make contributions to future generations by supporting, teaching, nurturing, and serving children or other adults. One can achieve generativity through involvement with the welfare of future generations [9], which may be obtained through community groups, work, and political involvement.

Many of the concerns that adults have about children and their role in childrearing have been discussed in the previous young adulthood section. The focus of the childrearing discussion for this section is recognition of the fears and frustrations that the adult experiences. The nurse can be an excellent resource to the family, assisting members with their questions and finding resources for their answers. One of the stressors experienced is the conflicting information offered by various resources. It is important that mother and father have the information and that they have discussed a unified plan and practice for childrearing, as consistency between parents is important to decrease distress of both the child and parents. With more women working, fathers are increasingly being recognized and accepted as important persons in the day-to-day socialization of children.

MANAGING A HOME

The task of organizing a household and home is defined by Havighurst [10] as one of the major concerns of adulthood. As discussed throughout this book, all family members have responsibilities in the home, and their joint decision making can strengthen family unity. To decrease the stress of this task, perhaps the single most important factor is that each knows one's task, role, and responsibilities so that all tasks are met. Smooth, efficient running of a household is a major organizational task. Thus, the family member with the best organizational skills should spearhead the task.

The adult goals of maintaining family ties with parents and siblings encompass adjusting to relationships with in-laws. In-law relationships require a certain amount of diplomacy, compromise, and sacrifice, even with the best of all possible parents-in-law. Feelings generated between husband and wife in regard to in-law situations should be discussed immediately and not permitted to "brew on the back burner." The husband and wife can help each other to understand and accept their parents better and help the parents to understand and accept the spouse better. A workable plan for in-law relations can be rewarding and probably challenging, too. An unbiased third person such as the nurse can facilitate understanding of the dynamics present in a given situation and help to develop a workable plan.

CAREER AND SOCIAL LIFE

About one half of one's waking hours are spent at work. As discussed in previous sections, men and women make career choices during their 20s, but the 30s are usually when they become stabilized in their jobs. Goals are set with a plan as to how to keep their places or take advantage of the right opportunity to advance.

A rigid timetable for this advancement can be quite stressful if it is not possible to keep to the timetable. Adults will be more satisfied with self and the job if they continue to assess goals relative to their job and to develop alternatives. The distresses experienced are often produced by the expectations of others and not of self.

Friends are another important aspect of social development as they can have a strong influence and impact on one's emotional adjustment. Friends do a great deal of data processing for one another. A friend's response can be comforting or upsetting, but it at least gives the individual additional data to consider. Harry Stack Sullivan [25] states that social approval has as great an influence on one's behavior as physical needs. Friends help to determine self-concept, self-esteem, perception of trust in others, and to some degree, the overall social climate in the community. The individual and couples can assess whether people are friends or just acquaintances, and whether they generate or facilitate positive aspects of the self.

ADAPTING TO PHYSICAL CHANGES

As a person advances into the middle years, one is faced with adjusting either to female menopause or to male climacteric, to bodily changes, to the spouse's confusion, one's own uncertainty, aging parents, and children leaving home. Both men and women in their 40s find that their reproductive organs begin to atrophy. For the woman, the end of the reproductive cycle is clearly distinguished by menopause, whereas the male climacteric is gradual and less obvious. The psychological impact of menopause is often exaggerated. The stereotypic picture of a woman going through menopause is that of a depressed, tired, tearful, frigid, unpredictable bundle of nerves, which is a misconception. A study by Newgarten reported that about 75 percent of women felt that menopause did not change them in any important way [20]. About 50 percent of them found the menopause unpleasant. The remaining 50 percent reported they were not troubled by it. Young women were more concerned about it than women actually experiencing it. Perhaps this concern was due to fear of the unknown and the "horror stories" of menopause that have been passed down through the ages. It is important that women have the facts about menopause and that the young adult woman has correct information while her attitudes are forming and while her own mother is experiencing it. She can thus be of more support to her mother and more able to eliminate her fear of the unknown.

Menopause often comes at the same time that children are leaving, and it can exacerbate the feelings that mothering and homemaking roles are coming to an end. The nurse can assist the menopausal woman in recognizing that these events do not mean an end but the beginning of new accomplishments. The nurse can help the family to be more supportive and tolerant of inconsistencies that may arise and can encourage them to continue to demonstrate their love and caring.

There is much discussion as to whether there is a male climacteric, and if so, just when it occurs. There does seem to be a definite transitional period for men in their 40s or 50s. They reexamine their lives and may make radical changes in the way they do things. The man will probably be better able to cope with these changes if he and the family know to anticipate them. The open lines of communication among family members are important in supporting the man in the process of evaluating his life.

LIFE GOAL REEVALUATION

The man and woman are each examining goals that they have not and probably will not reach. This period is an opportunity for the adult to decide which of these goals are no longer important, which can be discarded, and which can be replaced with new goals. This process does not have to be perceived as an adjustment to failure. In order for the adult to cope with this reassessment period, one needs to keep the   goals and changes in perspective. Goals that continue to be important but cannot be achieved can be modified. Modifying rather than discarding a valued goal is important to the mental wellness of an individual. This time can be very positive in one's life as one looks forward to middle age.

To assist the middle-age family member in assessing stressors, the nurse can suggest that he complete the following sentences.

1. What I most want to change about my life is ———————————.
2. What I most want to keep the same in my life is ———————————.
3. What is most lacking in my life is   ———————————.
4. What I most need in my life is ———————————.
5. What I am willing to do to change my life is ———————————.

A careful assessment of these answers will allow the middle-age adult to gain direction for making alterations in life to meet one's goals and to continue a creative and productive life.

The Self-Contract. In order to maintain the perspective sets for the reevaluated goals, self-contracting can be a useful wellness behavior for the middle-age individual to develop. The family member takes responsibility for self, participates in the decision-making process, and becomes his own problem solver by self-contracting. Self-discovery is much more rewarding than being told what to do.

Before writing the contract, one must give some thought to goal setting in order to provide for creative management of stressors. The goals set should be unique to the family member. Becoming goal conscious does not have to take spontaneity out of life. Goals can be enjoyed at every step of the process if they are specific, totally achievable, practical, and unique to the individual.

A number of rules must be followed while self-contracting for wellness. The family member should pick the right time to begin, set one goal at a time, and plan the day accordingly. No one can be perfect every day, so one day a week should be set aside for permission to be imperfect. This practice is called the "free day" rule. Because most individuals have grandiose initial plans, it is recommended that the actual goal be set at 50 percent so that it can more realistically be accomplished. For example, if an individual wishes to lose 40 pounds, he sets the goal for 20 pounds. Some individuals choose a reward for themselves if the goal is achieved, as well as a cost if the contract is not fulfilled. Record keeping by a graph or calendar is helpful in identifying patterns of behavior. Reevaluation can be scheduled at specific intervals so that these behaviors can be reviewed. Many individuals sign their contracts in order to psychologically formalize them and to make them more meaningful.

Maintaining Wellness Behaviors. Exercise and the use of leisure time are of specific importance to the middle-age adult in maintaining high-level mental well-being. It is especially important for the middle-age adult to develop a reper-toire of energizers at this time in preparation for retirement and future life experi-ences. All of the psychosocial strategies and techniques discussed in the young adult section are useful for the middle-age adult to encourage mental wellness behaviors through relaxation.

During middle age one has the realization that he as well as his parents are aging. According to Newgarten [20], some adults during this period come to sympathize with parents in a new way. At the same time (around 40) that the person may be acquiring a new sympathy for his parents, the parents may be turning to him for aid—financial, emotional, physical, and social. How one responds to this request for assistance depends not only on that person's maturity and moral values but also on the extent of the request, the previous relationship with one's parents, other responsibilities, and resources available for the aging parents. Dependence versus independence is a conflict that both sets of adults are experiencing as the relation-ship with parents and the adult child is being reevaluated. It is essential that the elderly adult parents be as independent as possible in the dependent state. Some decisions may have to be made regarding the care and safety of aging parents when and if they can no longer care for themselves. The nurse can assist with resources available and with exploring the stresses, joys, and ramifications of having parents move into the home. Mental wellness need not be compromised if alternatives are well understood before implementation. An understanding of the later years discussed in the next section will help the adult parents to understand better the goals of their parents. Table 4-7 summarizes the stresses and wellness behaviors for the middle adult years.

Table 4-7. Stressors and Wellness Behaviors for the Middle-age Adult

A. *Common stressors*	2. Establish selves in community groups
1. Physical signs of aging	3. Make contributions to future generations
2. Childrearing problems	
3. Children leaving home	4. Utilize resources beneficial to childrearing practices
4. Unmet life goals	
5. In-law relationships	5. Recognize individual family members' tasks
6. Job pressures	
7. Status in social group	6. Establish positive expectations of aging process
8. Use of leisure time	
9. Dependence of aging parents	7. Evaluate and revise life goals
10. Organizing and managing the household	8. Use positive coping mechanisms for dealing with aging parents
B. *Wellness behaviors*	9. Provide time for leisure activity
Middle-age adults should	10. Adjust to physical and psychosocial changes
1. Maintain open communications with important other people	

Later Adulthood

When does old age begin? At what point is the term "elderly" properly applied? In considering mental wellness, the answer varies since some consider old age a state of mind despite well-recognized physical signs of aging. For many, the reality of being old starts with attaining eligibility for senior citizens' clubs or discounts (as early as age 55), with signing up for Social Security or Medicare benefits in the 60s, or when deteriorating health necessitates hospitalization or a change of residence. The emotional realization of old age helps to guide the adaptation to it.

INTEGRITY VERSUS DESPAIR

Mental wellness in the older family can be understood in terms of Erikson's conceptualization of integrity versus despair. The older person attempts to come to terms with himself as he begins to contemplate the remaining span of life. Erikson describes this task as "acceptance of one's one and only life cycle and of the people who have become significant to it as something that had to be and that, by necessity, permitted no substitutions." Integrity requires the wisdom to accept the fact that there are no "ifs" in life. One was born with certain genetic characteristics into a certain family, into a certain set of circumstances, and at a particular point in history. One makes certain decisions throughout life, and none of these circumstances can be altered. One need not waste energy speculating about what might have been *if.* Past happenings cannot be altered and a life cannot be lived over. One of the beauties of old age that can enhance the mental wellness of the elderly person as well as those around him is the use of past experiences, knowledge, and mature judgment to round out his own life and to improve the path for others to follow [16].

During the "September years," the elderly person seeks to bring a sense of closure to his life. Most spend time rounding out their accomplishments or even seeking new avenues of interest. There is usually time for leisure and for catching up on hobbies and other activities that took a backseat during working years. Contentment, emotional peace, and mental well-being can come to the person who derives pleasure from leisure activities, a sense of fulfillment, the growth and development of children and grandchildren, and the accomplishments of the institutions one helped to create. The person can use senior citizen years as a time of relaxed integration of past years into successful closure. This integration is fundamental to achieving and maintaining mental wellness during this psychosocial stage. The alternative is a sense of despair, of standing at the fringes of life with nothing to hope for.

ADAPTING TO RETIREMENT

Maintaining quality of life during old age requires adaptation to certain changes, which may be perceived as losses. Loss of income is a change usually associated with retirement. As the person goes to the social security office, he may well wonder what the next years hold. Many seniors have reasonable pensions supplemented by social security, while others have to manage on social security alone. Times of rapid inflation have hit the elderly especially hard for they are often unable to seek a job for higher wages as many in preretirement years can do. Income holds the key to mental wellness in many ways by influencing or even dictating many of life's choices for the elderly person. Housing, food and nutrition, illness care, and social activities are all greatly influenced by the older person's income. A major task of this country and its communities is to assure adequate income and to provide services that maximize its effectiveness.

The person's attitude toward retirement is important in promoting wellness. If one sees retirement as a change from one mode of activity to another, he will not be likely to perceive it as a loss. If one feels he is "being retired" against his will, he will see it as a negative influence in his life. As time passes and the increasingly female work force face retirement along with spouses, mutual sharing of feelings and support for one another can enhance both partners' facing changes in work situations.

ADAPTING TO PHYSICAL CHANGES

Physical changes frequently accompany old age and may require considerable adaptation as the person seeks to regain equilibrium. Vaillant [27, 28] in a longitudinal study of men obtained data suggesting that positive mental health significantly retards irreversible midlife decline in physical health. Thus the person who strives to maintain a high level of mental wellness throughout life experiences a doubling of its long-term effects. One is able to better maintain both mental and physical wellness throughout the remainder of life. Nurses need to realize the tremendous importance of promoting both physical and mental wellness in earlier stages. The habits, values, and attitudes pay big dividends as the person reaches later years.

CHANGING LIVING CIRCUMSTANCES

Older people may face changes in their home environments. Many persons choose to move from a large house to a smaller one or to an apartment, or from their home in a cold winter climate to one in the Sun Belt. Even when changes are not forced by circumstances, considerable adaptation is required as new communities and new friends present themselves.

DEATH OF LOVED ONES

At some time during the period of old age, the person faces the death of a spouse or other important loved ones. Persons may react differently to life events depending on when they occur during the life cycle. Death of a mother is certainly perceived differently by the 7-year-old and the 60-year-old. The older person comes to expect the death of a parent or a spouse; Eisdorfer and Wilkie [6] speculate that death of a spouse may not constitute so severe a stress because it is expected. Because of the experience of peers, the older person is more prepared to deal with his own loss of a spouse. Women are conditioned to become widows and probably are better prepared emotionally for this event than men.

MAINTAINING WELLNESS BEHAVIORS

The mentally well older person, in general, can cope successfully with most anticipated stressful situations. He has had many years to learn coping skills and to anticipate and deal with life's stressors. He has the wisdom of years of experience in making judgments in a variety of situations and is a veteran of his numerous mistakes and successes. The older person needs the support of family and the nurse to maintain self-assurance, self-esteem, and competence. The older person need not fear the changes that occur in old age. Chances are in his favor that he will belong to the majority of older Americans who live independently and happily for many postretirement years. The perception that days are too short for all one wants or needs to do is a positive sign of mental wellness. Old age can be a time of enrichment as one reviews one's life and selects activities that will round out experiences.

An important ingredient to successful adaptation to life events during old age is the presence of effective support groups. One of these, of course, is the family. Distance need not prevent the family from maintaining its bonds with letters and telephone calls to make frequent contacts. Elderly persons find self-help groups to be effective support networks. They foster collective group adaptation and assurance that one is a socially important person. The system of peers is another important support network, and many older persons who live far from their families find neighbors and friends to be helpful and supportive. Some cite friends as more important than family members in making adaptations to life situations. It seems that many elderly persons avoid and even resent having to rely on their families. Perhaps the perceived threat to their independence is too great. If the peer network is effective in helping older people meet their needs, mental wellness will be preserved. Family members need not feel hurt if the loved one's friends seem to assume greater importance than they do. They need simply to understand that independence and self-esteem are prized possessions for mental wellness and that the older person has found a means of coping that is most effective. The nurse should be alert for such potential conflicts and mediate appropriately.

The peer network serves another important function, that of helping the elderly person avoid loneliness. Aguilera [1] cites loneliness as a major threat to a healthful old age. Communities should help older citizens by providing opportunities for useful activities in the company of others. Given a place and some direction, older citizens can have meaningful activities in the community, in age-integrated groups as well as senior citizens' clubs. Older family members should be encouraged to participate. Many of these organizations offer companionship, support, and help in locating community services that may be of help. Most important, they offer person-to-person contact, which assures the older person that he is still important in this world. Social and psychological needs can be met effectively and consistently by peer groups and friends of all ages.

ACCEPTING MORTALITY

The older person is well aware that death is near [11]. Death is the final stage of living, to be faced by one and all at some appointed hour. Ecclesiastes tells us that "to every thing there is a season, and a time to every purpose under the heaven: a time to be born, and a time to die."

The older person faces the death of friends and perhaps the spouse. Eventually, one must face the eventuality of one's own death, accept it as part of life, or face the despair of uncertainty. Nurses have tremendous potential for helping older persons and their families to accept the eventuality of death. Mental wellness until the end of life requires integration of all life experiences into a purposeful, meaningful whole. The experience of death is but one component of what is to be integrated. Family members, friends, and self-help groups can all provide insight and direction for the older person seeking meaning in life's end. The highest level of mental wellness is achieved when the older person comes to view death as a deeply personal experience that has meaning for others as well. As others have left their mark on him through their living and dying, so will he leave his mark on others. The nurse can facilitate this developmental process, assuming a pivotal role by helping the older person derive perspective and meaning from death. As Lidz [16] has stated: "The way in which they lead their last years provides an example and a warning to their descendants and influences how they provide for their own

Table 4-8. Stressors and Wellness Behaviors in Later Adulthood

A. *Common stressors*	B. *Wellness behaviors*
1. Physical changes	Older adults should
2. Fear of growing old	1. Maintain self-sufficiency and independence
3. Retirement	2. Experience an interest in "well aging"
4. Changes in sexuality	3. Share feelings regarding changes with important other people
5. Fear of helplessness	4. Experience feelings of love from family and important other people
6. Change in financial situation	5. Utilize past experiences in present adulthood
7. Change in residence	6. Continue to develop work and leisure-time activities
8. Expectations of growing old	

later years. Further, how the old people are treated by their children commonly furnishes an illustration to grandchildren of how persons treat parents. The aged may be close to the end of life, but the way in which they live and let live will continue to influence life." It is crucial that family support be full of the mutual caring, warmth, and respect that characterized earlier times with the family. Mental wellness of all family members demands it, and for the elderly family member who faces the end of his years, the support itself is life giving.

Successful aging may depend as much on expectations as it does on health and financial base [23]. What the elderly person expects to happen may well determine in reality what does happen. But in recognizing these expectations, the individual is in a position to influence positively what will happen. A person is only as old as one expects to be. The saying, "You are as old as you feel" certainly seems to be true. Most older persons fear helplessness and sickness. But in the absence of poor health, why should growing older be an ordeal? The concept of *old* tends to be associated with the concept of illness, but it need not be so [5]. The stressors and wellness behaviors for later adult years are summarized in Table 4-8.

References

1. Aguilera, D. C. Stressors in late adulthood. *Fam. Community Health* 2:61, 1980.
2. Baumrind, D. Child care practices anteceding three patterns of preschool behavior. *Genet. Psychol. Monogr.* 75:43, 1967.
3. Baumrind, D. Current patterns of parental authority. *Dev. Psychol. Monogr.* 1:1, 1971.
4. Benjamin, H., and Ihlenfeld, C. Transsexualism. *Am. J. Nurs.* 73:457, 1973.
5. Dangott, L. Aging and high level wellness. *Health Values* 2:40, 1978.
6. Eisdorfer, C., and Wilkie, F. L. Stress and Behavior in the Aging. In *Issues in Mental Health and Aging*, Vol. 1, *Research*. Washington, D.C.: National Institute of Mental Health, Center for Studies of the Mental Health of the Aging.
7. Erikson, E. *Childhood and Society* (2nd ed.). New York: Norton, 1963.
8. Erikson, E. *Identity: Youth and Crisis*. New York: Norton, 1968.

9. Freiberg, K. L. *Human Development: A Life-Span Approach.* N. Scituate, Mass.: Duxbury, 1979.
10. Havinghurst, R. *Developmental Tasks and Education* (3rd ed.). New York: McKay, 1972.
11. Jahoda, M. *Current Concepts of Positive Mental Health.* New York: Basic Books, 1958.
12. Jahoda, M. Toward a Social Psychology of Mental Health. In A. M. Rose (Ed.), *Mental Health and Mental Disorder.* New York: Norton, 1955.
13. Jourard, S. M. *The Transparent Self.* New York: Van Nostrand, 1971.
14. Kieren, D., Henton, J., and Marotz, R. *His and Hers: A Problem-Solving Approach to Marriage.* Hinsdale, Ill.: Dryden, 1975.
15. Kliman, G. *Psychological Emergencies of Childhood.* New York: Grune & Stratton, 1968.
16. Lidz, T. *The Person* (rev. ed.). New York: Basic Books, 1976.
17. Maslow, A. H. *Motivation and Personality.* New York: Harper, 1954.
18. Menninger, K. *The Human Mind.* New York: Knopf, 1946.
19. Mental Health Association. *Mental Health is One, Two Three.* Arlington, Va. (zip 22209).
20. Newgarten, B. (Ed.). *Middle Age and Aging.* Chicago: University of Chicago Press, 1968.
21. Reres, M. E. Stressors in adolescence. *Fam. Community Health* 2:31, 1980.
22. Selye, H. *Stress Without Distress.* New York: Lippincott, 1974.
23. Smith, B. K. *Aging in America.* Boston: Beacon Press, 1973.
24. Starr, B. D., and Goldstein, H. S. *Human Development and Behavior.* New York: Springer, 1975.
25. Sullivan, H. S. *The Interpersonal Theory of Psychiatry.* New York: Norton, 1963.
26. Tubesing, D. A. *Stress Skills Participant Workshop.* Duluth, Minn.: Whole Person Associates, 1979.
27. Vaillant, G. *Adaptation to Life.* Boston: Little, Brown, 1977.
28. Vaillant, G. Natural history of male psychologic health. *N. Engl. J. Med.* 301:1249, 1979.
29. Westley, W. A., and Epstein, N. B. *The Silent Majority.* San Francisco: Jossey-Bass, 1969.
30. Whaley, L. F., and Wong, D. L. *Nursing Care of Infants and Children.* St. Louis: Mosby, 1979.
31. Wu, R. Stressors at birth. *Fam. Community Health* 2:1, 1980.

Assessment Tool

The nurse should indicate for each item whether the family or family member accomplishes the item according to criteria indicated in the columns. If an item or section does not apply, the points represented by that item or section should be so indicated by marking the "not applicable" column. In scoring at the end of each section, the category "total points possible" means the total number of points that could be attained if every item applied. The "total not applicable" category shows the total items or sections that do not apply to the family at this time; this number should be subtracted from the "total points possible" to obtain the "total applicable" score. When comparing "total applicable" with the "total points attained," the nurse and the family can see the numerical difference in what should or could be achieved and what does exist at the present time. Scores in each section should be transferred to the summary section at the end of the chapter's assessment tool.

	Usually (2 pts)	Sometimes (1 pt)	Never (0 pt)	Not applicable
I. The *infant* develops wellness by experiencing				
A. A warm and protective environment	____	____	____	____
B. Caring role models who fulfill				
1. Physical needs	____	____	____	____
2. Social needs	____	____	____	____
3. Psychological needs	____	____	____	____
C. A close attachment to the mother immediately following birth	____	____	____	____
D. Stranger anxiety	____	____	____	____
E. Oral satisfaction through nourishment and sucking	____	____	____	____
F. Minimal distress during weaning exhibited by acceptance of cup and spoon	____	____	____	____
G. Visual stimulation	____	____	____	____
H. Touch stimulation	____	____	____	____
I. Verbal stimulation	____	____	____	____
J. Increased mobility during the second half of infancy	____	____	____	____
K. Exploration of body by self	____	____	____	____
L. A relationship with important people in his environment	____	____	____	____
M. Secure feelings as exhibited by				
1. Smiling	____	____	____	____
2. Cooing	____	____	____	____
3. Sleeping comfortably	____	____	____	____
N. A wellness-monitoring system under the guidance of parents and health-care professionals	____	____	____	____

Total points possible   *36*

Total not applicable   ____

Total applicable   ____

Total points attained   ____

	Usually (2 pts)	Sometimes (1 pt)	Never (0 pt)	Not applicable
II. The *toddler* develops wellness by experiencing				
A. A sense of autonomy as exhibited by making choices about activities of daily life	____	____	____	____
B. An increasing ability to control his body	____	____	____	____
C. Psychological and physical readiness for toilet training	____	____	____	____
D. New and changing attitudes toward sex differences	____	____	____	____
E. Feelings of a sense of right and wrong	____	____	____	____
F. A beginning mastery of language	____	____	____	____
G. Emotional relationships with others	____	____	____	____
H. New and different types of foods	____	____	____	____
I. Changing eating patterns	____	____	____	____
J. Adequate time for play and self-expression activities	____	____	____	____
K. Life events through play	____	____	____	____
L. Reduction of tension through play	____	____	____	____
M. A role within the family system	____	____	____	____
N. Acceptance by adults	____	____	____	____
O. Participation in family activities	____	____	____	____
P. A wellness-monitoring system under the guidance of parents and health-care professionals	____	____	____	____

Total points possible _32_

Total not applicable ____

Total applicable ____

Total points attained ____

	Usually (2 pts)	Sometimes (1 pt)	Never (0 pt)	Not applicable
III. The *preschooler* develops wellness by experiencing				
A. A sense of initiative as exhibited by acceptance of a greater responsibility in daily activities	———	———	———	———
B. Enthusiasm for learning	———	———	———	———
C. Wellness role models	———	———	———	———
D. Family relationships and sex-role functions	———	———	———	———
E. Life events through play and self-expression activities	———	———	———	———
F. Pride in accomplishments	———	———	———	———
G. Development of conscience	———	———	———	———
H. Acceptance of the moral behavior of others	———	———	———	———
I. Self-control	———	———	———	———
J. A positive attitude toward life events	———	———	———	———
K. Differentiation of self from others	———	———	———	———
L. Sexually appropriate behaviors	———	———	———	———
M. Development of a sexual identity	———	———	———	———
N. An "inner-directed" feeling of accomplishment	———	———	———	———
O. Increased psychomotor control	———	———	———	———
P. A wellness-monitoring system under the guidance of parents and health-care professionals	———	———	———	———
Q. A greater cooperativeness with others	———			

Total points possible   *34*
Total not applicable   ———
Total applicable   ———
Total points attained   ———

	Usually (2 pts)	Sometimes (1 pt)	Never (0 pt)	Not applicable
IV. The *school-age child* develops wellness by experiencing				
A. Meaningful challenges at school and at home	_____	_____	_____	_____
B. Learning new skills	_____	_____	_____	_____
C. Failures as well as successes	_____	_____	_____	_____
D. Acceptance of responsibility for actions	_____	_____	_____	_____
E. Increased self-control	_____	_____	_____	_____
F. The acceptance of the adult value system	_____	_____	_____	_____
G. The appreciation of social implications of behavior	_____	_____	_____	_____
H. Belonging to an identified peer group	_____	_____	_____	_____
I. Increasing independence	_____	_____	_____	_____
J. Expressed sexual curiosity	_____	_____	_____	_____
K. Growth of a positive self-concept	_____	_____	_____	_____
L. Relationship with a "best friend"	_____	_____	_____	_____
M. Consideration for feelings of others	_____	_____	_____	_____
N. Expression of feelings about sexuality	_____	_____	_____	_____
O. Regular participation in play and exercise activities	_____	_____	_____	_____

Total points possible   _30_
Total not applicable   _____
Total applicable   _____
Total points attained   _____

	Usually (2 pts)	Sometimes (1 pt)	Never (0 pt)	Not applicable
V. The *adolescent* develops wellness by				
A. Recognizing vascillating feelings about body and emotional changes	_____	_____	_____	_____
B. Coping effectively with changes in self	_____	_____	_____	_____
C. Moving toward reorientation of re-				

	Usually (2 pts)	Sometimes (1 pt)	Never (0 pt)	Not applicable
lationships with parents	⎯⎯	⎯⎯	⎯⎯	⎯⎯
D. Experiencing successes in directing own life	⎯⎯	⎯⎯	⎯⎯	⎯⎯
E. Identifying with peer group	⎯⎯	⎯⎯	⎯⎯	⎯⎯
F. Maintaining a sense of humor	⎯⎯	⎯⎯	⎯⎯	⎯⎯
G. Beginning to prepare for vocational choices	⎯⎯	⎯⎯	⎯⎯	⎯⎯
H. Achieving socially responsible behaviors	⎯⎯			⎯⎯

Total points possible　　*16*
Total not applicable　　⎯⎯
Total applicable　　⎯⎯
Total points attained　　⎯⎯

VI. The *young adult* develops wellness by

	Usually (2 pts)	Sometimes (1 pt)	Never (0 pt)	Not applicable
A. Assuming responsibility for decision making in life experiences	⎯⎯	⎯⎯	⎯⎯	⎯⎯
B. Committing oneself to a career choice	⎯⎯	⎯⎯	⎯⎯	⎯⎯
C. Selecting a mate	⎯⎯	⎯⎯	⎯⎯	⎯⎯
D. Establishing goals leading to an independent life	⎯⎯	⎯⎯	⎯⎯	⎯⎯
E. Becoming financially independent	⎯⎯	⎯⎯	⎯⎯	⎯⎯
F. Assuming responsibility for reorientation with family of origin	⎯⎯	⎯⎯	⎯⎯	⎯⎯
G. Continuing to develop own identity	⎯⎯	⎯⎯	⎯⎯	⎯⎯
H. Fusing own identity with that of an important other person	⎯⎯	⎯⎯	⎯⎯	⎯⎯
I. Maintaining self-identity as well as couple identity	⎯⎯	⎯⎯	⎯⎯	⎯⎯
J. Seeking advice from friends, family, and professionals regarding life experiences	⎯⎯	⎯⎯	⎯⎯	⎯⎯
K. Experiencing a sense of importance, ac-				

	Usually (2 pts)	Sometimes (1 pt)	Never (0 pt)	Not applicable
complishment, uniqueness, and self-directedness in the work setting	___	___	___	___
L. Utilizing a systematic assessment in choosing a career	___	___	___	___
M. Experiencing a sense of job stability	___	___	___	___
N. Coping effectively with job changes	___	___	___	___
O. Coping effectively with multiple roles	___	___	___	___
P. Committing self to a relationship	___	___	___	___
Q. Strengthening the commitment to the partner	___	___	___	___
R. Experiencing a sense of belonging, love, and self-esteem	___	___	___	___
S. Maintaining open communication with important other people	___	___	___	___
T. Identifying feelings regarding parenthood	___	___	___	___
U. Preparing for children	___	___	___	___
V. Modeling a flexible well life-style	___	___	___	___
W. Acquiring knowledge of effective stress management	___	___	___	___
X. Creatively managing stress	___	___	___	___

Total points possible   *48*
Total not applicable   ___
Total applicable   ___
Total points attained   ___

VII. The *middle-age adult* develops wellness by
  A. Maintaining open communications with important other people ___ ___ ___ ___
  B. Establishing self in community groups ___ ___ ___ ___

	Usually (2 pts)	Sometimes (1 pt)	Never (0 pt)	Not applicable
C. Guiding the next generation	____	____	____	____
D. Having concern for and belief in others	____	____	____	____
E. Supporting, teaching, nurturing, and serving children or other adults	____	____	____	____
F. Being productive at work	____	____	____	____
G. Being productive at home	____	____	____	____
H. Utilizing resources beneficial to child-rearing practices	____	____	____	____
I. Developing a unified plan between parents for childrearing	____	____	____	____
J. Valuing consistency as a practice of child-rearing	____	____	____	____
K. Establishing household tasks for each family member	____	____	____	____
L. Recognizing individual members' tasks	____	____	____	____
M. Maintaining open communications about in-law relations	____	____	____	____
N. Establishing a workable plan for family interaction with in-laws	____	____	____	____
O. Assessing goals relative to job and developing alternatives	____	____	____	____
P. Having friends that generate or facilitate positive aspects of self	____	____	____	____
Q. Adjusting to physical and psychosocial changes	____	____	____	____
R. Woman recognizing that menopause does not change self in any important way	____	____	____	____
S. Seeking information about menopause	____	____	____	____

	Usually (2 pts)	Sometimes (1 pt)	Never (0 pt)	Not applicable
T. Man recognizing that he may be experiencing a transitional period	____	____	____	____
U. Modifying rather than discarding valued life goals that cannot be accomplished	____	____	____	____
V. Providing time daily for leisure activity	____	____	____	____
W. Utilizing relaxation techniques daily	____	____	____	____
X. Utilizing positive coping mechanisms for dealing with aging parents	____	____	____	____
Y. Reassessing relationship and role with aging parents	____	____	____	____
Z. Encouraging independence in aging parents within their physical and mental abilities	____	____	____	____
ZZ. Utilizing self-contract	____	____	____	____

Total points possible   *54*

Total not applicable   ____

Total applicable   ____

Total points attained   ____

VIII. The *older adult* develops wellness by	Usually (2 pts)	Sometimes (1 pt)	Never (0 pt)	Not applicable
A. Integrating past experiences into present adulthood stage	____	____	____	____
B. Deriving pleasure from leisure activities	____	____	____	____
C. Experiencing a sense of fulfillment	____	____	____	____
D. Enjoying the accomplishments of the institutions one helped to create	____	____	____	____
E. Adapting positively to physical changes	____	____	____	____
F. Adapting positively to community or residence changes	____	____	____	____

	Usually (2 pts)	Sometimes (1 pt)	Never (0 pt)	Not applicable
G. Effectively dealing with loss of spouse or important other person	——	——	——	——
H. Coping successfully with anticipated stressors	——	——	——	——
I. Maintaining self-sufficiency and independence	——	——	——	——
J. Experiencing effective support systems (groups, family members, friends)	——	——	——	——
K. Maintaining positive self-esteem	——	——	——	——
L. Avoiding loneliness	——	——	——	——
M. Accepting the possibility of own death	——	——	——	——
N. Experiencing feelings of love from important other people	——	——	——	——
O. Sharing feelings with important other people	——	——	——	——

Total points possible		_30_
Total not applicable		——
Total applicable		——
Total points attained		——

Assessment Tool Summary

	Subtotal points possible	Subtotal not applicable	Subtotal applicable	Subtotal points attained
I. Infant	_36_	——	——	——
II. Toddler	_32_	——	——	——
III. Preschooler	_34_	——	——	·——
IV. School-age child	_30_	——	——	——
V. Adolescent	_16_	——	——	——
VI. Young adult	_48_	——	——	——
VII. Middle-age adult	_54_	——	——	——
VIII. Older adult	_30_	——	——	——

Total points possible		_280_
Total not applicable		——
Total applicable		——
Total points attained		——

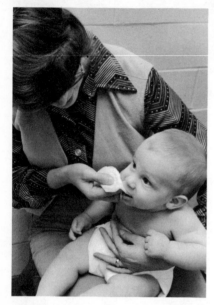

FIVE

Dental Wellness Across the Life Span

Today more than ever before, family wellness care requires the skills of many professions and their practitioners. Coordinated communication among professionals in various disciplines strengthens each profession while improving the relationship among practitioners as each acknowledges the skills of the others. The recipient of care benefits from the joint efforts of professionals dedicated to enhancing wellness. Nurses and dental professionals have long recognized the role of dental health in total family health and have shown much potential for working together. To capitalize on a belief in this concept of collegial relationships between professionals, the nursing role in dental wellness as a component of family wellness will be explored.

It is ironic that the nurse often has the initial as well as continuing contact with family members who need dental wellness guidance, and yet fears her knowledge is inadequate to provide comprehensive guidance. This chapter is directed toward filling this gap. The nurse encounters family members in the home, at school, as inpatients or outpatients, and many are in need of dental wellness guidance. Her access to family members of all ages in need of dental guidance indicates the need for a comprehensive look at dental wellness. While dental hygienists and dentists, both general and specialized, offer a range of services to enhance or restore dental wellness, the nurse's ongoing contact with families puts her in a position to teach and reinforce daily behaviors to promote dental wellness. The nurse is often involved in follow-up activities of programs begun in the dental office, school, or other community agency. Continuity of care can be promoted by the nurse and dental professionals working together with family members from agency to home. The aim of this chapter is to provide information and tools to enable the nurse to work with families and dental professionals to improve dental wellness of families.

The chief components necessary for the family to achieve dental wellness at any stage of development include (1) daily care of the teeth through brushing and rinsing to remove food substances that may lead to decay; (2) eating a well-balanced diet and avoiding high-sugar foods; (3) regular exposure to fluoride systemically or topically; and (4) regular visits to a dental hygienist or dentist for cleaning and assessment.

The nurse's main objectives while helping the family achieve dental wellness are to (1) assess dental wellness of all family members; (2) share knowledge of health-care practices and resources to promote dental wellness; and (3) help the family assume the highest possible degree of self-responsibility in dental wellness. To achieve these objectives, the nurse must again realize that the self-care behaviors necessary for dental wellness depend to a great extent on previous life-style patterns, attitudes and values of the family, and the cultural beliefs and practices that guide family members in their daily lives.

While dental problems incur low mortality, their very commonness makes them important economic and social concerns in the maintenance of a well family. Many dental problems are largely preventable, and methods of doing so will be considered in this chapter. More important, factors and behaviors contributing to dental wellness will be addressed.

The developmental framework is used to provide structure to the concepts and practices related to dental wellness. As with many aspects of wellness, behaviors that promote or hinder wellness begin early in life and continue throughout the years. At each stage there are specific factors and behaviors, but some commonalities exist in all age groups. Because nutrition plays such an important role in developing and maintaining dental wellness, food and eating practices will be given special emphasis for each developmental group. Concerns, myths, and commonly asked questions relative to dental wellness throughout the life cycle will be covered for each developmental stage.

The nurse is a key person in the community to help the family locate resources needed to achieve and maintain dental wellness. These resources are covered in the latter part of the chapter for the nurse to suggest to the family as needed. Because paying for dental services can often be a barrier to receiving professional care, various payment plans and insurance programs are also discussed.

Nutritional Aspects of Dental Wellness

Nutrition is an important factor in many aspects of wellness, and so it is with dental wellness in the family. Although nutrition is discussed in Chapter 6, how it relates specifically to dental wellness will be addressed here. Proper nutrition contributes to dental wellness, along with regular and correct oral hygiene techniques, and professional cleaning with assessments on a regular basis. A poor diet can lead to a variety of dental problems, including dental caries and periodontal disease. A diet high in sugar promotes tooth decay. Sugar is quickly broken down in the mouth to form acids, which in turn break down tooth enamel and begin the process of tooth decay. Whether this process will destroy the enamel depends on (1) the hardness of the tooth enamel, (2) the strength of the acids formed, and (3) the length of time the acids are actually in contact with the teeth. The greatest damage is done within the first 20 minutes of eating sweet foods. The tooth can take only so many repeated attacks until it breaks down. Teeth should be brushed or the mouth rinsed within the first 20 minutes after eating sweet foods [1]. Even more importantly, concentrated sweet foods should be avoided.

THE EFFECTS OF SUGAR

The potential for tooth decay from high-sugar foods is compounded by the sticky texture of these foods. The stickiness makes removal of the substance by brushing or rinsing just that much more difficult. Liquids are easier to remove than solids. Homemade or commercially prepared foods should be assessed for sugar content, and high-sugar foods avoided. If the food is prepared at home, often the sugar can be reduced during preparation. The careful consumer should learn to read labels, realizing that ingredients are listed in the order of the amount present in the item.

Table 5-1. Foods and Dental Wellness[a]

Satisfactory[b]	Unsatisfactory[c]
Fruits, preferably fresh without added sugar	Jellies
	Pies, cakes, cookies, donuts
Vegetables, preferably fresh	Chocolate milk
	Candy
Meat	Juices, soda pop, or other beverages with sugar added
Eggs and cheese	
Milk, without added syrups	Syrups, such as maple and honey
	Chewing gum with sugar

[a]Some foods, such as raisins, are nutritious for the body but do not promote dental wellness. Other foods, such as pretzels, can promote dental wellness but are not necessarily nutritious.
[b]Natural cleansing foods with less sugar.
[c]Sticky, fermentable, sugary foods.

In this way, the shopper can become aware of what foods contain sugar and in what relative amounts. Four main principles for dental wellness in relation to nutrition are

1. Avoid foods high in concentrated sugar
2. Eat foods that promote natural cleansing
3. Eat a diet adequate in protein
4. Brush or rinse the teeth within 20 minutes after eating

Table 5-1 shows foods that do and foods that do not promote dental wellness.

THE IMPORTANCE OF PROTEIN

Another important aspect of nutrition in dental wellness is protein. Protein substances make up the majority of the organic portions of enamel and dentin [12]. Protein deficiency manifested by kwashiorkor (a syndrome occurring in children who eat a diet adequate in calories but deficient in protein) in preschool Nigerian children may have been one reason for delayed eruption and hypoplasia of deciduous teeth [7]. When borderline protein-deficient diets are used throughout the reproductive cycle of rats, the offspring show several dental defects [9]. Children who suffer from protein-calorie malnutrition have crowded and rotated teeth, which may be the result of inadequate development or retarded growth of the jawbone matrix. Normal-size teeth in an undersize jaw would give the appearance of a mouthful of jumbled teeth [12]. In humans no direct correlation has been shown between dental caries and supplemental protein [13]. However, experimentally induced caries in rodents have been reduced significantly by adding casein, a protein, to the diet [12]. Therefore, protein does seem to have an influence on caries development. For proper growth and development of the whole body, including teeth and oral bony structures, each family member should receive a diet adequate in protein.

FLUORIDE

Fluoride is a mineral around which controversy still exists. It strengthens tooth enamel and supporting bones, thus making teeth more resistant to the action of acids. It occurs naturally in some water supplies, affording its residents important protection against tooth decay. It can be added to municipal water supplies, taken as a dietary supplement in the form of tablets or in vitamins, and topically applied to teeth through fluoride toothpastes, professional fluoride applications, and mouth rinses [1]. The dental community has long recognized the value of fluoride in preventing tooth decay.

There is unequivocal evidence that fluoridation of water supplies will reduce dental caries by as much as 60 percent. It is safe and inexpensive, costing only 20 cents per person annually to prevent dental decay in children. The political controversy that has arisen in some communities concerning whether to add fluoride to the water supply has prevented many citizens, particularly children, from receiving this beneficial mineral [8].

Fluoride is now believed to be essential to the mineralization of the teeth, especially in the erupting and maturing stages. The consumption of fluoride in the water at the optimal concentration of 1 part per million (ppm), depending on the temperature, reduces dental caries prevalence by 50 to 60 percent in permanent teeth [18]. Even with these statistics, a high percentage of the water supplies in the United States remain unfluoridated. The nurse should find out whether the community's water supply is fluoridated and, if fluoride is not already present, should work through appropriate channels in the community to have it added.

FOOD SELECTION

The food, diet, and nutrition needs of each family member at each developmental level should be considered as part of the nursing role in promoting dental wellness. The daily diets should include foods from the six food exchange groups (see Chap. 6) with emphasis on complex carbohydrates, vegetables, proteins, and fruits—and less emphasis on fats, and simple sugars. The family member can become aware of daily food habits by filling out diet diary sheets. Each item eaten at or between meals should be written down with reference to when and why the food was eaten. Since damage to the teeth can begin within 20 minutes after eating, multiply the number of times the person ate foods containing sugar by 20 to obtain a general idea of the cumulative length of time that acid has been working on the teeth. The nurse can assist the family in analyzing the results of the diary and in evaluating individual food habits. With a combination of proper food selection, eating habits, regular professional care, and oral hygiene measures at home, each family member can reduce the risk of dental disease and promote dental wellness. Each individual has the responsibility for maintaining oral health so that one may keep the natural teeth for his whole life and enjoy the healthful benefits of dental wellness.

The dental wellness assessment tool at the end of this chapter has been developed to help the nurse and family assess each member's dental wellness status, the need for additional wellness teaching, and the family's use of dental resources in the community. The tool should be the basis for ongoing assessment, planning, and interventions in the family. Ideally, it will reveal beneficial behaviors and practices the family members now incorporate into their life-style, which the nurse can positively reinforce.

Dental Wellness During Infancy

Dental wellness in the infant begins with the development of the 20 primary teeth during the prenatal period. The enamel of the permanent 6-year molars forms shortly before birth, and at birth the crowns of the primary teeth are almost completely formed. When the baby is 6 to 8 months of age, the central incisors are usually the first to erupt. The child should have all the primary teeth by 24 to 30 months of age [5]. The lower teeth usually erupt before the upper teeth. After the central incisors come the lateral incisors, then the first molars, canines, and second molars. Remember, however, that each child is an individual, and the rate of tooth development may vary considerably among children. Some babies may not get their first tooth until 9 months or even later, but parents should not be concerned.

Even though teething is a natural process, it can be a very frustrating time for parents and baby. Most babies experience some discomfort while teething. Sometimes the only evidence of an erupting tooth is an inflamed gum. At other times, the gum can become painfully swollen resulting in crying and irritability in the baby. The baby may want to chew on anything within reach. A teething ring or hard food may relieve this discomfort. In more severe cases, a physician may prescribe a soothing pain-relief medication, which should be used with caution. Commercial teething lotions that briefly numb the baby's gums are also available. The discomfort passes with the eruption of the tooth.

Teething is often blamed for various illnesses, yet it is a normal, well process; therefore, illness should not be expected during teething. If the baby is experiencing prolonged, abnormal symptoms that indicate an illness, such as fever, diarrhea, or vomiting, a physician should be called immediately to examine the child for the real cause of the illness.

PROMOTING OPTIMAL DEVELOPMENT OF TEETH DURING INFANCY
The infant's mouth deserves careful attention during this early period to promote wellness of teeth and oral cavity structures and to prevent dental problems from developing later on. Because the jaw continues to develop after birth as part of the normal growth process, parents should take this factor into account when deciding how to feed the infant. Breast-feeding exercises the baby's jaws naturally and aids in the development of a properly shaped, strong dental arch, essential to

properly positioned teeth. Bottle-feeding, while nutritionally sound, may be a factor in crooked teeth, tongue thrust, and finger-sucking. Parents who wish to bottle-feed should use nipples that are shaped to simulate the shape and action during breast-feeding. Several types are available. The dentist, pediatrician, or pharmacist can help the parents select one that is best for the child [2].

During infancy the child's mouth and teeth should be cleaned regularly to discourage the formation of acids, which can decay the newly erupting teeth. Regular cleaning of the baby's mouth not only controls acids that form in the mouth but introduces the infant to what will become a lifelong habit—tooth-brushing. On a daily basis, parents should clean the infant's teeth using soft gauze wrapped around the parent's finger. The gums and teeth can be gently wiped to remove milk coating and food residues. Eventually a soft, small toothbrush can be used. Toothpaste is not essential during infancy and may be a hindrance. The infant will probably object to the strong taste of most toothpastes [18].

During infancy as with all other developmental stages, prolonged contact of the teeth with sugars should be avoided. The infant who drinks from a bottle is subject to "nursing bottle mouth," in which teeth are decayed through contact with fermentable substances on the nipple of the bottle. It occurs when the child is put to bed with a bottle containing milk, fruit juice, or a nonnutritious high-sugar beverage such as a soft drink. Bacteria change the sugar in these liquids (lactose, fructose, or sucrose) into decay-causing acids. The nursing bottle mouth syndrome has also been documented in breast-feeding infants; it is believed to occur when the child falls asleep at the breast for long periods of time. The prolonged contact of the teeth with these liquids during sleep assures sufficient time for the process of decay to begin [2]. This practice can continue for months, until the child no longer drinks from a bottle and until most of the child's teeth are decayed and beyond repair. To avoid this problem, all nutrients, including liquids, should be consumed during the child's feeding time and before bedtime. The infant should not need additional nourishment after he is in his crib. If he needs additional sucking or comforting, he may be offered a pacifier, a soft stuffed animal, or a few minutes of cuddling, rocking, or soothing talk from the parents.

Parents of the infant may ask if teeth can have cavities when they erupt. Teeth decay only when exposed to acids, which form as a result of bacterial action on sugars present in the mouth. Easily fermentable, sticky carbohydrates are especially responsible for the development of a substance called plaque, which contains bacteria and which sticks to the teeth if it is not removed. The bacteria in the plaque act on the carbohydrates to produce acid. A large amount of plaque along with a diet high in carbohydrates can lead to a high level of acid production. While experts do not agree on how the acid affects the teeth, they do agree that the acid slowly destroys the surface enamel. Once the outer harder enamel is destroyed, the decay progresses through the softer dentin layer of the tooth [11]. All dental decay in children occurs after the tooth has erupted.

Fluoride is an important compound in the infant's diet for the development of decay-resistant teeth. While the child's teeth are forming, fluoride ingested from food and water or as a dietary supplement enters the bloodstream. It is carried to the enamel-forming cells of the developing teeth, where it combines with substances that make up the tooth enamel. The tooth is then more resistant to attack by acids in the mouth that contribute to tooth decay. The fluoride that is applied externally to the teeth by the dentist or dental hygienist also strengthens the tooth and makes it more resistant to decay. Such treatments have been shown to reduce cavities by 30 to 50 percent [4].

Fluoride, like other substances, can be beneficial when taken in proper dosages. Trace elements found in multivitamins are recommended in small dosages because they are beneficial to nutritional health. In larger dosages, they could prove to be fatal. Except for "mottled enamel," which has occurred when water supplies exceeded the recommended concentration, there is no documentation of danger from fluoride [6]. The benefits of fluoride in promoting dental wellness have been well documented, on the other hand, and deserve to be considered by parents in promoting dental wellness in themselves and their children. Early in the child's life, during infancy, is the time to begin the child's exposure to fluoride through the community water supply, or by daily multivitamins with fluoride if it is not present in the water, or is present in concentrations below 0.7 ppm. When the community water supply has no naturally occurring fluoride, it can be added at a level of 1 ppm. Topical application of fluoride will begin in the next developmental stage.

Some infants have a tendency to suck their fingers or thumbs, and parents often wonder whether this practice will result in crooked or protruding teeth. Thumb-sucking is a natural instinct, an inborn reflex. It creates a happy, secure feeling within the baby. By the age of 2 or 3 years, the child usually outgrows this need. However, if the child continues to thumb-suck past the age of 3 or 4, the sucking may affect the position of incoming permanent teeth and the shape of the jaw-bone. This habit may then result in the need for corrective orthodontic treatment to restore natural function, structure, and appearance [18].

Because thumb-sucking is fulfilling such an inborn security need for the child, excessive scolding and punishment for it may create much embarrassment and increased anxiety for the child, which could lead to more frequent and prolonged thumb or finger-sucking. Instead, the potential harm can be explained to the older child, and other pleasurable pastimes such as play activities can be substituted when the need to thumbsuck is obvious.

Another threat to dental wellness during infancy comes from exposure to tetracycline drugs. These drugs can cause permanent discoloration to the developing teeth and should be avoided if possible during infancy [9]. They should also be avoided during pregnancy, as discoloration to the developing teeth can also occur before birth.

NUTRITION AND DENTAL WELLNESS IN INFANCY

"What we eat, and how we eat, is determined by a complex learning process that begins in infancy" [18]. Indeed, one of the most important roles for a parent to fill is that of nutrition educator, and this role is most effectively accomplished through daily behaviors on behalf of the infant and the parent. What the parent feeds the child during infancy not only nourishes the child for the short term, but sets the pattern for a lifetime of nourishment. How this process is accomplished has considerable influence on both the dental and nutritional wellness of the child.

It is important for the parent to feed nutritious foods in accordance with the child's needs throughout the infancy period. Fluids should include breast milk or formula, and milk and fruit juices when appropriate. Soft drinks, whether carbonated or uncarbonated, should be avoided. During warm weather when the infant may need extra fluids, cool water can be offered. Some fruit juices contain natural fluoride, which is an added benefit [11].

The infant's diet early includes strained solid foods. Parents, when tasting these foods, often try to counteract the bland taste by adding sugar to cereals, vegetables, or even meats. This added sugar is unnecessary nutritionally, for the infant can and should receive all nutrients and calories from the food groups without resorting to added sugar or highly sweet foods. During teething periods, the parents should offer hard baby toast, which is low in sugar, and not cookies or graham crackers.

As the infant becomes more mobile, he becomes more active and may require a small snack between mealtimes. Snacks should come from one of the food groups, such as toast, cheese, or a soft fruit. It is easy to offer a high-sugar, empty-calorie cookie, but this simply perpetuates a bad habit of the parent while contributing to an environment conducive to tooth decay.

If children are not exposed to diets high in sugar, they will not develop a taste for sweets. From a nutritional and dental point of view, children do not "need" candy and other high-sugar foods. By offering such items, parents may be responding to their own needs to meet some arbitrary standard or role expectation as a parent. Careful consideration of what one hopes to accomplish as a parent should be a guiding principle as parents plan all aspects of the child's care. If they wish to raise a child who is well in mind and body with a fresh, beautiful smile, they will think twice before initiating a pattern of empty, high-sugar foods. Practices that encourage dental wellness behaviors during infancy include the following:

PARENTS SHOULD

1. Breast-feed infant in order to enhance a more properly shaped, strong dental arch.
2. Provide safe objects for chewing during teething.
3. Provide fluoride through foods or the water supply. Check with local health department about fluoridation of local water supply.

4. Discourage bottles of milk, juices, or sugar beverages at bedtime.
5. Offer water for extra fluids instead of sugar drinks.
6. Clean infant's teeth daily.
7. Care for primary teeth as if they are the permanent teeth.
8. Encourage adequate nutrition for age level, and minimize daily sugar challenges to teeth.
9. Take child for first dental visit between the ages of 9 months and 2 years.
10. Model dental wellness behaviors.

Dental Wellness in the Preschool Child

Between 1 and 5 years of age, children learn many behaviors that affect their level of dental wellness. They move from a state of being totally dependent on adults to one in which they begin to learn to do for themselves. They move from a period of acquiring teeth, with parents wiping gums and new teeth with soft gauze, to one in which they will learn to brush their own teeth with supervision from parents. This transition necessitates several important decisions from the parents, which apply to all age groups as well.

TEACHING PROPER ORAL HYGIENE

Among the first decisions the parent must make are what kind of toothbrush and toothpaste the child should use, how the teeth should be brushed, and who should do the brushing. It is most important that preschoolers be encouraged to brush their own teeth after each meal with the parent assisting, which will help children develop self-care skills and "learn by doing." Young children usually enjoy being encouraged to do things for themselves and delight in learning to use a toothbrush. The brush should be small enough in size to reach all the teeth and have soft bristles to prevent damage to the gums while still gently stimulating them [11]. These are the only requirements for a toothbrush, and many brands of manual toothbrushes meet these requirements. A parent should not feel the need to purchase an expensive electric toothbrush with a commercial theme in order to provide a good toothbrush for the child. The power of advertising through all media is great, but a simple, small, soft brush, perhaps in a color the child selects, will suffice. Nylon and natural bristles work equally well, though natural bristles are usually more expensive. As soon as the bristles begin to flare and show signs of wear, the toothbrush should be replaced. It is generally necessary to replace toothbrushes four or five times a year.

It is easy to become confused about what kind of toothpaste to buy. Advertising urges us to select certain colors and flavors. The toothpaste should be acceptable to the child flavorwise, not be highly abrasive, and contain fluoride. Most flavors will appeal to young children. They generally do not like too much of a flavor, so the parent can avoid a strong taste by putting toothpaste on only half the length of the bristles. This amount is generally sufficient to clean the teeth adequately. Parents should avoid purchasing toothpastes that claim to "whiten and brighten."

These contain either strong abrasives that whiten or polish the teeth or a chemical that dissolves plaque from the teeth. Both types of toothpaste are strongly abrasive and should be avoided by preschoolers and older people [11].

The preschool child should use a fluoride toothpaste every time he brushes, for every time he does so he is applying a very low concentration of fluoride. After a great deal of research, it is now known that fluoride toothpaste does help prevent decay, but it is not as effective as is fluoride in the water supply [11]. Scientific studies have shown that certain fluoride toothpastes will reduce tooth decay by as much as 20 to 35 percent [4]. Fluoride toothpastes have a progressively diminishing effect on children's teeth as they grow older. Whether fluoride in toothpaste or any form prevents decay after 25 years of age is debatable; however, there is some evidence that its use will halt the development of cavities already begun [11]. All children should use fluoride toothpastes.

In teaching the preschool child to assume increasing responsibility for brushing his own teeth, the parents must know the proper technique to teach. Certain principles apply to all methods. The handle should be grasped firmly for control during all movements. Direct the bristles in the direction needed for placement on the teeth and overlap strokes to avoid missing any area. A sequence of back to front, top and then bottom in brushing is helpful in preventing omissions. Time and concentration on the part of the parent are important. Counting strokes often aids in concentration and continuous movement, and helps develop the technique into an automatic one. The parent can teach the preschool child a little jingle to help him remember all the places to brush.

Top teeth back, top teeth front,
Inside, underneath, and then we go down.
Bottom teeth back, bottom teeth front,
Inside, underneath, rinse and we're done.

A very effective toothbrushing method for well children and adults, the *back-and-forth scrub* method consists of brushing all tooth surfaces with a back-and-forth scrub action, counting 8 to 10 strokes for each area of tooth surfaces.

The American Dental Association recommends the *rolling* method, which is similar to the scrub method except that the stroke of the brush is different. The brush is placed closer to the gingiva at a 45-degree angle so that when the brush is rolled up or down on the tooth, the side of the bristles will massage and clean the soft tissue. When the brush rolls down to the crown of the tooth, it is perpendicular to the tooth surface, so a hard stroke will clean the hard tissue of the tooth [16]. In teaching the preschool child to care properly for teeth, the parents must teach an effective technique using a soft brush and fluoride toothpaste. The teeth should be brushed after every meal.

VISITING THE DENTIST

Parents often wonder, "When should I first take my child to a dentist?" Professional dental care begins during the preschool period and continues throughout life. The preschool child should visit the dentist by the time all primary teeth have erupted, which means a visit to the dentist should occur sometime around the age of 2 years. Early examinations for cleaning and topical fluoride are important because surveys have shown that 50 percent of 2-year-olds have one or more decayed teeth [2]. Parents are particularly receptive to preventive and wellness-promotion activities during this early period of life when the child is receiving immunizations and regular growth and development appraisals. A collaborative effort of health team members with the family is both important and effective in promoting wellness in the young child.

The first visit to the dentist should be a pleasant experience in which favorable attitudes are established toward the dentist and the dental staff. Some explanation and description of the equipment and sounds, cleaning procedures, and x-rays should be given to the child before the first visit. Only cleaning and emergency procedures are generally performed during these early visits, and fluoride is applied on a 6-month to 1-year schedule. The dentist should be seen as a helpful person to the child, and parents should prepare the child in every way possible to foster this view. Restorative work may be necessary at some time in the future, and a good relationship between child and dentist from the beginning sets the stage for minimal or no trauma when less pleasant procedures are performed.

A preschool child may require repair of a carious tooth, and the parents may question the importance of filling primary teeth, since they are lost eventually anyway. The primary teeth are very important in many aspects of the child's life. They are important to appearance, to speaking, to chewing, and they hold the space necessary for the second set of permanent teeth. Primary teeth that become carious and are not repaired may be lost prematurely, making it possible for an adjacent tooth to drift into the open space and cause irregularities in the forming of permanent teeth. If primary teeth are out of alignment, there will usually be a space problem with the permanent teeth, since the primary teeth guide the buds of the permanent teeth into their proper position in the jawbones. Premature loss due to accidents or severe, unrepaired decay can cause dental problems as well as disfigurement in later stages of development. Furthermore, as in infancy, tetracycline drugs should be avoided to prevent discoloration.

PROMOTING DENTAL WELLNESS HABITS

The preschool period is an excellent time to influence food habits because children at this age are interested in everything around them and are influenced by family experiences. Eating habits are established and attitudes about food and the body are developed at this time. It is crucial that these habits and attitudes be ones that promote wellness.

The preschool nutrition survey of the nutritional status of 3441 children in the United States, from 1 to 6 years old, indicated the effect nutrition can have on dental health. Iron was found to be the nutrient most likely to be lacking in the diet. There also seemed to be a direct relationship between the iron intake of infants and socioeconomic level of families [18]. Furthermore, the study showed that although 95 percent of children were caries-free at 1 year of age, only 30 percent were caries-free at 5 years of age. The caries attack rate was greater in the lower level socioeconomic group.

The survey reported a greater willingness to try new foods during this preschool-age period. Permissive attitudes of parents and use of food as a reward or punishment may have a negative effect on children in developing self-care behaviors that promote wellness. Generally, nutritional deficiencies are less likely to occur if children enjoy a variety of foods. It is wise for the parents to introduce one new food at a time and in small amounts. Most children prefer simple foods that they can recognize easily; therefore, they usually like to separate foods and eat one part at a time. If the child develops a poor eating habit at an early age, it is wise to ignore it and show approval of more desirable habits. If there is a period when the child refuses food, it may be due either to a growing independent attitude or a slower growth rate leading to a need for fewer calories.

Preschoolers love to snack, and snacktime can be used to the preschooler's advantage. Candy and other sweets can be replaced by nutritious foods such as juice, pretzels, peanut butter, cheese, or fresh vegetables like carrots and celery. Infants and preschoolers are exposed to sugar early in our culture; however, parents can control the child's diet at this early age. Sticky, easily fermentable carbohydrates are the worst enemies in that they are quickly changed to acid in the mouth, which in turn destroys tooth enamel. Examples of easily fermentable carbohydrates are soda pop, nonsugarless gum, pies, cookies, cakes, candy, and heavy syrup [11]. Protein snacks may not be supplemented for those high in carbohydrates. Table 5-1 summarizes nutritious foods that promote dental wellness.

Some foods, called *detergent* foods, actually tend to cleanse the teeth and are particularly helpful when the person is unable to brush the teeth. These foods are fibrous and high in water content. Because they are fibrous, they encourage the act of chewing. Some examples of detergent foods are celery, carrots, radishes, pickles, apples, pears [11]. Many are also rich in vitamins so they add a bonus to one's wellness.

A diary sheet can be kept for 3 to 5 days while the child is eating his routine diet in order to learn what snack or other food habits need to be changed. Note the time he eats, the type of foods, and the amount of foods he eats each day. Are they the more fermentable carbohydrates or detergent foods? How many natural, whole-grain products are included in his daily diet? Natural foods cause less decay in general than do refined foods [11]. Natural foods include fresh meats, vegetables, and fruits, as well as foods with less refined sugars.

Preschool children are exposed to television and all its unhealthful advertising directed toward children. Parents can easily become pawns in the game consisting of the child's plaintive pleas for "Mr. Mike's Razzle Dazzle" (but high-sugar) cereal, candy, or soda pop. On shopping trips to the supermarket, the parent may be tempted to buy these products to satisfy a whining tired child or to buy him what the next-door neighbor's child might be eating for breakfast or snacks. One of the biggest favors a parent can do for a child is to minimize the high-sugar, sticky snacks and breakfast foods and have on hand the nutritious, naturally cleansing foods. Children need not develop a junk-food habit that robs them of valuable nutrients they could be eating while destroying their teeth. Parents can set an example by maintaining a wellness life-style and by not eating these foods themselves or allowing them into the house. Friends and relatives may need to be reminded that lollipops are not a good snack, but a juicy red apple is a welcome food. It is often very hard for parents to do the healthful thing when pressured from so many sides to do otherwise. Decayed areas in teeth do not repair themselves like cuts or scrapes on the skin. It is imperative to ensure dental wellness that the early mealtime and snacking habits developed by the child be ones that promote development and maintenance of the teeth. Dental wellness during the preschool period requires the following:

PARENTS SHOULD
1. Be dental wellness role models.
2. Provide soft toothbrush and nonabrasive fluoride toothpaste.
3. Provide nutritious diet for developmental stage.
4. Avoid high-sugar foods.
5. Provide regular dental visits for assessment and prophylaxis every 6 months to 1 year or as needed.
6. Monitor advertising for dental wellness teaching.
7. Allow child to increasingly assume responsibility for dental wellness.

CHILDREN SHOULD
1. Brush own teeth with parental supervision.
2. Choose own snacks from a nutritious selection.
3. View dental professionals as helping people.

Dental Wellness in the School-Age Child

The school-age child experiences two important milestones in terms of dental wellness. He acquires his set of permanent teeth and assumes nearly all the responsibility for their care. The 6-year molars are usually the first permanent teeth to erupt. There are four of these teeth, two in the upper and two in the lower jaw. They do not replace any primary teeth and appear behind the primary teeth. Because they are farther back in the mouth, they are more difficult for the child to reach with the toothbrush. Grooves in the surface of these teeth tend to hold food particles, which can lead to decay. For these reasons, the child should make a special effort to clean these molars very carefully [2]. Some dentists prefer placing a protective sealant on these molars.

LOSS OF PRIMARY TEETH
Loss of the primary teeth usually begins around the age of 5 or 6 and continues until all primary teeth have been replaced, around the age of 12 or 13. Losing teeth may prove awkward for the child, who may wonder what to do if a tooth comes

out while at school or at a friend's home. He should be reassured that adults are willing to help a youngster when he loses a tooth. Some may be concerned about the blood, the "hole" in the mouth, and the altered appearance of the face. Reassurance about the normality of these events as well as the normality of the feelings is usually all that is needed to alleviate the uneasiness.

The child in this age group has a growing awareness of his body, an ability to reason, and a willingness to learn. He must begin to realize the importance of the new set of permanent teeth that he is acquiring and his role in keeping them in good condition for a lifetime. Dental caries seem to constitute primarily a disease of childhood, so the child assumes primary responsibility for preventing them.

ASSUMING RESPONSIBILITY FOR ORAL HYGIENE

Careful brushing twice a day with a fluoride toothpaste and rinsing after lunch at school are requisites for oral hygiene. The parent should check periodically on the child's toothbrushing technique and condition of the toothbrush. Professional cleaning and fluoride application every 6 months are also recommended. Some school districts provide a weekly fluoride rinse program for children whose parents give consent to participate. This program is useful for helping to prevent tooth decay.

At this age the child has acquired the small muscle control to floss his teeth. Flossing helps to remove adherent food particles and plaque that are missed by the toothbrush. It is a relatively easy procedure to perform and can be done before or after toothbrushing. Waxed and unwaxed floss are available. Unwaxed floss removes plaque more effectively. A strand of floss about 18 inches long should be wrapped around two fingers until a section of about 1 inch is left between the thumb and index finger of each hand. The two fingers guide the floss between and around the teeth so that the gingival tissue is not harmed. With a small sawing motion, the floss should be gently moved between the teeth. A diagonal motion will allow smooth insertion. A thumb or finger can be used as a fulcrum to maintain control [16]. Once the floss is down between the teeth, it can be moved up and down along the sides of the tooth five or six times, which will remove plaque as well as polish the surface of the tooth. Both index fingers can be used as guides when flossing the lower teeth [11]. A plastic Y-shaped holder is now available to wrap the floss around instead of the finger. This device is particularly helpful for cleaning the back teeth and hard-to-reach areas.

The school-age child can realize and appreciate the results of his tooth-cleaning efforts by using disclosing tablets, which can be purchased in the pharmacy. The coloring agent in the tablets is absorbed by the plaque so the child and his parents can see exactly where the toothbrush and floss should be more carefully directed.

ACCIDENT PREVENTION

Certain hazards present themselves to the school-age child who is involved in learning skills required for individual team and individual sports. Anyone who has observed a group of children playing in a playground or neighborhood yard realizes the risk of accidents from bodies colliding either with each other or with objects such as swings, baseball bats, and the ground or pavement. Children can be taught the risks and hazards of accidents. They need to know about the appropriate use and handling of playground equipment and the proper way to walk, not run, up and down stairs. Dental wellness teaching discourages placing foreign objects into the mouth and biting pencils. Shoving and pushing at water fountains can cause chipping of teeth and other mouth injuries.

Sometimes despite reasonable care by the child and supervision by adults, a tooth will be knocked out, a traumatic experience usually for the parents as well as the child. First, the parents should remain calm. It may be possible to save the tooth. It should be kept clean and moist by putting it in water or under the tongue. If it is clean, it may be replaced into the socket. Replacing the tooth may require endodontic root canal therapy, but it can be attempted only if the clean, moist tooth and the child are taken to the dentist immediately [11].

If a child receives a blow to a tooth and it darkens in color, such a change does not necessarily mean the tooth is dead. Internal bleeding into the tooth may be causing the dark color. In this case, it may take several months for the dark color to disappear [11]. The dentist should be seen as soon as possible since he may wish to follow the child for observational purposes for several months.

To prevent accidents that may cause injury to the teeth, nurses should assist the family in assessing risks in and around the home and school, in light of specific behaviors of the child. For example, the nurse in the school or in the home who observes a child running with an object in his mouth or trying to bite a very hard object should point out the hazards of this behavior to the child, teacher, and parents to try to discourage it. Nail-biting, thumb and finger-sucking, tongue thrusting, and bruxism (grinding the teeth) should be discouraged because they can cause damage to the teeth or malformations in the mouth. Using seat belts while riding in the car will minimize injury to the mouth as well as to other parts of the body in case of a collision. The nurse's role in accident prevention is a very important one as she helps the child and the family become aware of risks and how to prevent them. Another hazard to the child's teeth can occur from drugs of the tetracycline class. They can cause permanent discoloration of the teeth and should be avoided until age 8 [9].

ORTHODONTIA

The acquisition of the permanent set of teeth during the school years sometimes presents the need for orthodontia. Preventive orthodontic appliances to maintain space and prevent malocclusion are becoming more readily available to a greater number of children. Prosthetic appliances to replace missing teeth, restore function, and improve appearance are also available. In order for the parents to accept the need for orthodontic aid, they must understand the purposes of this type of care. The orthodontist, a specialist in preventing and correcting malocclusion and irregularities of the teeth, can explain the individual child's needs to the parents before treatment.

Parents must understand that chewing ability is dependent on the proper closure of the teeth. Furthermore, malocclusion—that is, any deviation from the proper relationship of the maxillary arch and/or teeth and the mandibular arch and/or teeth—can play a role in the development of caries and periodontal disease [19]. Poor nutrition, early loss of primary teeth, and keeping primary teeth too long can lead to improper fitting together of the upper and lower teeth.

Are orthodontic treatments painful? Even though everyone's pain threshold varies, orthodontic treatment is generally considered painless. The fitting of appliances can cause discomfort and some aching of the teeth, which usually disappears in 1 to 2 days.

Orthodontic treatment can be a very slow process that can continue for 2 years or longer. Sometimes the orthodontist requires the child to wear an appliance for a period of time after the correction has taken place in order to prevent regression of the condition.

Home care of the child receiving orthodontic care is most important. Gums, teeth, and appliances must be tended very carefully. The good habits of brushing will have to be continued meticulously during orthodontic treatment, since the bands and wires on the teeth, and other appliances as well, make cleaning the teeth somewhat difficult. Avoidance of hard or sticky foods is especially important because they are difficult to remove from the teeth and can damage the appliances and hardware. To aid in removing food particles, special toothbrushes have been designed for children with orthodontic appliances. One design has a single row of bristles to be used above and below the wires of the appliance. A second design has three rows of bristles, the middle row being shorter, so that the brush reaches the tooth surface above and below the appliances and removes plaque from the bands at the same time. Probably the most effective toothbrushing method with these brushes and appliances is the multitufted or circular scrub technique [16]. This method involves a small circular cleansing stroke. The toothbrush is placed at a 90-degree angle at the gingival crest, and the brush is rotated in small circles to a slow count of five. The brush is slowly moved throughout the mouth by overlapping the strokes [16].

Irrigation is sometimes a helpful adjunct to toothbrushing for the child with appliances. This method utilizes a device that flushes water through the teeth and appliances to remove food particles. The irrigator can be particularly helpful in removing food particles loosened by flossing. This procedure is an adjunct, not a replacement for toothbrushing [16].

PROPER NUTRITION

Nutrition continues to play an important part in dental wellness during this stage. The child should be served balanced nutritious meals at home and at school and should be taught to prepare nutritious snacks as described earlier in this chapter. Children at this age enjoy taking responsibility for their own care and should be encouraged to do so once they demonstrate the ability and willingness to snack nutritiously.

Children at this age are targets for advertising and other promotional schemes that encourage them to eat junk food. At the supermarket, the high-sugar cereals and other nonnutritious foods are placed at the eye level of the smaller person, while the unsweetened high-fiber cereals are on the higher or lower shelves. Combating the efforts of corporations and businesses who would have the child eat not for his own well-being but for theirs is a constant struggle. Education of and by the parents as to these ploys is necessary to help the child become an informed, responsible, and wellness-oriented consumer.

Many schools incorporate dental education into the school health curriculum. Parents should find out what is taught and how. The school health curriculum should emphasize the child's responsibility in promoting his own dental wellness, and should teach and reinforce the necessary skills. Behaviors for parents and child to promote dental wellness during the school-age stage include the following:

PARENTS SHOULD
1. Continue educating the child about dental wellness care.
2. Encourage a positive attitude toward dental professionals.
3. Stress accident prevention.
4. Take child to a dental professional for assessment, cleaning, and fluoride treatment every 6 months to 1 year or as needed.
5. Discourage poor dental habits such as thumb-sucking, nail-biting, and bruxism.
6. Obtain orthodontic assistance if recommended.
7. Encourage appropriate nutrients for developmental stage, de-emphasizing high-sugar foods.
8. Assure fluoride through water supply, topical application, diet, and toothpastes.
9. Use appropriate first-aid procedures if permanent tooth is lost.

CHILDREN SHOULD
1. Incorporate dental wellness practices into life-style.
2. Know principles of sound nutrition in dental wellness.
3. Use correct toothbrushing and flossing techniques.
4. Prepare nutritious snacks.
5. Participate in dental wellness programs at school.
6. Be aware of accident hazards to teeth and mouth.
7. Wear seat belt when car is in motion.
8. Realize importance of fluoride in dental wellness.

Dental Wellness During Adolescence

Adolescents have a higher incidence of dental decay than any other group of school children [17]. Girls have a higher dental caries incidence than boys of the same age. This difference may be due to the usually earlier eruption of teeth in girls, so the teeth are exposed to a cariogenic environment for a longer time [16].

Of children over 14 years of age, 75 to 80 percent have some form of gum disease [3]. The high incidence of dental caries and other problems during this age period points to the need to assist adolescents in promoting wellness-oriented practices.

Adolescents are usually so active and healthy that it is sometimes difficult to persuade them to practice disciplined wellness practices. Yet the teenage years are a critical time for developing good dental wellness habits or maintaining those already acquired. Except for third molars, the child probably has all his permanent teeth. Meticulous self-cleaning, regular professional care, and good dietary conduct continue to be essentials of dental wellness.

Unfortunately, the beginning symptoms of periodontal disease can occur as early as the teenage years. The most frequent sign is swollen gums that bleed easily, particularly during flossing or brushing [2]. As the disease progresses, the gums separate from the teeth leaving spaces between the gums and teeth where bacteria can accumulate. Eventually, the disease attacks the bone that supports the teeth, and the teeth must be removed [2]. This is a sad state of affairs since it could have been prevented by personal and professional care of the teeth and by good diet in earlier years.

Adolescents are usually quite interested in their appearance. Therefore, dental wellness counseling can focus on the need for adequate nutrition, which can result in clear skin, mental alertness, and a healthy mouth. Along with sound dietary practices, the teenager should appreciate the effects of fluoride, proper toothbrushing techniques, and flossing methods. If the adolescent is concerned about the intake of sugar as it relates to obesity, then this can be a motivating factor toward dental wellness as well.

ACCIDENT PREVENTION

Accidents reach a high incidence during adolescence. Among major hazards to the teeth are beginning the use of shop tools, car and motorcycle accidents, and competitive sports. Safe driving practices and use of seat belts are important wellness behaviors. Mouth protectors and face-guards have contributed greatly to the reduction of oral injuries in some contact sports. Before the introduction of face-guards and mouth protectors, oral injuries caused 50 percent of all football injuries. The use of these protectors may now prevent more than 100,000 oral injuries annually among 1 million players in high school, junior college, and college games [17]. School regulations requiring the use of proper equipment should be encouraged.

PROMOTING DENTAL WELLNESS

Adolescence is a period of transition. Many adolescents will be parents themselves someday. Therefore, attitudes and practices developed at this time will influence future families. Wellness teaching should be directed more toward the adolescent than the parent so as to encourage self-responsibility as he moves toward the adult role. Obviously, working with this age group offers a real challenge.

Teenagers are very conscious of how they look. Body image is crucial and can be threatened in several ways. The adolescent whose orthodontic therapy continues into adolescence may feel awkward, out of place, and unattractive. He may need much support to feel reassured about worth and attractiveness during the treatment period. However, in some peer groups orthodontic appliances are well accepted and are viewed as "in."

The teenager who has experienced years of dental neglect may realize during the teenage years that decayed, discolored, or maloccluded teeth are detrimental to appearance as well as overall level of wellness. The nurse can be of help to the teenager and the parents by attempting to locate resources for restorative dental care. Educational strategies and financial resources will probably be necessary to prevent the occurrence of similar problems in other family members such as younger siblings. Dental wellness often takes low priority in families who have a difficult time meeting basic needs, and the results of this priority setting, while evident in the younger years, become a vivid reality during adolescence. The nurse's skill in finding resources to help families will pay off in the teenager's building a positive body image as he moves toward adulthood.

NUTRITIONAL NEEDS

Nutritional needs assume major importance as one realizes that next to infancy, adolescence is the period of greatest growth spurt. For boys the nutritional requirements are the highest of any time in their lives, while for girls the nutritional needs are higher than ever before and will be superseded only during pregnancy and lactation. According to the Recommended Dietary Allowances (RDA), teenage boys need more calories and more of every nutrient except iron and vitamin D than girls of the same age [12].

Given the special importance of nutrition during the teenage years, it is not surprising that the most prevalent health problems among teenagers are obesity, iron deficiency, and dental caries. The nutritional practices of teenagers simply do not meet the demands. Given the hectic pace of the teenager's life, including the tendency to skip breakfast and to skimp on other meals, it is no surprise that between-meal snacks provide 25 percent of the daily caloric intake of teenagers [18]. Therefore, it is extremely important that these between-meal snacks be health-providing, nutritious foods that tend to have a cleansing effect, thus inhibiting bacterial fermentation. Even the "fast foods" that are extremely popular can have these qualities if the person is knowledgeable and cares about those foods that increase the wellness state. The caloric and sodium values of many fast foods are high, whereas these values in natural fruits and vegetables can be quite low. Needless to say, once the child has developed poor eating habits it becomes very difficult to change these habits during adolescence and adulthood. Peer pressure and conformity to group norms militate against changing nutritional practices. Perhaps the current popular interest in physical fitness will help alter some poor nutrition as well as exercise practices.

Although it may not be possible to change the teenager's eating practices at home, attempts have been and are being made to limit access to unhealthful foods in school. There is a movement by the American Dental Association as well as other concerned groups, such as PTAs, to ban sweets or "junk foods" in school lunch programs as well as to ban television commercials that encourage consumption of high-sugar foods. Federal government officials are slowly picking up this idea and are beginning to encourage changes in the federally funded school hot-lunch programs. Juice machines are being installed at schools along with or in place of soda pop machines. Soft drinks contain acid as well as sugar: what a combination! Community-based efforts such as these may prove effective, along with school health education from early school years on. Most important in converting the sad prevalence of dental disease to a high prevalence of dental wellness is early and continuous education by the parents by word and example. Dental wellness practices during adolescence require the following:

PARENTS SHOULD
1. Emphasize proper nutrition for developmental stage.
2. Encourage dental wellness by appropriate flossing, toothbrushing, and regular visits to the dental professional.
3. Encourage self-responsibility in dental wellness.
4. Encourage accident prevention.
5. Assure fluoride through water supply, topical application, diet, and toothpastes.

ADOLESCENTS SHOULD
1. Practice proper toothbrushing and flossing techniques.
2. Incorporate dental wellness practices into life-style.
3. Assume major responsibility for dental wellness.
4. Avoid potential accident hazards to teeth and mouth.
5. Eat nutritious diet according to developmental stage.
6. Participate in school dental wellness programs.

Dental Wellness in the Adult

Adults play a variety of roles; they must practice dental wellness behaviors for themselves as individuals as well as take on the responsibility of educating and encouraging dental wellness attitudes and practices in children. The bases for developing and practicing dental wellness habits are parental example, guidance, and encouragement. The dental wellness state in the adult is the result of all the previous years of daily self-care, proper diet, professional cleaning and assessment, exposure to fluoride, and a nutritious noncariogenic diet. Whether these dental wellness practices were incorporated in the person's life through the childhood years will be evident in the adult years. If dental wellness practices were followed faithfully in childhood, then the adult years will be evidenced by a high level of dental wellness. If not, much restorative work will be necessary along with attitudinal, value, and behavioral changes on the part of the adult.

Of every 100 Americans, fewer than 5 go through life without tooth decay. By middle age, 2 out of 3 people will have serious gum disease [3]. However, an informed, knowledgeable adult will more likely practice wellness-oriented self-care measures.

As people grow older, periodontal disease becomes more prevalent. Many older adults have accepted this condition as a normal part of aging because of the lack of knowledge and unavailability of professional care in previous years. It can, however, be prevented with oral hygiene measures that prevent the buildup of plaque and encourage care of the gingiva. Gum disease is a nearly universal ailment that strikes 95 percent of the population at some time, and after the age of 35 it is the chief cause of loss of teeth [6]. Some common symptoms of periodontal disease are red, swollen, bleeding gums, persistent bad breath, and loosening of teeth [6]. Besides plaque buildup in the gum pockets, poor-fitting dentures, malocclusion, mouth breathing, bruxism, and biting of toothpicks, bobby pins, and other sharp objects can also contribute to the development of periodontal disease [11].

For those with periodontal problems, the Bass method of toothbrushing is recommended. This sulcular method is particularly good for removing food particles trapped in the sulcus, the area between the teeth and the gums. The toothbrush is directed toward the gingiva at a 45-degree angle. Some pressure is applied, allowing the bristle ends to slide into the sulcus. A slight back and forth vibration is then made with the brush while it is still in the sulcus. The vibration movement should be repeated four or five times, followed by a thorough rinsing [16].

During adulthood, the person may notice teeth stains. Coffee, tea, tobacco, and some drugs can cause stains or discolorations. These stains are sometimes rough and can accumulate plaque. It is generally recommended that individuals have their teeth cleaned every 6 months to prevent the buildup of calculus, which is plaque that has hardened over a period of time. This removable type of stain is usually an external or extrinsic type. Certain drugs may alter normal oral flora, allowing the growth of bacteria that produce discoloration. As a result, orange and red hues may sometimes be found on tooth surfaces. Occupational exposure to metal dusts may also cause color changes in the worker's teeth [16].

Some stains are intrinsic and not removable. One of the common reasons for this type of stain is pulp-tissue damage. Pigments from the blood in persons suffering from disease such as jaundice may cause stains. If the fluoride level in the water supply is too high, brown staining may occur on the teeth. Tetracycline is a drug that may cause intrinsic staining, particularly in small children and in the fetus if taken by the pregnant woman [16]. The nurse should know the origin of all stains, but more health guidance will be necessary in relation to the extrinsic stain because it may be an indication of inadequate oral hygiene. Proper daily self-care should be stressed.

With the emphasis on dental wellness practices for children, sometimes one may believe such behaviors are not important for adults. In order to last a lifetime, however, the teeth must be cared for during all developmental stages. The regular toothbrushing and flossing practices developed during childhood, regular professional visits, and proper diet should be integral components of the adult family member's life-style. Nutrition is important for preventing obesity as well as for maintaining dental wellness. The nurse can accomplish several wellness goals through encouraging proper eating habits. Adults can accomplish many dental wellness goals. They can care for their teeth on a daily basis; they can eat foods that enhance dental wellness and prevent caries; they can visit a dental professional on a regular basis. Adults can take actions so that they may enter the geriatric years with a full set of teeth in a high level of wellness. The behaviors listed here serve as a guide to the adult for dental wellness:

ADULTS SHOULD
1. Provide an appropriate role model, as well as guide and encourage children toward dental wellness practices.
2. Practice dental self-care measures.
3. Visit a dental professional every 6 to 12 months or more often as needed.
4. Eat a well-balanced diet based on the RDA exchanges.
5. Practice correct toothbrushing and flossing techniques.
6. Expose teeth to fluoride through toothpastes and water supply.

THE PREGNANT ADULT
The pregnant woman has a responsibility for caring for herself as well as the fetus. This responsibility extends to the teeth as part of the total domain of physical health. Even as early as the sixth week of embryonic life, tooth bud formation and calcification of the primary teeth begin [18]. Therefore, nutrition in the pregnant woman is very important for the developing primary teeth, which are in turn important to the development of the permanent teeth, in which calcification of the crowns begins at birth and continues until age 16 for the third molars [18]. It is essential that pregnant women receive a nutritionally balanced diet, particularly in vitamins A and D, calcium, and phosphorus. Deficiency in these nutrients can result in poor development of tooth enamel in the fetus.

Some pregnant women are concerned about the saying, "for every baby a tooth." Contrary to this old belief, the baby does not absorb calcium from the mother's teeth [2]. The composition of adult teeth does not change once established. The expectant mother should continue dental wellness practices during this period of her life just as she does at any other time. The nutrients for her body and the developing fetus must be provided by the foods she eats. As in the nonpregnant state of health, she needs to have dental checkups regularly, to restrict her intake of sugars and junk foods, and to clean her teeth, gums, and tongue daily. Poor oral hygiene can lead to gingivitis, an infection in the gums that is due to bacterial plaque and may be exaggerated by the pregnant woman's hormonal system. Most problems, however, can be avoided by brushing within 20 minutes of eating, flossing daily, eating a well-balanced diet, and utilizing professional care [2].

The pregnant woman's altered state of health does not seem to pose a threat to her state of dental wellness. In 1936, W. A. Price, a field-study expert with primitive tribes, found that no natural stresses such as rapid growth or pregnancy seemed to disturb the dental health status of these tribal groups, contending that these groups of people have considerable reserves of minerals stored in their bodies. He attributes dental wellness entirely to diet. Having studied Canadian, African, and Athabascan Indian tribes as well as Eskimos, he reports no signs of dental deformities and very few caries among those on an indigenous diet. However, once these tribes adopted the Caucasian diet, dental caries and deformities were noticed within 6 months [14,15]. An important key to dental wellness continues to be diet.

Other obstacles to the development of healthy teeth exist, however, that do not relate to proper diet. For example, German measles contracted during the first 4 months of pregnancy can result in the formation of weak enamel or even cleft palate [11]. Furthermore, certain medications may have an adverse effect on the teeth of the developing fetus. Since 1972, the package inserts for tetracycline medications have warned against their use in children under 8 years old. The warning is as follows: "The Use of Drugs of the tetracycline class during tooth development (last half of pregnancy, infancy, and childhood to the age of eight years) may cause permanent discoloration of the teeth (yellow-gray-brown)" [9]. Tetracyclines, therefore, should not be used during pregnancy unless other drugs are not likely to be effective or are contraindicated [9].

Parents are particularly receptive to dental wellness counseling during the prenatal period. Prenatal dental counseling teaches parents how to follow sound nutritional practices themselves and then how to encourage these practices in their children. It is best to include both parents in discussions about promotion of dental wellness and the causes of dental problems so that both will have the knowledge necessary to prevent problems such as nursing bottle caries and tetracycline staining, and to promote dental wellness through sound life-style practices beginning in infancy. Dental wellness considerations during pregnancy require the following:

PREGNANT WOMEN SHOULD
1. Eat a well-balanced diet.
2. Clean teeth, gums, and tongue daily.
3. Utilize professional dental services every 6 months or as needed.
4. Realize responsibility for dental wellness of the fetus.
5. Use caution in taking drugs during pregnancy.

Dental Wellness During Later Adult Years

Dental wellness assumes special importance during the later adult years because (1) dental wellness status in the later years is a result of the previous years' behaviors and their influence on dental wellness; (2) the growing number as well as proportion of older citizens makes their wellness status a concern to all society.

The older family member who has followed the recommended dental wellness behaviors for all the previous stages is very likely to progress through the later years with a high level of dental wellness, with gums and all the teeth in good condition. The elderly person should continue to brush after every meal, floss daily, and seek visits with a dental professional every 6 to 12 months. Fluoride toothpastes should continue to be used.

Certain changes during aging, however, may compromise the elderly person's ability to achieve the highest level of dental wellness by creating special needs. Taste changes occur that may be due to a decrease or change in the taste-bud nerve endings. The color of the teeth may become darker with yellow, brown, or gray hues, which may be due to changes in dentin or to food stains.

There may be decreased vascularity in the pulp, gum recession, and less saliva secretion due to atrophy of the salivary glands. The oral membranes may therefore be more sensitive to external pressures, such as poorly fitting appliances or coarse food. The healing ability of the oral membranes may be decreased. Furthermore, the decrease in saliva flow can enhance caries formation because the saliva's "washing" effect is reduced. The elderly often suck on small candies to alleviate this dryness, which in turn also increases caries incidence.

Tooth loss or damage to the tooth are more common in this stage of life than any other because the person has had more years of bad habits and also is subject to other factors that compromise dental wellness. Tooth-surface damage can appear as a result of years of bruxism or chewing hard foods or objects. Tooth loss due to periodontal disease is a more common threat at this time than tooth decay, whereas tooth decay is more prevalent in younger age groups.

Many senior citizens enjoy a high level of dental wellness throughout their entire life. Others, however, may not have been exposed to dental wellness education and may not have had access to professional dental services. These older persons do experience tooth loss. Some who have lost teeth wear dental appliances, while others simply do without because they lack either financial or geographic access to services.

DENTURE CARE

Wearing dentures necessitates some changes in dental wellness practices because the method of cleaning the oral cavity changes. The dentures should be cleaned periodically to prevent accumulation of irritants that could damage oral membranes. These irritants might be food particles or plaque debris that become trapped in the device. Cleaning should also prevent bad breath and, of course, enhance appearance. Dentures may be rinsed after meals and brushed periodically with a mild agent; coarse abrasives can scratch dentures. They can be soaked in a detergent that utilizes chemical action to loosen deposits and stains, then given a good rinsing. The immersion, or soaking method, also provides a safe place for dentures when they are not being worn. Dentures should not remain out of the mouth for extended periods of time because the configuration of the gums can change and cause dentures to fit improperly. The fit should be checked periodically by a dentist because a poor fit can cause abrasions on the gums as well as discomfort and perhaps embarrassment.

NUTRITION

Nutrition is closely associated with dental wellness in the elderly. Good eating practices should be characteristic of this stage as well as earlier periods of life. The basic six food groups should be reviewed with special emphasis on foods in each category that appeal to the elderly person in terms of previous food preferences, expense, ease of preparation, and consistency. A diet should be formulated that is as varied and balanced as possible.

Just as nutrition affects development and maintenance of the teeth, teeth affect development and maintenance of a good diet. The person with poor teeth or poorly fitting dentures may select only soft foods and avoid meats, fruits, and vegetables that require biting and chewing. The nurse may be able to help the person find resources to improve the dental problem or to suggest dietary modifications if professional dental care is not possible. Nonmeat protein substitutes, thoroughly cooked vegetables, and some fruits can be suggested. Fish, eggs, beans, and lentils offer more tender forms of protein. Enriched or whole-grain breads and cereals offer B vitamins as well as iron. Canned fruits are easier to chew than fresh. Citrus fruits can be replaced by orange or grapefruit juices with no loss in vitamin C content.

Certain psychosocial and environmental factors are associated with the elderly person's food selection and resulting dental wellness status. A lower socio-economic status, loneliness due to loss of family members or friends, a lack of appreciation of the need for adequate nutrition, inadequate cooking facilities, and lack of interest in foods are but a few reasons for poor nutritional and dental health in old age. By this age, food habits are well established and difficult to alter. The lack of a daily routine of job responsibility often negates the desire to keep oneself nutritionally fit. Community outreach programs, such as Meals-on-Wheels and senior nutrition programs, offer alternatives to older people that help them meet dental as well as nutritional wellness needs. The nurse can assist older persons in the community by making them aware of these resources and by helping stimulate interest in the development of such groups. Dental wellness factors in the older family member require the following:

ELDERLY PERSONS SHOULD
1. Practice dental self-care measures.
2. Brush teeth after every meal, and floss daily.
3. Eat a balanced diet according to RDA exchanges.
4. Adapt oral cleansing methods for dental appliances.
5. Maintain nutritious diet according to dental needs.
6. Visit a dental professional every 6 months to 1 year, or as needed.

Payment Plans for
Dental Wellness

Even though there has been an increase in the various types of dental payment programs, most Americans continue to use a private dentist. In 1974, 95 percent of the people who sought dental treatment went to one of 110,999 private dentists in this country [6].

But where do people go who cannot afford a private dentist? This is where free state and local governmental clinics enter the system. Many health departments provide dental care free or at a reduced cost for the low-income family. Head Start and Medicaid programs and some voluntary community organizations provide or finance dental care. Since 1975, all states have been required to have a comprehensive Medicaid program, which must include substantial dental services [16]. Medicare, a public health-insurance program for persons aged 65 or over, extremely limits dental care coverage. Routine dental treatment and dentures are not included. Only oral surgical procedures that are performed in the hospital are covered [16].

But what about the family in the middle—the one who has difficulty paying the private dentist but who is not eligible for the free clinics? One answer for this group is the private clinic that is a benefit offered by a union or employer. The company or union group sets up its own clinic and hires its own dental staff in order to reduce costs. Does this work? Sometimes the client runs into the same problems that a free governmental agency client faces. Some of these problems are (1) poor care provision by salaried staff members who may have less incentive to give maximum care; (2) unsatisfactory facilities; (3) different dentists at each visit and therefore, less than optimal dentist–patient relationships. Because of these problems, some employers are allowing employees to choose their own dentist, with a percentage of the fee being paid by the employer.

Another alternative is the fast-growing health maintenance organization (HMO), a prepaid health plan in which an individual or family pays a fixed fee at regular intervals. The fee remains the same regardless of the extent of therapy performed. Most HMOs are medically oriented with little dental coverage, but the dental HMO is a new concept that seems to be growing. A group of dentists form a group practice and charge a fixed fee regardless of the number of patient visits. These health plans have been developed because of the increasing costs of dental care. The philosophy behind HMOs is that the HMO makes more money if it assists the client in preventing illness and maintaining wellness. Furthermore, the goal of the HMO is to give comprehensive dental health care. The client who needs preventive dental care is more likely to see the dentist early because there will be no additional charge. Patient-education programs are a vital part of the HMO system in order to provide this comprehensive, preventive dental health care.

Until recently, few people had dental insurance coverage. Estimates for 1980 indicated that 60 million people would carry some form of dental plan, with 1 out of 4 Americans being covered, as opposed to about 2 out of 100 Americans who had any kind of dental coverage in 1963 [6]. Most of this dental health coverage is available through groups rather than on an individual basis. Much of this growth has occurred because large companies, such as United Auto Workers, through union and management efforts have begun to include dental coverage as benefits for their employees. Various organizations have evolved that offer dental prepayment plans. Their services vary widely. Private programs are only one part of the system. The federal government plays a large part in dental programs, of which Medicaid is the largest sector. Much coverage, however, is through employee–employer sponsored group arrangements with commercial insurance companies, dental service corporations, Blue Cross, Blue Shield, or other independent plans [10].

There are different types of payment plans, including deductibles, limitations, and exclusions. Some individuals become confused by the terms used. The client must be able to read the small print. Does the insurance company pay for 100 percent of the fees or is there a deductible? Is there a maximum coverage for each individual per year? Are only certain services covered? Is there a "waiting period" before benefits begin? Does payment include hospitalization? If not, perhaps the client's medical policy covers hospital dental care.

Because many dentists are concerned about third-party insurance plans dictating treatment and regulating fees, the Delta dental plans have come into existence. These plans are run by dentists in order to prevent interference with the dentist–patient relationship by "outsiders." If incongruities such as inappropriateness of fees arise, a peer-review committee examines the issue. This action reflects professional accountability on the part of dentists. Many employee groups and schoolchildren are being covered by these plans.

Some people believe that a larger, more comprehensive health-care plan called national health insurance is needed. Because of the high costs of medical and dental care, they think that federal government intervention is necessary to provide less expensive care to all citizens. This plan is a "hot" political issue, and there are many snags in the presently proposed system. Since the majority of citizens cannot seem to agree on one plan, it remains to be seen how this issue will turn out in the next several years. If a national health insurance is eventually implemented, one of the debatable topics will be which health services, including dental care, should be covered.

Community Role in Dental Wellness

Community agencies, both voluntary and official, play a role in encouraging dental wellness through education and direct services. The voluntary agencies are able to take more independent action in establishing clinics and providing funds for the treatment services. These groups usually include citizen representatives who guide the groups' policy making and make them as relevant as possible to the needs of the target group. Voluntary organizations are frequently responsible for bringing community problems to the attention of official agencies and encouraging development of services in the official sector.

Official agencies may provide services such as surveying the dental status of the larger population, appraising and interpreting the information gathered, and disseminating dental information to appropriate groups and individuals. The official agencies may be involved in research and coordination of efforts for a large number of community agencies. Evaluation is an important part of all agency programs because it stimulates greater community effort and provides a challenge to the unsolved areas of dental needs. Evaluation should be an integral and ongoing part of all agency programs, whether voluntary or official.

The preventive aspects of dental health have gained an important place in community dentistry and may lead to a true wellness orientation in dental health. Dental care is a vital part of the public health program. These public health programs provide care to those people who are economically unable to secure care, as well as to those people living in isolated areas who are unable to utilize conventional community resources. Local dentists have developed contracts with local health departments. In isolated areas, trailers equipped with modern dental equipment may be utilized.

The school dental-health program has gradually evolved. In 1903 the first dentist was employed to do dental examinations in the schools of Reading, Pennsylvania, and in 1914 10 dental hygienists were introduced into the schools of Bridgeport, Connecticut, for the purpose of cleaning children's teeth in order to prevent tooth decay [17].

Ever more schoolchildren are receiving dental care through government programs such as the Maternal Child Health Service and Head Start, as well as the school system in which they are involved. The school nurse and the teachers can bring the school life of the child closer to the parent. Through home visits, the nurse can share information with parents. The nurse can gain insight into parents' attitudes toward dental wellness and may also be a source of information for referral of the family to needed treatment centers. If better rapport is established between home and school, parents will understand the need for dental care and will secure treatment earlier.

Today the school nurse is instrumental in detection and referral of dental health needs as well as in the provision of dental health education. Dentists and dental hygienists alone cannot expect to provide all the care needed by an ever-increasing population. By case finding in the schools, the nurse can make follow-up home visits to view the total family functioning as a unit. She can assess the local neighborhood in order to ascertain resources available to the family as well as the general economic status of the neighborhood and family. She can assess whether the general economic and ethnic status of the neighborhood is congruent with that of the family. During the home visit, additional health education can be provided while involving the family members in the goals related to dental wellness.

The SHARP (School Health Additional Referral Program) study indicated the influence of home visits on the increased number of corrected defects. Decay was a major problem; in fact, this particular area of Philadelphia, Pennsylvania had the lowest rate for correction of defects. Community resources were available but not utilized. Home visits and telephone calls were made to parents encouraging them to utilize the resources. Only 30 percent of the children in that district had corrections in the year preceding the initiation of the SHARP program. During the first year of the program, 54 percent of defects were corrected; in the second year, 63 percent. This program certainly seems to indicate that close one-to-one guidance to increase parental knowledge and understanding improves correction of dental defects in children [17].

Social, cultural, and economic factors obviously have an influence on the dental care available to families. Those with greatest needs and least services available seem to be the nonwhite, poor, inner-city, or rural dwellers who have low educational backgrounds and are headed by one parent [17].

Problem family situations, lack of services, low income, and lack of a wellness approach seem to have great influence on utilization of services. Despite the resources in this country, a national health plan to care for all children's dental needs has not been developed. Children definitely need some form of dental care during their school years. Nurses can be active in legislative efforts and can encourage more and better programs for dental health care of children. The nurse can take action on the local community level by helping to solve problems on the level at which they arise.

In looking at provision of dental care, one must admit that there is more to cheer than to regret. The cost barrier is decreasing because of prepayment plans, and the trend in dentistry is toward preventive and comprehensive care. Because of concerns about high cost, quality care is being defined more carefully. The consumer movement has created a greater awareness of consumer needs. Human intervention, education, and concern continue to be important aspects of dental wellness.

The most important consideration for all age groups is that dental health problems *can* be avoided and dental wellness achieved with proper home and professional care. Tooth decay and gum disease can be eliminated. Dental wellness counseling is an important feature of the parental and health professional roles. Knowledge and self-care are the goals of dental wellness. As families learn about nutrition, fluoride, daily self-care, and professional services, programs of instruction and guidance related to the developmental stage of family members can be incorporated into the family's wellness program. Early exposure to dental-wellness teaching and development of dental wellness practices can positively affect the total family system.

Today there is a greater awareness that each person has the primary responsibility for one's own dental wellness and is responsible for daily health practices that do or do not promote dental wellness. Technology has its place in dental wellness but is not the major part of the picture. The day-to-day dental and nutritional practices from infancy through old age are the cornerstones and milestones of lifelong dental wellness.

References

1. American Dental Association. *Diet and Dental Health.* Chicago, 1975.
2. American Dental Association. *Your Child's Teeth.* Chicago, 1973.
3. Block Drug Corporation. *A Healthier Mouth—It's Up to You.* Jersey City, N.J., 1975.
4. Crest Professional Services. *Why Fluorides.* Services Division of Proctor & Gamble, Cincinnati, Ohio.
5. Davies, D. M. *The Influence of Teeth, Diet, and Habits on the Human Face.* London: Heinemann, 1972.
6. Denholtz, M., and Denholtz, E. *How to Save Your Teeth and Your Money.* New York: Van Nostrand Reinhold, 1977.
7. Enwonwu, C. O. Prevalence of Enamel Hypoplasia in Well-Fed and Malnourished Nigerians. In A. E. Nizel (Ed.), *Nutrition and Preventive Dentistry: Science and Practice.* Philadelphia: Saunders, 1972.
8. Flynn, P. A. *The Healing Continuum.* Bowie, Md.: Robert J. Brady, 1980.
9. Food and Drug Administration. *Drug Bulletin—Tetracycline Pediatric Drops to be Withdrawn From Market.* 8:3, 1978.
10. Ingle, J. I., and Blair, P. *International Dental Care Delivery.* Cambridge, Mass.: Ballinger, 1978.
11. McKeown, J. *Everybody's Tooth Book.* Santa Clara, Calif.: Entrepreneur, 1973.
12. Nizel, A. E. *Nutrition in Preventive Dentistry: Science and Practice.* Philadelphia: Saunders, 1972.
13. Nizel, A. E. Amino Acids, Proteins, and Dental Caries. In A. E. Nizel (Ed.), *Nutrition in Preventive Dentistry: Science and Practice.* Philadelphia: Saunders, 1972.
14. Price, W. A. Eskimo and Indian field studies in Alaska and Canada (caries). *J. Am. Dent. Assoc.* 23:417, 1936.
15. Price, W. A. Field studies among some African tribes on the relation of their nutrition to the incidence of dental caries and dental arch deformities. *J. Am. Dent. Assoc.* 23:876, 1936.
16. Steele, P. F. *Dimensions of Dental Hygiene.* Philadelphia: Lea & Febiger, 1975.
17. Stoll, F. A. *Dental Health Education.* Philadelphia: Lea & Febiger, 1977.
18. Sweeney, E. A. *The Food That Stays: An Update on Nutrition, Diet, Sugar, and Caries.* New York: MedCom, 1977.
19. Wilkins, E. M. *Clinical Practice of the Dental Hygienes.* Philadelphia: Lea & Febiger, 1971.

Assessment Tool

The nurse should indicate for each item whether the family or family member accomplishes the item according to criteria indicated in the columns. If an item or section does not apply, the points represented by that item or section should be so indicated by marking the "not applicable" column. In scoring at the end of each section, the category "total points possible" means the total number of points that could be attained if every item applied. The "total not applicable" category shows the total points for items or sections that do not apply to the family at this time; this number should be subtracted from the "total points possible" to obtain the "total applicable" score. When comparing "total applicable" with the "total points attained," the nurse and the family can see the numerical difference in what should or could be achieved and what does exist at the present time. Scores in each section should be transferred to the summary section at the end of the chapter's assessment tool.

	Yes (2 pts)	No (0 pt)	Not applicable

I. Family Awareness of Dental
    Wellness Principles

	Yes (2 pts)	No (0 pt)	Not applicable
A. Brushing teeth within 20 minutes of each meal	____	____	____
B. Flossing daily	____	____	____
C. Eating a well-balanced diet according to the RDA exchange list	____	____	____
D. Avoiding foods high in concentrated sugars	____	____	____
E. Regular exposure to fluoride systemically and/or topically	____	____	____
F. Visiting a dental professional once a year, or more often based on the judgment of the family or professional	____	____	____
G. Awareness of dental wellness resources	____	____	____
H. Practicing self-responsibility in dental wellness appropriate to developmental stage	____	____	____
I. Eating foods that promote dental cleansing	____	____	____

Total points possible   *18*
Total not applicable   ____
Total applicable   ____
Total points attained   ____

	Usually (2 pts)	Sometimes (1 pt)	Never (0 pt)	Not applicable

II. Dental Wellness Practices During
    Developmental Stages

A. Parents promote dental wellness during
   infancy by

	Usually (2 pts)	Sometimes (1 pt)	Never (0 pt)	Not applicable
1. Recognizing primary tooth development	____	____	____	____
2. Providing comforting solution/ measures for baby's gums during teething	____	____	____	____
3. Providing safe objects for the baby to chew during teething	____	____	____	____
4. Recognizing that teething is a natural process and should not be associated with illness-related symptoms	____	____	____	____
5. Breast-feeding, in that this process aids in the development of a properly shaped, strong dental arch	____	____	____	____
6. Purchasing nipples, if bottle-feeding, that simulate the shape and action of breast-feeding	____	____	____	____
7. Cleaning infant's teeth daily	____	____	____	____
8. Utilizing a soft-bristled toothbrush while brushing the older infant's teeth	____	____	____	____

	Usually (2 pts)	Some-times (1 pt)	Never (0 pt)	Not appli-cable
9. Encouraging bottles of milk, juices, or other sugar-containing beverages during mealtimes and *before* bedtime	____	____	____	____
10. Ensuring fluoride in the infant's diet or water supply	____	____	____	____
11. Substituting other pleasurable pastimes for thumb or finger-sucking	____	____	____	____
12. Modeling dental wellness behaviors	____	____	____	____
13. Providing adequate nourishment for the child's developmental stage based on the RDA exchange list	____	____	____	____
14. Avoiding high-sugar foods	____	____	____	____
15. Taking the child for his first dental visit between the ages of 9 months and 2 years	____	____	____	____
16. Giving only medications that will not discolor teeth	____	____	____	____

Total points possible   *32*

Total not applicable   ____

Not applicable   ____

Total attained   ____

B. Parents promote dental wellness in the *preschool child* by

	Usually	Some-times	Never	Not appli-cable
1. Allowing increased independence in dental self-care activities	____	____	____	____
2. Providing a soft-bristled, small toothbrush	____	____	____	____
3. Providing a nonabrasive, fluoride toothpaste	____	____	____	____
4. Replacing toothbrushes every 3 months	____	____	____	____
5. Teaching correct toothbrushing technique	____	____	____	____
6. Taking child to dental professional by 2 years of age	____	____	____	____
7. Preparing child in a positive manner for the first dental visit	____	____	____	____
8. Restoring primary teeth that have dental caries	____	____	____	____
9. Providing a nutritious diet according to developmental needs	____	____	____	____
10. Avoiding high-sugar foods	____	____	____	____
11. Providing naturally cleansing foods	____	____	____	____
12. Positively using child's requests for high-sugar foods as a wellness-teaching experience	____	____	____	____

	Usually (2 pts)	Some-times (1 pt)	Never (0 pt)	Not appli-cable
13. Giving only medications that will not discolor teeth	___	___	___	___

Total points possible   *26*
Total not applicable   ___
Total applicable   ___
Total points attained   ___

C. Parents promote dental wellness in the *school-age child* by

	Usually	Some-times	Never	Not appli-cable
1. Recognizing development of secondary teeth	___	___	___	___
2. Reassuring child about what to do if tooth loss occurs away from home	___	___	___	___
3. Capitalizing on child's willingness and ability to learn dental wellness behaviors	___	___	___	___
4. Periodically checking child's toothbrushing technique	___	___	___	___
5. Encouraging child to rinse mouth after meals at school	___	___	___	___
6. Teaching child correct technique for flossing	___	___	___	___
7. Periodically checking adequacy of toothbrushing technique by using disclosing tablets	___	___	___	___
8. Teaching child risks and hazards of accidents to teeth	___	___	___	___
9. Providing first-aid measures in case of tooth loss	___	___	___	___
10. Seeking dental care if tooth darkens in color	___	___	___	___
11. Assessing child's accident potential in home and school setting	___	___	___	___
12. Discouraging nail-biting, thumb and finger-sucking, bruxism	___	___	___	___
13. Encouraging use of auto seat belts	___	___	___	___
14. Consulting dentist as necessary for orthodontia needs	___	___	___	___
15. Modifying oral hygiene practices if orthodontic appliances are worn	___	___	___	___
16. Providing adequate nourishment for child's developmental needs based on the RDA exchange list	___	___	___	___
17. Teaching child to prepare nutritious snacks	___	___	___	___
18. Teaching awareness of detrimental advertising	___	___	___	___

	Usually (2 pts)	Some-times (1 pt)	Never (0 pt)	Not appli-cable
19. Supporting dental wellness education in the school curriculum	___	___	___	___
20. Giving only medications that will not discolor teeth	___	___	___	___
Total points possible				40
Total not applicable				___
Total applicable				___
Total points attained				___

D. The *school-age child* practices dental wellness by

	Usually (2 pts)	Some-times (1 pt)	Never (0 pt)	Not appli-cable
1. Incorporating dental wellness practices into life-style	___	___	___	___
2. Eating nutritious foods based on the RDA exchange list	___	___	___	___
3. Using correct toothbrushing and flossing techniques	___	___	___	___
4. Preparing nutritious snacks	___	___	___	___
5. Participating in dental wellness programs at school	___	___	___	___
6. Recognizing potential for accident hazards to teeth and mouth	___	___	___	___
7. Wearing the seat belt while car is in motion	___	___	___	___
8. Obtaining fluoride systemically and topically	___	___	___	___
Total points possible				16
Total not applicable				___
Total applicable				___
Total points attained				___

E. Parents promote dental wellness in the *adolescent* by

	Usually (2 pts)	Some-times (1 pt)	Never (0 pt)	Not appli-cable
1. Recognizing the high prevalence of dental caries in teenagers	___	___	___	___
2. Relating dental wellness to personal appearance	___	___	___	___
3. Recognizing the risks of periodontal disease in teenagers	___	___	___	___
4. Assessing accident potential in the adolescent's environment	___	___	___	___
5. Supporting the use of protective equipment in contact sports	___	___	___	___
6. Encouraging self-responsibility in dental wellness practices	___	___	___	___
7. Assessing influence of orthodontic equipment on body image and self-esteem	___	___	___	___

	Usually (2 pts)	Some- times (1 pt)	Never (0 pt)	Not appli- cable
8. Seeking appropriate resources for restorative care	——	——	——	——
9. Providing adequate nutrition for de- velopmental stage based on the RDA exchange list	——	——	——	——
10. Encouraging nutritious snacks	——	——	——	——
11. Supporting efforts to ban junk foods in schools	——	——	——	——
12. Supporting dental wellness education in the school	——	——	——	——
13. Taking child to dental professional every 6 to 12 months	——	——	——	——

Total points possible _26_
Total not applicable ——
Total applicable ——
Total points attained ——

F. The *adolescent* practices dental wellness by

	Usually (2 pts)	Some- times (1 pt)	Never (0 pt)	Not appli- cable
1. Utilizing proper toothbrushing and flossing techniques	——	——	——	——
2. Assuming the major responsibility for dental wellness	——	——	——	——
3. Incorporating dental wellness prac- tices into life-style	——	——	——	——
4. Avoiding potential accident hazards to teeth and mouth	——	——	——	——
5. Eating a nutritious diet according to developmental stage and ac- cording to RDA exchange list	——	——	——	——
6. Participating in dental wellness programs at school	——	——	——	——

Total points possible _12_
Total not applicable ——
Total applicable ——
Total points attained ——

G. The *adult* practices dental wellness by

	Usually (2 pts)	Some- times (1 pt)	Never (0 pt)	Not appli- cable
1. Incorporating dental wellness be- haviors into life-style	——	——	——	——
2. Encouraging dental wellness at- titudes and practices in children	——	——	——	——
3. Realizing risks of periodontal dis- ease during adulthood	——	——	——	——
4. Practicing Bass method of tooth- brushing if periodontal disease is present	——	——	——	——

	Usually (2 pts)	Some-times (1 pt)	Never (0 pt)	Not appli-cable
5. Visiting dental professional every 6 to 12 months for assessment and prophylaxis	____	____	____	____
6. Brushing teeth within 20 minutes of a meal	____	____	____	____
7. Flossing daily	____	____	____	____
8. Eating a nutritious diet according to the RDA exchange list for age	____	____	____	____

Total points possible ___16___
Total not applicable _____
Total applicable _____
Total points attained _____

H. The *pregnant woman* practices dental wellness by

	Usually (2 pts)	Some-times (1 pt)	Never (0 pt)	Not appli-cable
1. Accepting responsibility for dental wellness of fetus	____	____	____	____
2. Recognizing tooth development in fetus	____	____	____	____
3. Eating nutritionally balanced diet according to RDA exchange list for pregnancy	____	____	____	____
4. Visiting dental professional during pregnancy	____	____	____	____
5. Brushing teeth within 20 minutes of eating meals	____	____	____	____
6. Flossing daily	____	____	____	____
7. Avoiding use of tetracycline drugs during pregnancy	____	____	____	____

Total points possible ___14___
Total not applicable _____
Total applicable _____
Total points attained _____

I. The *elderly family member* practices dental wellness by

	Usually (2 pts)	Some-times (1 pt)	Never (0 pt)	Not appli-cable
1. Realizing how some normal changes during old age may threaten dental wellness	____	____	____	____
2. Using appropriate cleansing methods for dental appliances	____	____	____	____
3. Brushing teeth within 20 minutes of eating	____	____	____	____
4. Flossing daily	____	____	____	____
5. Seeking visits with a dental professional every 6 to 12 months	____	____	____	____
6. Exposing teeth to fluoride through water supply and fluoride toothpastes	____	____	____	____

	Usually (2 pts)	Sometimes (1 pt)	Never (0 pt)	Not applicable
7. Eating nutritious diet according to RDA for age	___	___	___	___
8. Avoiding high-sugar foods	___	___	___	___
9. Seeking community nutrition programs as necessary to supplement home diet	___	___	___	___

Total points possible		*18*
Total not applicable		___
Total applicable		___
Total points attained		___

	Yes (2 pts)	No (0 pt)	Not applicable
III. Family Awareness of Dental Payment Plans			
A. Headstart	___	___	___
B. Dental insurance	___	___	___
C. HMO	___	___	___
D. Employer-sponsored clinics	___	___	___
E. Delta dental plans	___	___	___

Total points possible		*10*
Total not applicable		___
Total applicable		___
Total points attained		___

	Yes	No	Not applicable
IV. Family Awareness of Community Role in Dental Wellness			
A. Voluntary organizations	___	___	___
B. Official agencies	___	___	___
C. School dental health programs	___	___	___
D. Headstart	___	___	___

Total points possible		*8*
Total not applicable		___
Total applicable		___
Total points attained		___

Assessment Tool Summary

	Subtotal points possible	Subtotal not applicable	Subtotal applicable	Subtotal points attained
I. Family Awareness of Dental Wellness Principles	*18*	___	___	___
II. Dental Wellness Practices During Developmental Stages				
A. Infancy	*32*	___	___	___
B. Preschool	*26*	___	___	___

	Subtotal points possible	Subtotal not applicable	Subtotal applicable	Subtotal points attained
C. School age: Parents	40			
D. School age: Child	16			
E. Adolescence: Parents	26			
F. Adolescence: Child	12			
G. Adult	16			
H. Pregnant Woman	14			
I. Elderly Family Member	18			
III. Family Awareness of Dental Payment Plans	10			
IV. Family Awareness of Community Role in Dental Wellness	8			

Total points possible   236

Total not applicable   ____

Total applicable   ____

Total points attained   ____

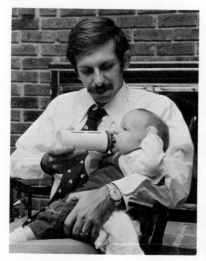

SIX

Nutritional wellness encompasses food and nutrients and their relationship to the growth, development, and well-being of each person in the family. Many factors influence the nutritional wellness of family members. Nutrition is important to the overall wellness of the family in that the eating pattern of each family member will influence to a great extent one's ability to stay well, to work, to feel good about oneself, and to live longer. A primary goal of this chapter is to introduce and reinforce concepts and facts associated with a nutritionally balanced eating habit throughout the life span. The family that is knowledgeable about nutritional wellness factors will be able to make informed decisions to influence their position on the nutritional wellness continuum (Fig. 6-1).

Framework for Nutritional Wellness

The framework for nutritional wellness establishes the physiologic requirements of the body as its foundation. The age, sex, genetic makeup, temperature of the environment, and activity level greatly influence the energy and nutrient demands of the body. That the body needs specific nutrients to meet its physiologic demands appears to be a simple concept. It becomes more complex when we consider the factors that influence what foods are eaten in each person's attempt to meet those physiologic requirements. Values, knowledge about foods and nutrition, eating habits that have been forming and changing since childhood, finances, mealtime environment, exercise level, and self-concept, all influence what foods we eat to meet the body's physiologic requirements (Fig. 6-2).

PHYSIOLOGIC REQUIREMENTS

The body needs sufficient amounts of carbohydrate, protein, fat, water, vitamins, and minerals to function. The specific needs are very individualized, depending on the age and sex of the individual, rate of growth, genetic makeup, activity level, and temperature of the environment. The nutritional requirements for meeting physiologic demands have been established for each age group; they are called the Recommended Dietary Allowances (RDA) (Table 6-1).

Recommended Dietary Allowances are established by the Committee on Dietary Allowances of the Food and Nutrition Board of the National Research Council. Every 4 or 5 years, the committee publishes an update of the RDA. The RDA are defined as "levels of intake of essential nutrients which, based on current knowledge, are considered to be adequate to meet the nutritional needs of most healthy persons in the United States" [15]. Because of the many influences on the nutritional requirements of individuals, the Recommended Dietary Allowances are estimated for both sexes and for various age groups. In order to overcome the lack of knowledge concerning differences in the individual requirements, the estimated Recommended Dietary Allowances are *not minimum* requirements. Rather, they exceed the needs of most individuals, thereby ensuring that the needs of nearly all

Figure 6-1. Nutritional wellness continuum. (Definitions adapted from M. V. Krause and L. K. Mahan [13].)

Poor Nutrition
Family member is deprived of an adequate amount of the essential nutrients over an extended period of time.

Good Nutrition
Family member benefits from the intake of a well-balanced diet.

Optimum Nutrition
Family member has ingested and utilized all of the essential nutrients (carbohydrates, proteins, fats, minerals, vitamins, and water) to maintain health and well-being at the highest possible level.

individuals are met [2]. One must keep in mind that there are many dietary unknowns and that human requirements for many nutrients have not been established. Many people may attain adequate growth, development, and wellness with nutrient intakes below those suggested by the RDA; it is nonetheless important for the nurse and other health personnel to remember that an individual whose diet consistently maintains levels of nutrients below RDA is at greater risk for a nutritional deficiency. The nurse should provide the well family with knowledge about Recommended Dietary Allowances and about how they can adjust these to be congruent with the other influences, so that the nutritional requirements of all

Figure 6-2. A model for family nutritional wellness.

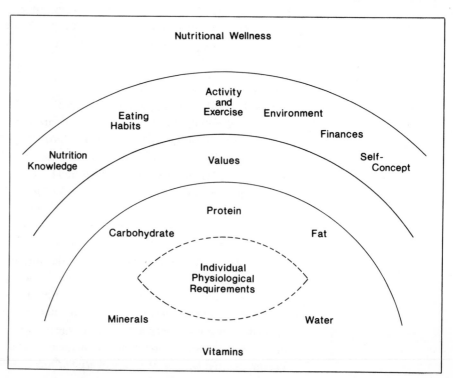

Nutritional Wellness

Activity and Exercise

Eating Habits

Environment

Finances

Nutrition Knowledge

Values

Self-Concept

Protein

Carbohydrate

Fat

Individual Physiological Requirements

Minerals

Water

Vitamins

family members are met. Families should be informed that RDA is a useful guide for estimating caloric needs of population groups but that it should not be used at face value to determine individual caloric needs. However, RDA can assist families by demonstrating to them how caloric needs change throughout the life span and by influencing their choice of a proper balance of foods from each food group. The best guide for adequate intake of calories is maintenance of desired body weight [13].

The activities, responsibilities, and goals of the individual change as he grows and develops throughout the life span. Therefore, energy expenditures and caloric needs are also changing. One's need for essential nutrients throughout life continues, but caloric intake must change along with changes in energy expenditure and growth and development. To alter that caloric intake effectively, the family must understand the nature of the nutritionally balanced eating habit.

DEVELOPING A NUTRITIONALLY BALANCED EATING HABIT

The basis of a family's nutritionally balanced eating habit is a well-prepared meal that meets the nutrition needs of all members. For many years, the guide for good nutrition has been the Basic Four Food Groups. The use of the Basic Four Food Groups has been quite effective in assuring adequate food intake in the four major categories.

The six food exchange lists were developed by The American Dietetic Association and American Diabetes Association, Inc. The new grouping differs from the old one in five major areas: (1) a separate list for fat is provided that is not found in the Basic Four; (2) the Basic Four fruit-vegetable group is split to form two exchange groupings, one fruit and one vegetable; (3) the vegetable list includes only nonstarchy vegetables; (4) starchy vegetables are included in the bread group; and (5) meats are divided into three categories according to fat content. Within the Basic Four, foods of similar nutritive value are grouped together, but this grouping really gives no information regarding caloric content. The advantage of the six *Exchange Lists for Meal Planning* is that they provide a quick method for determining approximate caloric content within the nutrient group; they also assure more variety in the diet by separating the fruits from the vegetables. The comparison is shown in Table 6-2.

Table 6-3 gives examples of foods in each category of the six food exchange lists, which can be helpful to the family in planning daily menus that will meet the needs of all family members. Table 6-4 gives exchanges for common "fast foods." A very essential part of the nursing role is teaching the nutritionally balanced eating habit. It is the nurse who interacts with the well family and who can provide the correct information so that the family can make informed decisions about nutrition. Food exchange guides are given for each age group in the specific section for that group.

Eating the proper foods is a major part of the nutritionally balanced eating habit.

Table 6-1. Recommended Daily Dietary Allowances, Revised 1979[a]

	Age in years	Weight		Height		Protein (gm)	Fat-Soluble Vitamins			Water-Soluble Vitamins		
		kg	lbs	cm	in.		Vitamin A (μg R.E.)	Vitamin D (μg)	Vitamin E (mg a T.E.)	Vitamin C (mg)	Thiamin (mg)	Riboflavin (mg)
Infants	0.0–0.5	6	13	60	24	(kg × 2.2)	420	10.0	3	35	0.3	0.4
	0.5–1.0	9	20	71	28	(kg × 2.0)	400	10.0	4	35	0.5	0.6
Children	1–3	13	29	90	35	23	400	10.0	5	45	0.7	0.8
	4–6	20	44	112	44	30	500	10.0	6	45	0.9	1.0
	7–10	28	62	132	52	34	700	10.0	7	45	1.2	1.4
Males	11–14	45	99	157	62	45	1000	10.0	8	50	1.4	1.6
	15–18	66	145	176	69	56	1000	10.0	10	60	1.4	1.7
	19–22	70	154	177	70	56	1000	7.5	10	60	1.5	1.7
	23–50	70	154	178	70	56	1000	5.0	10	60	1.4	1.6
	51+	70	154	178	70	56	1000	5.0	10	60	1.2	1.4
Females	11–14	46	101	157	62	46	800	10.0	8	50	1.1	1.3
	15–18	55	120	163	64	46	800	10.0	8	60	1.1	1.3
	19–22	55	120	163	64	44	800	7.5	8	60	1.1	1.3
	23–50	55	120	163	64	44	800	5.0	8	60	1.0	1.2
	51+	55	120	163	64	44	800	5.0	8	60	1.0	1.2
Pregnant						+30	+200	+5.0	+2	+20	+0.4	+0.3
Lactating						+20	+400	+5.0	+3	+40	+0.5	+0.5

[a]Designed for the maintenance of good nutrition of practically all healthy people in the United States. The allowances are intended to provide for individual variations among most normal persons as they live in the United States under usual environmental stress. Diets should be based on a variety of common foods in order to provide other nutrients for which human requirements have been less well defined.

[b]The RDA for vitamin B_{12} in infants is based on average concentration of the vitamin in human milk. The allowances after weaning are based on energy intake (as recommended by the American Academy of Pediatrics) and consideration of other factors such as intestinal absorption.

[c]The increased requirement during pregnancy cannot be met by the iron content of habitual American diets nor by the existing iron stores of many women; therefore, the use of 30–60 mg of supplemental iron is recommended. Iron needs during lactation are not substantially different from those of nonpregnant women, but continued supplementation of the mother for 2–3 months after parturition is advisable in order to replenish stores depleted by pregnancy.

Source: Food and Nutrition Board, National Academy of Sciences, National Research Council [15]. Adapted by Suitor and Hunter [22].

In addition to proper food intake, the nutritionally balanced eating habit is also based on the following assumptions:

1. Each family member has three regular meals a day or six smaller meals a day.
2. Each meal is eaten at approximately the same time each day.
3. With each meal each person drinks a minimum of 1 glass of water/fluid, as well as 1 glass of water between meals to ensure adequate fluid intake.
4. Each meal is eaten slowly in a relaxed atmosphere to aid in the digestion and utilization of the nutrient.

The past eating habits and values of family members greatly influence their motivation to improve or change to achieve the described nutritionally balanced eating habit. These habits are undergirded by the values about food and eating that one has developed since childhood. All behaviors, including nutritional behaviors, pass through one's personal value screen.

Eating Habits. Eating habits comprise the responses of individuals or groups to social and cultural pressures in selecting, consuming, and utilizing portions of the available food supply [12]. In this technologic society, elaborate systems of food processing, preparation, and refrigeration have made available a variety of foods

Table 6-1. (continued)

Water-Soluble Vitamins				Minerals					
Niacin (mg N.E.)	Vitamin B (mg)	Folacin (µg)	Vitamin B$_{12}$ (µg)	Calcium (mg)	Phosphorus (mg)	Magnesium (mg)	Iron (mg)	Zinc (mg)	Iodine (µg)
6	0.3	30	0.5[b]	360	240	50	10	3	40
8	0.6	45	1.5	540	360	70	15	5	50
9	0.9	100	2.0	800	800	150	15	10	70
11	1.3	200	2.5	800	800	200	10	10	90
16	1.6	300	3.0	800	800	250	10	10	120
18	1.8	400	3.0	1200	1200	350	18	15	150
18	2.0	400	3.0	1200	1200	400	10	15	150
19	2.2	400	3.0	800	800	350	10	15	150
18	2.2	400	3.0	800	800	350	10	15	150
16	2.2	400	3.0	800	800	350	10	15	150
15	1.8	400	3.0	1200	1200	300	18	15	150
14	2.0	400	3.0	1200	1200	300	18	15	150
14	2.0	400	3.0	800	800	300	18	15	150
13	2.0	400	3.0	800	800	300	18	15	150
13	2.0	400	3.0	800	800	300	10	15	150
+2	+0.6	+400	+1.0	+400	+400	+150	—[c]	+5	+25
+5	+0.5	+100	+1.0	+400	+400	+150	—[c]	+10	+50

Table 6-2. Comparison of Basic Four and Six Food Exchange Lists

Basic Four	Food Exchange Lists	Carbohydrate (gm)	Protein (gm)	Fat (gm)	Calories
1. Milk group[a]	1. Milk exchange	12	8	trace	80
2. Meat group[b]	2. Meat exchange	0	7	5	75
	Lean meat	0	7	3	55
	Medium-fat meat	0	7	5	75
	High-fat meat	0	7	8	100
3. Bread-cereal group	3. Bread-cereal-starchy vegetable exchange	15	2	0	70
4. Fruit-vegetable group	4. Fruit exchange	10	0	0	40
	5. Vegetable exchange	5	2	0	25
	6. Fat exchange	0	0	5	45

[a]The milk group in the Basic Four is based on 10 gm fat as contained in whole milk products. In the Six Food Exchanges the amount of fat is based on the use of nonfat milk and milk products.
[b]The Basic Four meat group consists of the nutrient values in the medium-fat group.
Source: Lewis [14] and *Exchange Lists for Meal Planning*. The exchange lists are based on material in the *Exchange Lists for Meal Planning* prepared by Committees of the American Diabetes Association, Inc. and The American Dietetic Association in cooperation with the National Institute of Arthritis, Metabolism and Digestive Diseases and the National Heart and Lung Institute, National Institutes of Health, Public Health Service, U.S. Department of Health, Education and Welfare.

year round. Also, the transportation improvements make it possible for more people to consume more fresh fruits and vegetables. Attitudes and preferences developed because of one's geographic location also influence eating habits. One who lives along the seacoast is more likely to eat seafood, while farmers and those who live inland are more likely to eat meat.

Table 6-3. Six Food Exchange Lists

List 1

Milk Exchanges	Amount
Nonfat fortified milk	
Skim or nonfat milk	1 cup
Powdered (nonfat dry, before adding liquid)	⅓ cup
Canned, evaporated—skim milk	½ cup
Buttermilk made from skim milk	1 cup
Yogurt made from skim milk (plain, unflavored)	1 cup
Low-fat fortified milk	
1% fat fortified milk (omit ½ Fat Exchange)	1 cup
2% fat fortified milk (omit 1 Fat Exchange)	1 cup
Yogurt made from 2% fortified milk (plain, unflavored) (omit 1 Fat Exchange)	1 cup
Whole milk (omit 2 Fat Exchanges)	
Whole milk	1 cup
Canned, evaporated whole milk	½ cup
Buttermilk made from whole milk	1 cup
Yogurt made from whole milk (plain, unflavored)	1 cup

Note: This list shows kinds and amounts of milk or milk products to use for one Milk Exchange. Low-fat and whole milk contain saturated fat.

List 2

Vegetable Exchanges

Asparagus
Bean sprouts
Beets
Broccoli
Brussels sprouts
Cabbage
Carrots
Cauliflower
Celery
Eggplant
Green pepper
Greens
  Beets
  Chards
  Collards
  Dandelion
  Kale
  Mustard
  Spinach
  Turnips
Use as desired
  Chicory
  Chinese cabbage
  Cucumbers
  Endive
  Escarole

Mushrooms
Okra
Onions
Rhubarb
Rutabaga
Sauerkraut
String beans, green or yellow
Summer squash
Tomatoes
Tomato juice
Turnips
Vegetable juice cocktail
Zucchini

Lettuce
Parsley
Pickles, dill
Radishes
Watercress

Note: One-half cup serving equals one exchange. Starchy vegetables are found in the Bread Exchange list.

Table 6-3. (continued)

List 3

Fruit Exchanges	Amount	Fruit Exchanges	Amount
Apple	1 small	Grape juice	¼ cup
Apple juice	⅓ cup	Mango	½ small
Applesauce (unsweetened)	½ cup	Melon	
Apricots, fresh	2 medium	Cantaloupe	¼ small
Apricots, dried	4 halves	Honeydew	⅛ medium
Banana	½ small	Watermelon	1 cup
Berries		Nectarine	1 small
Blackberries	½ cup	Orange	1 small
Blueberries	½ cup	Orange juice	½ cup
Cranberries (unsweetened)	as desired	Papaya	¾ cup
Raspberries	½ cup	Peach	1 medium
Strawberries	¾ cup	Pear	1 small
Cherries	10 large	Persimmon, native	1 medium
Cider	⅓ cup	Pineapple	½ cup
Dates	2	Pineapple juice	⅓ cup
Figs, fresh	1	Plums	2 medium
Figs, dried	1	Prunes	2 medium
Grapefruit	½	Prune juice	¼ cup
Grapefruit juice	½ cup	Raisins	2 tablespoons
Grapes	12	Tangerine	1 medium

Note: This list shows the kinds and amounts of fruits to use for one Fruit Exchange.

List 4

Bread Exchanges	Amount	Bread Exchanges	Amount
Bread[a]		*Popcorn (popped, no fat added, large kernel)*	3 cups
White (including French and Italian)	1 slice	*Cornmeal (dry)*	2 tablespoons
Whole wheat	1 slice	*Flour*	2½ tablespoons
Rye or pumpernickel	1 slice	*Wheat germ*	¼ cup
Raisin	1 slice	*Crackers*	
Bagel, small	½	*Arrowroot*	3
English muffin, small	½	*Graham, 2½" sq.*	2
Plain roll, bread	1	*Matzoth, 4" × 6"*	½
Frankfurter roll	½	*Oyster*	20
Hamburger bun	½	*Pretzels, 3⅛" long × ⅛" dia.*	25
Dried bread crumbs	3 tablespoons	*Rye wafers, 2" × 3½"*	3
Tortilla, 6"	1	*Saltines*	6
Cereal		*Soda, 2½" sq.*	4
Bran flakes	½ cup	*Dried beans, peas, and lentils*	
Other ready-to-eat unsweetened cereal	¾ cup	*Beans, peas, lentils (dried and cooked)*	½ cup
Puffed cereal (unfrosted)	1 cup	*Baked beans, no pork (canned)*	¼ cup
Cereal (cooked)	½ cup		
Grits (cooked)	½ cup	*Starchy vegetables*	
Rice or barley (cooked)	½ cup	*Corn*	⅓ cup
Pasta (cooked), spaghetti, noodles, macaroni	½ cup	*Corn on cob*	1 small

Table 6-3, List 4 (continued)

Bread Exchanges	Amount	Bread Exchanges	Amount
Lima beans	½ cup	Corn muffin, 2″ dia. (omit 1 Fat Exchange)	1
Parsnips	⅔ cup	Crackers, round butter type (omit 1 Fat Exchange)	5
Peas, green (canned or frozen)	½ cup	Muffin, plain small (omit 1 Fat Exchange)	1
Potato, white	1 small	Potatoes, french fried, length 2″ to 3½″ (omit 1 Fat Exchange)	8
Potato (mashed)	½ cup		
Pumpkin	¾ cup		
Winter squash, acorn, or butternut	½ cup	Potato or corn chips (omit 2 Fat Exchanges)	15
Yam or sweet potato	¼ cup	Pancake, 5″ × ½″ (omit 1 Fat Exchange)	1
Prepared foods			
Biscuit 2″ dia. (omit 1 Fat Exchange)	1	Waffle, 5″ × ½″ (omit 1 Fat Exchange)	1
Corn bread, 2″ × 2″ × 1″ (omit 1 Fat Exchange)	1		

Note: This list shows the kinds and amounts of breads, cereals, starchy vegetables, and prepared foods to use for one Bread Exchange. Those that appear in italics are *low-fat*.

[a]Whole grain and enriched breads and cereals, germ and bran products, and dried beans and peas are good sources of iron and among the better sources of thiamin. The whole grain, bran, and germ products have more fiber than products made from refined flours. Dried beans and peas are also good sources of fiber. Wheat germ, bran, dried beans, potatoes, lima beans, parsnips, pumpkin, and winter squash are particularly good sources of potassium. The better sources of folacin in this listing include whole wheat bread, wheat germ, dried beans, corn, lima beans, parsnips, green peas, pumpkin, and sweet potato.

Starchy vegetables are included because they contain the same amount of carbohydrate and protein as one slice of bread.

List 5

Meat Exchanges	Amount
Low-fat	
Beef: Baby beef (very lean), chipped beef, chuck, flank steak, tenderloin, plate ribs, plate skirt steak, round (bottom, top), all cuts rump, spare ribs, tripe	1 oz.
Lamb: Leg, rib, sirloin, loin (roast and chops), shank, shoulder	1 oz.
Pork: Leg (whole rump, center shank), ham, smoked (center slices)	1 oz.
Veal: Leg, loin, rib, shank, shoulder, cutlets	1 oz.
Poultry: Meat (no skin) of chicken, turkey, cornish hen, guinea hen, pheasant	1 oz.
Fish: Any fresh or frozen	1 oz.
Canned salmon, tuna, mackerel, crab and lobster	¼ cup
Clams, oysters, scallops, shrimp	5 or 1 oz.
Sardines, drained	3
Cheeses containing less than 5% butterfat	1 oz.
Cottage cheese, dry and 2% butterfat	¼ cup
Dried beans and peas (omit 1 Bread Exchange)	½ cup
Medium-fat	
Beef: Ground (15% fat), corned beef (canned), rib eye, round (ground commercial)	1 oz.
Pork: Loin (all cuts tenderloin), shoulder arm (picnic), shoulder blade, boston butt, Canadian bacon, boiled ham	1 oz.
Liver, heart, kidney, and sweetbreads (these are high in cholesterol)	1 oz.
Cottage cheese, creamed	¼ cup
Cheese: Mozzarella, ricotta, farmer's cheese, Neufchatel, Parmesan	1 oz.
Egg (high in cholesterol)	1
Peanut butter (omit 2 additional Fat Exchanges)	2 tablespoons

Table 6-3, List 5 (continued)

Meat Exchanges	Amount
High-fat	
Beef: Brisket, corned beef (brisket), ground beef (more than 20% fat), hamburger, chuck (ground commercial), roasts (rib), steaks (club and rib)	1 oz.
Lamb: Breast	1 oz.
Pork: Spare ribs, loin (back ribs), pork (ground), country style ham, deviled ham	1 oz.
Veal: Breast	1 oz.
Poultry: Capon, duck (domestic), goose	1 oz.
Cheese: Cheddar types	1 oz.
Cold cuts	4½" × ⅛" slice
Frankfurter	1 small

Note: This list shows the kinds and amounts of low-, medium-, and high-fat meat and other protein-rich foods to use for one Meat Exchange. Trim off all visible fat.

List 6

Fat Exchanges	Amount
Margarine, soft, tub, or stick[a]	1 teaspoon
Avocado (4" dia.)[b]	⅛
Oil: Corn, cottonseed, safflower, soy, sunflower	1 teaspoon
Oil, olive[b]	1 teaspoon
Oil, peanut[b]	1 teaspoon
Olives[b]	5 small
Almonds[b]	10 whole
Pecans[b]	2 large whole
Peanuts[b]	
Spanish	20 whole
Virginia	10 whole
Walnuts	6 small
Nuts, other[b]	6 small
Margarine, regular stick	1 teaspoon
Butter	1 teaspoon
Bacon fat	1 teaspoon
Bacon, crisp	1 strip
Cream, light	2 tablespoons
Cream, sour	2 tablespoons
Cream, heavy	1 tablespoon
Cream cheese	1 tablespoon
French dressing[c]	1 tablespoon
Italian dressing[c]	1 tablespoon
Lard	1 teaspoon
Mayonnaise[c]	1 teaspoon
Salad dressing, mayonnaise type[c]	2 teaspoons
Salt pork	¾ inch cube

Note: This list shows the kinds and amounts of fat-containing foods to use for one Fat Exchange. To plan a diet low in saturated fat select only those exchanges that appear in italics. They are *polyunsaturated*.
[a]Made with corn, cottonseed, safflower, soy, or sunflower oil only.
[b]Fat content is primarily monounsaturated.
[c]If made with corn, cottonseed, safflower, soy, or sunflower oil can be used on fat modified diet.
Source: The exchange lists are based on material in the *Exchange Lists for Meal Planning* prepared by Committees of the American Diabetes Association, Inc. and The American Dietetic Association in cooperation with the National Institute of Arthritis, Metabolism and Digestive Diseases and the National Heart and Lung Institute, National Institutes of Health, Public Health Service, U.S. Department of Health, Education and Welfare.

Table 6-4. Exchanges for Fast Foods[a]

	Bread	Meat	Fat	Other	Calories
Arby's					
Regular	2	3	—	—	355
Junior	2	2	—	—	282
Super	3	3	1	1v	468
Ham 'N Cheese	2	4	—	—	428
Turkey Deluxe	2	3	1	—	400
Beef & Cheese	2	4	—	—	428
Potato Cake	1	—	1	—	113
Coleslaw	—	—	1	1v	70
Diet Dr. Pepper	—	—	—	f	0
Barbecue Sauce—1 pkg.	—	—	—	f	10
Horsey Sauce	—	—	1	—	45
Arthur Treacher's					
Treacher's Basket	2	3	4	—	531
Treacher's Boat	2	5	6	—	771
Krunch Pups	1½	1	3	—	312
Shrimp	2	2	3	—	421
Original Dinner	2	5	5	—	726
Mate	2	7	6	—	921
Coleslaw, 4 ozs.	—	—	2	1v	115
Milk	—	—	—	1m	160
Braum's					
Hamburger	2	3	1	—	420
Cheeseburger	2	4	2	—	540
Corndog	1½	1	3	—	312
French fries					
Small order	1½	—	2	—	192
Large order	3	—	5	—	339
Stk. Sandwich	3	4	3	—	639
Burger Chef					
Hamburger	2	1	2	—	321
Double Hamburger	2	2½	1	—	368
Super Chef	3	3½	2	—	556
Big Chef	3	3	3	—	564
French Fries	2	—	2	—	226
Fish Sandwich	2	2	3	—	421
Mariner Dinner	2	4	5	—	651
Rancher Dinner	1	5	3	—	578
Casa Bonita					
Dinner #1—2 beef enchiladas, 1 cheese	6	2	8	—	908
Dinner #2—3 tacos	6	3	5	—	848
Dinner #3—1 tamale, 1 beef enchilada, 1 taco	6	3	8	—	983
Dinner #4—1 beef enchilada, 1 cheese enchilada, 1 taco	6	2	7	—	863
Deluxe	8	4½	6	—	1141
American	5	6	12	—	1330

Table 6-4. (continued)

	Bread	Meat	Fat	Other	Calories
Dairy Queen Stores, Inc.					
King Burger	4	4	—	—	572
Beef Burger	4	2	—	—	422
Jiffy Burger	2	1	—	—	211
Stk. Sandwich	4	2	2	—	512
Fish Sandwich	4	3	3	—	632
Grilled Cheese	2	2	2	—	376
Hot Dog	2	1	—	—	211
Tacos	1	1½	—	—	182
Stk. Finger Basket	4	4	6	—	832
French Fries	1½	—	2	—	192
Onion Rings	2	—	4	—	306
Burrito	2	2	2	—	376
Sugar Free Dr. Pepper	—	—	—	f	0
Der Wienerschnitzel					
Hot Dog	2	1	1	—	256
Chili Dog	2	1½	1	—	293
Kraut Dog	2	1	1	—	256
Cheese Dog	2	2	1	—	331
Mustard Dog	2	1	1	—	256
French Fries					
Large order	2	—	4	—	306
Small order	1	—	2	—	158
Polish Sandwich	2	3	4	—	531
Dickies Fish and Chips					
Fish, French Fries, and Coleslaw	3	4	8	—	854
Shrimp, French Fries, and Coleslaw	3	2	6	—	614
El Chico					
Nooner 1—enchilada, chili, fried rice, taco	4½	3	8	—	881
Nooner 2—enchilada, cheese taco, chili, chili con queso, beans	3	3	3	—	564
Nooner 3—chalupa, chili con queso, meat taco, rice	4½	3	3	—	666
Nooner 4—chalupa, refried beans, taco salad, enchilada, chili, rice	6	2	4	—	728
Burrito Lunch—1 burrito & refried beans	3	4	5	—	719
Burrito Dinner—2 burritos and refried beans	4	8	9	—	1267
Poblano Chili Relleno Dinner	3	3	3	—	564
Quesdaillas	5	4	5	—	855
Chalupas Jalisco Style	3½	4	5	—	753
Chicken Enchiladas	4½	3	3	—	666

Table 6-4. (continued)

	Bread	Meat	Fat	Other	Calories
Kentucky Fried Chicken					
Fried Chicken, Mashed					
Potato, Coleslaw, Roll					
3-Piece Dinner					
Original	4	5	4	—	817
Crispy	4	5	6	—	907
2-Piece Dinner					
Original	3	3	3	—	564
Crispy	3	3	5	—	664
McDonald's					
Hamburger	2	1	—	—	260
Cheeseburger	2	1½	—	—	306
Quarter Pounder	2	3	—	—	420
Filet-O-Fish	2½	1½	3½	—	400
Egg McMuffin	1½	2	1	—	350
Pork Sausage	—	1	1½	—	185
Scrambled Eggs	—	1½	1	—	160
100% Orange Juice—6 oz.	—	—	—	1½ fr	60
Sirloin Stockade					
Dinners served w/baked					
potatoes w/butter and					
Texas toast					
Club Stk.	4	4	3	—	707
Sizzling Sirloin Stk.	4	6	3	—	857
Stockade Strip Stk.	4	7	3	—	932
Rancher Stk.	4	9	3	—	1082
Filet Stk.—Tenderloin	4	6	4	—	892
Chicken Fried Stk.	5	4	4	—	810
Kabob	4	4	3	—	707
Ground Sirloin Stk.	4	6	3	—	857
Hamburger	2	3	—	—	361
Fish Platter	4	5	4	—	817
Shrimp	4	2	3	—	557
German Sausage	4	4	7	—	877
Taco Bell					
Taco	½	1	1	—	154
Bell Burger	2	1½	1	—	283
Bell Burger w/cheese	2	2	2	—	376
Beef Burrito	2	3	3	—	496
Bean Burrito	3	—	3	—	339
Enchirito	2	2	3	—	421
Burrito Supreme	2½	2	3	1v	480
Tostado	1½	1	2	—	267
Combination Burrito	2½	2	2	—	410
Frijoles	1½	½	4	—	309
Taco Bueno					
Taco	1	1	1	—	188
Bean Burrito	2	1	1	—	256
Combination Burrito	2	3	2	—	451
Meat Burrito	1	4	2	—	458
Deluxe Burrito	1	2	1	—	263

Table 6-4. (continued)

	Bread	Meat	Fat	Other	Calories
Chili Burger	2	2½	—	—	323
Frijoles	1½	—	3	—	237
Frito Pie	2½	½	3	—	362
Chalupa	2	1	1	—	256
Deluxe Chalupa	1	3	1	—	338
Taco Tico					
Taco	½	1	1	—	154
Burrito	3	2	2	—	444
Taco Burger	2	2	1	—	331
Sancho	2	3	2	—	451
Soft Taco	½	1	1	—	154
Refried Beans	2	—	2	—	226
Tostado	2½	—	3	—	305
Enchilada	½	2	2	—	274
Tamale	1½	1	1	—	222
Chili	1½	2	1	—	297
Tamale Pie	2	1½	2	—	338
Taco Dinner Plate	3½	4	5	—	756
Nacho	1½	—	1	—	150
Salad w/dressing	—	—	2	1v	115
Wendy's					
Hamburger	3	3	1	—	474
Double Hamburger	3	6	1	—	699
Cheeseburger	3	4	1	—	549
French Fries	2	—	4	—	306
Frostie	4	—	3	—	407
Diet Pepsi	—	—	—	f	0

[a]Key to Abbreviations: Vegetable v; milk m; free f; fruit fr. The food groups listed are based on the exchange system developed by the American Diabetes Association and The American Dietetic Association.

Source: Adapted from St. Francis Hospital, Diabetes Center, Tulsa, Oklahoma, *Eating Out Made Simple*, 1979.

The close relationship between food and cultural belief patterns passed on from generation to generation cannot be ignored. The value of food varies among different groups. Individuals acquire a taste for certain foods prepared in certain ways, under considerable influence from their ethnic, social, school, work, and professional groups. The number and distribution of meals each day are also based on tradition and culture.

Regional dietary variations are recognized across the United States. Southerners are apt to use cornmeal, grits, rice, and biscuits. Salt pork, kale, and black-eyed peas are popular. The black person's "soul" food has gained prominence. Much feeling and soul go into the preparation of these foods, such as pork snout, ribs, and chicken wings. People of the Midwest have taken advantage of available ingredients by using fish from the Great Lakes and corn from the plains. Wisconsin has become famous as a dairy state. Fowl, fish, corn, fish cakes, lobster, and turkey represent traditions in the New England states.

Food has an important social, and for some a ceremonial, significance. After all, eating is a social event. People enjoy the company of others during a meal. Holidays rate special meals, and often business is transacted over food. Many milestone events such as weddings are celebrated in gourmet fashion. Serving food in style is a custom of most cultural and social groups.

Also involved in the nutritionally balanced eating habit is the financial aspect, a less voluntary type of influence. Today, approximately one half of the family's income is spent on food [13], which definitely can have a great impact on the types and variety of foods the family can afford. The nurse is often able to assist a family in eating more nutritiously within the family food budget by increasing the family's nutrition knowledge. The Six Food Exchange Lists provide many alternatives with equal nutrient value, allowing families to select items within their financial ability.

MEALTIME ENVIRONMENT

Mealtime is a social event, a time for sharing the day's happy events, successes, problems, and failures, and a discussion time for family decision making. It seems that the evening mealtime has taken on this role, probably due more to convenience than to any other factor. The reason this event has become so important is that in many families it is the only time that the family is together for a common purpose. Because of its decision-making role, mealtime has lost some of the former atmosphere of a quiet, pleasant, relatively nonstressed time for the enjoyment of eating and conversing in a congenial atmosphere.

A quiet, relaxed atmosphere is more conducive for digestion and the savoring of each morsel eaten. Also, mealtime is an opportunity for loving, caring, and sharing in the family. In order for this atmosphere to exist, all family members will have to work together to support such a happening. One way is for the family to share in establishing guidelines for what *they* want *their* mealtime atmosphere to be. Some simple suggestions follow that can foster a "well" atmosphere at mealtime.

The family can designate time for specific meals to be "family" meals, when all will be present. This reservation of time is becoming increasingly more difficult to achieve with the complex schedule of family members. The family can, however, strive to make mealtime a pleasant and relaxed occasion. To this end, the family may decide to ban interruptions that may not support the relaxed atmosphere, such as personal telephone calls. Perhaps soft, quiet music would help to promote this environment. Guidelines could be established so that the conversation would center around the pleasures and successes of the day and would not be the time for family arguments. Another time could be set aside for the more in-depth and difficult discussions and decisions. A more pleasant atmosphere is well lighted, bright, and adequately ventilated. A goal the nurse can assist the family in establishing is that mealtime be a valued family event and not just a habit.

EXERCISE AND ACTIVITY

Exercise and activity assist the person in achieving a nutritionally balanced eating habit by providing an outlet for excess energy and thus achieving a more relaxed internal environment. Exercise is the closest thing to an anti-aging pill now available. It has effects like a miracle drug, and it's free for the doing. About 45 percent of adult Americans—that is, 49 million of 109 million men and women—are sedentary and not engaging in physical exercise [11]. Substantial evidence supports the value of exercise in maintaining health, in improving circulation, respiration, and sleep, in diminishing stress, and in improving appetite. Exercise can reduce the risk of heart attack and enhance survival following an attack by increasing collateral circulation. Just as regular meal patterns are important, so is it beneficial to exercise daily. One with a busy schedule may feel he is receiving enough exercise or that he does not have the time for planned exercise events. There are many ways family members can increase exercise in their usual daily activities such as walking instead of taking the car, and bending and stretching when reaching for items. Swimming, walking, running, bicycling, and ropejumping are especially good and inexpensive forms of exercise since they actively strengthen the circulatory and respiratory systems. Age need not be an impediment for bicycling and other forms of exercise. Tolstoy learned to ride a bicycle at age 67. A bicycle with side wheels can be used by older people who worry about balancing but want the exercise. Bicycles can also be used for going distances too long to walk. Gardening is another fine hobby and moneysaver. Handyman activities, bird-watching, fishing, and hiking interest many members of the family. Dancing is an activity that combines social, interpersonal, and physical pleasure. Sexual activity is a useful form of exercise for the relief of tension, mild tuning up of circulation and muscles, and emotional well-being. When suggesting activity ideas, it is important for the nurse to start with interests and current habits of the family members and then to assist with adaptations if necessary.

Activities that involve the entire family provide opportunities to share the pleasure of each other's company as an added bonus to the benefits of physical exercise. The self-concept of the family is thus enhanced as they engage in more opportunities to meet the goals of caring, loving, and sharing with one another.

SELF-CONCEPT

How an individual feels about himself can influence the nutritionally balanced eating habit. The value one places on self can influence what he eats, whom he eats with, and what meaning that food has for himself. The force that guides family members in supporting growth on the nutritional wellness continuum is the *value* the family places on nutritional wellness. Does the family place value on the premise that environment and exercise can enhance nutritional wellness? Does the family value eating the right foods in the right amounts for each family member as a means of enhancing one's ability to remain well, to work, and to be happy?

All the concepts that contribute to the nutritionally balanced eating habit are manifested uniquely by each family. They can interact to achieve the highest possible level of nutritional wellness in the family. As the nurse works with the family in relation to each member's developmental stage, she assists the family in synthesizing the knowledge about nutrition and the dynamics of family interaction to effect another dimension of family wellness.

Nutritional Wellness in the Infant

Infancy is the most crucial period for development of sound eating practices in the human being. The infant in utero depends wholly on the mother's nutritional status and eating practices. The woman who eats well before and during pregnancy helps ensure that her infant will fully develop his potential prior to birth.

After birth the responsibility for nutritional wellness remains with the parents, but the feeding of the infant takes on importance. Not only do the foods provide nutrients for the immediate physiologic needs of the child, but the act of eating contributes to an important psychological phenomenon—the development of a sense of trust. The parents in their role as leaders of the family unit develop new eating practices as the new member is incorporated into the family network. How they develop their particular style of family eating, including such variables as times for meals, foods served, and the atmosphere at mealtimes, establishes precedents and practices that become habits. Habits at this age are shaped by the parents and it is of utmost importance that habits be developed that maximize wellness. The habits established in early life often last a lifetime. Sound practices promote wellness; whereas, detrimental practices have the opposite effect.

It has been recognized for generations that the nutrients in human milk meet the nutritional requirements of the infant. In fact, the commercial infant formulas have been prepared to resemble as closely as possible the constituents of human milk. The Recommended Dietary Allowances for infants have been determined primarily through analysis of the nutrients in human milk. Thus, breast-feeding during the early months of infancy can be supported on nutritional grounds alone. While some controversy still exists about the ideal ratio of carbohydrate, fat, and protein for the infant, the ratio of 42 percent carbohydrate, 50 percent fat, and 8 percent protein supplied by human milk is generally considered ideal for the well infant. Human milk provides added physiologic benefits. It stimulates formation of antibodies against such diseases as chicken pox, mumps, measles, and polio, provided the mother has developed immunity to these diseases. Further, the incidence of respiratory infections is lower during the second 6 months of life for the breast-fed baby than for the child who is not breast-fed [24]. From a physiologic point of view, human milk is the choice to promote optimal nutritional wellness.

Psychological wellness of the infant is best encouraged through holding the baby close while feeding so he can feel the warmth and comfort of the adult's body. This feeling can be accomplished whether the infant is breast-fed or bottle-fed, and it is an important contribution to the development of trust. The infant should be fed promptly when the parent notices he is hungry. The common belief held years ago that one should let the child cry for a while before feeding is now believed to be detrimental to the infant's establishment of trust in his world.

How often the infant requires feeding is a common concern of parents. Newborns need frequent feeding, and most physicians and nurses recommend a flexible self-demand schedule. Newborns initially feed six to eight times a day, every 2 to 4 hours, and consume 2 to 3 ounces per feeding. Generally by 2 weeks of age, most infants have increased the amount at each feeding and have reduced the number of daily feedings to six. By 2 months, most infants sleep through the night and are fed five times a day. The next milestone is at age 6 months, and by this time most infants consume three small meals and four milk feedings a day [18].

Solid foods are added in the form of infant cereals, strained foods, and finger foods during the first year of life. While human milk and commercially prepared formulas provide adequate amounts of major nutrients, they are deficient in iron. (Some commercial formulas are prepared with iron added.) Because iron stores acquired prenatally gradually diminish by 4 to 5 months of age in the full-term infant, iron should be added [24]. Infant cereals fortified with iron are an excellent source of iron.

Solid foods meet both physiologic and psychological needs and can contribute to wellness in both dimensions. The child's development provides cues to the family as to when to introduce solid foods. The sucking reflex is strongest during the first 2 months when the child receives all his nutrients from human milk or commercial formula. By age 3 or 4 months, the extrusion reflex diminishes so that food placed on the tongue is not pushed out but is carried to the back of the mouth. This reflex reduction is a cue to introduce solid foods such as cereal and fruit, especially in the larger infant. When the infant begins chewing motions, around age 6 months, he should be given foods to develop this action further. When the infant can handle strained foods well, one may introduce thicker textured foods, including home-cooked cereals and soft mashed fruits and vegetables. Parents should carefully add thicker foods and gradually introduce small pieces of soft foods as the child becomes more able to chew and swallow them without difficulty. When the infant begins pincer movements, he may be given finger foods such as hard toast and crackers [18].

Texture and color are important curiosities to the child. He needs to feel differently-textured foods with his hands as well as in his mouth. The opportunity to feel different types of foods as well as to taste them assists the child in learning about his world and trusting it.

Certain foods should be avoided during infancy. Cow's milk and eggs may provoke an allergic response. Each new food should be introduced separately so that the family can observe for rashes or other signs of intolerance.

As new foods are introduced, the child should eat only the amounts he desires. The family is often tempted to force the infant to eat and thereby overfeed him. Growth rate and level of activity are the most valid influences on the child's hunger at mealtimes and thus should be trusted to guide the child in the "right" amounts to consume.

During the first year of life, the infant is developing skills in self-feeding. By 7 months of age, the infant in a sitting position is able to help with his bottle. By 8 months, he is quite adept at tipping the bottle to the last drop. An infant by the end of the first year can completely manage bottle-feeding alone. With spoon-feeding, by 8 months of age he can bring his head forward to meet the spoon. The tongue has developed increased motility, which allows for more manipulation of food in the mouth. By the end of the first year, the child has developed chewing motions. Also by this time, he has a well-developed pincer grasp and can understand how to get food to his mouth. He is ready and able to feed himself.

Because food habits are forming at this early age, the balanced nutrition habit is especially important. Foods should be offered from all six food exchanges by the end of the first year. This balance of foods will furnish the child with all essential nutrients for growth and nutritional wellness and will set the stage for the toddler period. Food habits and eating practices developed during this important first year provide the foundation for nutritional wellness for the balance of life. Important nutritional guidelines for the infant are as follows:

1. Allow child to determine quantities of food.
2. Provide adequate amounts of fluids and nutrients according to developmental age.
3. Introduce solid foods according to developmental cues.
4. Introduce new foods one at a time.
5. Add iron supplements by age 4 to 5 months.
6. Follow infant's cues for self-feeding.

Nutritional Wellness in the Toddler

The toddler period is the bridge between infancy and childhood extending from 1 to 3 years of age. It is essential that the nurse assist the family with an understanding of growth and development, as knowledge of this process serves as a guide for fostering good eating habits. With the second year of life, growth slows so that the toddler gains only about 2.5 to 5 kg (5 to 10 lb.) in weight and 7.5 cm (3 in.) in height per year. The child thus requires less food and is less hungry than he was during infancy [22]. It is crucial that parents understand this phenomenon because they will have to alter their expectations of the child's food consumption and serve smaller portions accordingly.

Two important developments occur during the toddler stage: (1) hand coordination and control become evident and the toddler eats with utensils more than fingers and hands; and (2) teething continues with the eruption of molars at 2 to 3 years of age. Therefore, the child should be encouraged to use favorite dishes and utensils (fork and spoon) when eating, and praised for doing well. When the child has teeth that can grind food, he is able to chew more easily. Foods that require more chewing, such as large chunks of meat or raw, crunchy vegetables can be a welcome addition to the diet. The meat, however, should be of low fiber, such as chicken, fish, or ground beef because the child still has only a limited number of teeth for chewing.

Parents should capitalize on the child's developmental tasks during this period, promoting his autonomy by encouraging self-control and self-help activities. During this stage of development, parents continue to have a great deal of influence on the child's developing food habits. Because the toddler strives for control as part of his normal growth and development, this is a good time to begin allowing him to choose his food within the guidelines of the recommended food exchanges. Because the toddler's attention span is short, it may be difficult for him to remain seated during an entire meal. But he can enjoy the benefits of eating with the entire family if the parents allow him the freedom to move around the room and return to the table as he wishes.

Parents can encourage self-feeding by offering finger foods and including some of the toddler's favorite foods and utensils in the meal plan. Small servings rather than large ones will encourage intake. Setting up rituals of eating with the family, using favorite utensils, and eating favorite foods at special family gatherings builds on the trust established in infancy.

The toddler becomes absorbed in his food, both physically and mentally. He loves to mess and feel the texture and enjoy the color of foods. Exploring food with the hands and eyes is a positive, wellness-promoting behavior for the child and should be allowed and encouraged by the family. Plastic sheets can be placed under the child's chair to protect floors, and large bibs can be used to help protect clothing.

Supervision is an important aspect of the eating process because toddlers tend to put small pieces of food into their body orifices, such as the ear or nose. Excessively hot or cold foods should be avoided because the toddler may be uncomfortable with extreme temperatures. Poisonous substances should be kept out of reach. With the toddler's increasing mobility, he is more likely to find hazardous substances that he can ingest.

While maintaining a watchful eye, parents need to display a flexible attitude in dealing with their child. Recognizing the child's changing growth and developmental patterns can create a greater awareness of the child's nutritional needs. Meeting these needs in a calm, relaxed, and knowledgeable manner can lead to greater security for the child in his environment.

Table 6-5 indicates the food exchanges appropriate for toddlers. These exchanges should provide the needed nutrients for toddlers while preparing them for the next stage of development—the preschool period.

Nutritional Wellness in the Preschooler

Food habits continue to develop during the 3 to 5-year-old age period. This period is the time to focus on simple health teaching about nutritious foods and their relationship to the body. Initiative and inquisitiveness characterize the preschool child, who is enthusiastic about increasing his knowledge about the world around him.

One of the child's methods of learning is imitating those around him. If he sees

Table 6-5. Recommended Food Exchanges for Toddlers: Meat = 2–3, Bread = 2, Vegetable = as desired (2–3 tablespoons per serving), Starchy vegetable = 2 (2–3 tablespoons per exchange), Fruit = 2–3, Milk = 2, Fat = 2.

Daily Meal Plan Exchanges

Breakfast	Lunch	Dinner	Evening Snack
1 Meat	½ Meat	1½ Meats	½ Milk
½ Bread	1 Bread	½ Bread	½ Fruit
½ Fat	1 Veg.	1 Fat	
½ Milk	1 Starchy veg.	1 Veg.	
1 Fruit	½ Milk	1 Starchy veg.	
	½ Fruit	½ Milk	
	½ Fat		

Note: Any exchanges not used for meals can be used for planned snacks. Portions are smaller than on those listed on six food exchange lists of Tables 6-3 and 6-4.

parents and older siblings eating wholesome foods, he too will most likely choose nutritious foods. Parents and siblings can avoid eating in front of the television set, encourage a relaxed atmosphere at mealtime, and discourage the use of food as a bribe.

During this time period, preschoolers are becoming socialized in group process by virtue of experiences such as nursery school. Children are mindful of the eating habits of peers as well as of teachers. Parents should inquire into the school's practices and attitudes toward food as well as its provision of food within the school system. If a parent visits the school during snack time, he will gain an awareness of the wellness aspects of the school's nutrition program. Snack time is an excellent opportunity for the child to be introduced to nutritional education. The Children's Nutrition Education Project, a 2-year study conducted at California State University, emphasizes this point. The 2½ to 5-year-old preschoolers who participated in the program increased their consumption of fruits and vegetables by 25 percent and milk by 21 percent, while cutting down on breads and desserts [22].

Parents and siblings also have an important role in nutrition education. Parents and older siblings can read storybooks to children that depict colorful pictures of nutritious foods; they can encourage role playing with dolls and play games with children that relate to nutrition education. Children are almost constantly bombarded with food advertisements on television and are profoundly influenced by the catchy rhymes and cartoons. It is the responsibility of adults to help children sort out the foods that are truly nutritious from those that are not. The parent may do this by discussing the advertisement with the child and by taking the child to the grocery store and allowing him to help select foods for the family.

Many of the problems that parents encounter in feeding preschoolers are related to their lack of insight into normal child development. Appetites and rates of growth decrease during the preschool years as they do in the toddler period. Milk intakes are rather inconsistent at this time and change with age. A reduction in milk intake usually begins at approximately 6 months of age [18]. Intakes of milk between ages 1 and 4 years are approximately 1 to 2½ cups per day. After this age the total volume of milk increases. Between the ages of 3 and 8 years, there is a slow, steady, and relatively consistent increase in the intake of all nutrients.

Familiarity with food is believed to influence its acceptance; therefore, new foods, even though they have been previously refused, should be offered periodically and early in the meal. Parents often become concerned because the preschooler eats little meat, but this is often related to difficulty in chewing. The nurse can assist the family in looking at softer, easier-to-chew forms of meat and meat substitutes.

Preschoolers frequently respond more favorably to small amounts of foods. Finger foods can be cut into bite-size portions, such as wedges of apples, oranges, and carrots. Keeping foods simple, mild tasting, and at room temperature makes them more acceptable to preschoolers. Foods should complement each other: Serve a dry food with a moist food or a soft food with a crunchy food. In order to promote these wellness behaviors, Table 6-6 explains the appropriate exchanges for the preschooler.

During the preschool period, children develop more skills in self-feeding. While learning to be more independent, preschoolers quickly learn that they can gain attention with food. When a child does not eat, the parents tend to encourage and cajole him to eat. By dropping napkins and putting his hands in the food, the child gains additional attention. It is important that parents understand this behavior. Parents can change or establish a behavior by following a desirable act with a reward; therefore, it tends to occur more frequently. A reward can be a simple smile, a gold star for a star chart, or a material gift. Parents should avoid criticism and ignore undesirable behavior. Independence can be enhanced by allowing the

Table 6-6. Recommended Food Exchanges for Preschoolers: Meat = 4–5, Bread = 3–4, Vegetable = as desired (4 tablespoons per serving), Starchy Vegetable = 2–3 (4 tablespoons per exchange), Fruit = 2–3, Milk = 2–3, Fat = 3.

Daily Meal Plan Exchanges

Breakfast	Lunch	Dinner
1 Meat	1 Meat	2 Meats
1–2 Bread	Veg. as desired	Veg. as desired
1 Fat	1 Starchy veg. (4 Tbsp.)	1 Starchy veg. (4 Tbsp.)
1 Milk	1 Bread	1 Bread
1 Fruit	1 Fruit	1 Fat
	1 Fat	1 Milk
	1 Milk	

Note: Any exchanges not used for meals can be used for planned snacks. Portions are smaller than on those listed on six food exchange lists of Tables 6-3 and 6-4.

child some choice in the selection of the reward. Eventually, the child will enjoy the attention and praise given for desirable dinnertime behavior. To set up a behavior program, the nurse can assist the parents in (1) defining the desired behavior in specific terms; (2) keeping a record of how frequently the desired behavior occurs; (3) utilizing praise for desired behavior rather than criticism for the undesirable behavior; and (4) including the child in setting up the reward system.

Other important aspects of nutrition and development in the preschooler's life are exercise and the environment. Preschoolers, if allowed to use their environment, will exercise adequately. They are naturally curious and active. Good attitudes toward exercise, however, can begin at this early age. Children can begin enjoying toys that provide exercise, such as balls and bicycles. They may begin swimming and walking with other family members. The earlier these concepts are fostered, the greater the awareness level of these wellness activities throughout the life span.

Parents have the responsibility for taking the lead in promoting nutritious foods and avoiding nonnutritious items. The simplest way to limit the intake of nonnutritious foods is to keep them out of the home. Having nutritious, fresh, colorful foods available is the first step toward nutritional wellness. Second, good table manners can be encouraged by providing appropriate-sized utensils for the child, being a role model, and establishing attainable rules of behavior.

Nutritional Wellness in the School-Age Child

The school-age period is characterized developmentally by Erikson's concept of industry versus inferiority. At this time of his young life, the child has a great deal of interest in learning and doing. He is becoming more self-reliant and able to take responsibility for himself. In school he is learning innumerable facts, as well as skills in the cognitive, psychomotor and interpersonal areas. He is developing from a young child still dependent primarily on his parents into one who broadens his network of resources to include peers and teachers as well. The school-age child experiences new environments for eating as he goes to school and visits with friends in their homes.

His self-concept continues to develop, and the forces that stimulate its development now extend beyond the immediate family. The child's teacher and peers assume important roles that supplement the parental role in how the child sees himself in his world. What they say and do helps shape not only how he sees himself but the behaviors he learns and the values he develops. The child is receptive and eager to learn, and thus this time is opportune for him to acquire more knowledge about nutrition and eating and to develop and strengthen values that support the nutritionally balanced eating habit.

Physiologically, the school-age child between the ages of 6 and 10 is growing at a slow pace, marked by small increases and stabilization. His appetite may follow this growth pattern by peaking and dropping also. Parents should not expect the child to eat the same amounts of food during this entire period since fluctuation in appetite parallels fluctuation in growth rate. The child still needs servings of food from the six food groups as indicated in Table 6-3, but the amounts in each serving may vary (Table 6-7).

The values the child has been developing continue to grow in number and in kind. Although he may have deeply valued the social experience of eating with his family, he now comes to value eating with his friends at school and in settings outside the home. New foods and food habits are introduced to the school-age child through his ever-widening social circle. The well family who has not provided junk foods and many sweets may be faced with demands for these foods because the child's friends eat them. Children should be encouraged to understand why these foods are not provided in the lunch box, what alternatives exist, and why. Capitalizing on the child's eagerness to learn, parents can reinforce the notion that food is fuel and that it is important that it be of high quality. Parents should encourage the child to select foods for family meals as well as school lunches from a wide range of nutritious foods in the six food exchange lists.

Values during this stage of development confront the pervasive influence of television. In shaping values and teaching personal decision making, parents can work with the child to determine what information about foods (as well as other health subjects) is accurate, misleading, wellness-promoting, or harmful. The advertising, particularly on children's programs, should be scrutinized, and the child should be informed that the purpose of advertising is to sell a product, regardless of its effects on the consumer. Throughout the country, some parent groups have mobilized to raise the community's level of awareness about advertising and children's lives and to lobby for a more wellness-promoting approach by advertisers. As a subtle and ever-present value shaper, television advertising and pro-

Table 6-7. Recommended Food Exchanges for the School-Age Child: Age 6–9, Meat = 4–5, Bread = 4, Vegetable = as desired, Starchy Vegetable = 1–2 (⅓ cup), Fruit = 2–3, Milk = 2–3, Fat = 3. Age 9–12, Meat = 4–6, Bread = 4, Vegetable = as desired, Starchy Vegetable = 1–2 (regular portion), Fruit = 3, Milk = 3–4, Fat = 3.

Daily Meal Plan Exchanges

Breakfast	Lunch	Dinner
1 Meat	2 Meats	2–3 Meats
1 Bread	2 Breads	1 Bread
1 Fat	1 Fat	1 Fat
1 Fruit	1 Milk	1 Milk
1 Milk	1 Fruit	1 Fruit
	Veg. as desired	1–2 Starchy veg.
		Veg. as desired

Note: Any exchanges not used for meals can be used for snacks. Portions may be smaller than those listed in six food exchange lists of Tables 6-3 and 6-4.

gramming should be scrutinized very carefully for the school-age viewer who is interested and eager to learn.

Because the school-age child is beginning to get involved in after-school activities, the home environment as a force conducive to eating and digesting food may be compromised. With the child as well as older members of the family participating in scouts, lessons, and neighborhood games, an established mealtime can become a thing of the past. The family may find it important to sit down and figure out how they can all come together on a regular basis for a pleasurable eating experience. Each family member, including the school-age child, may have to modify his schedule or give up some activity occasionally so that a reasonably stable family meal pattern can be maintained.

Activity and exercise are valuable components of a nutritionally balanced eating habit. School-age children are full of vim, vigor, and vitality, thus physical activity and exercise should be an integral part of their lives. Exercise is necessary for growing bodies; also, the exercise will occupy their time, thereby reducing the possibility of nibbling before meals. Children who sit down to a meal after a period of strenuous exercise will have little difficulty eating from the six food groups that their parents have prepared.

Snack foods will probably become an integral part of the school-age child's life for several reasons: (1) increased interest in and ability to participate in a range of physical activities; (2) the influence of peers and social situations; and (3) the influence of television advertising and store merchandising practices. Extra nutrients and calories may be required by the school-age child, and it is crucial to his continued wellness that nutritious snacks be provided and encouraged. The junk-food habit, when established early, is difficult to break. As the school-age child learns more about self-responsibility, he learns to appreciate the simple but important practice of selecting fruits, raw vegetables, nuts, or enriched crackers as snack foods. Concentrated sugar should be avoided in food and beverages. Water is still the number one thirst quencher and does not have the unnecessary sugar, sodium, and sometimes caffeine of soft drinks. The child should be rewarded with praise when he selects nutritious snacks. He can also teach his peers about nutritious eating by serving nutritious snacks when they visit.

The well family has been teaching the child about nutrition all through his life thus far, both through example and through exposure to informal teaching-learning situations. Participating in the many activities at school exposes the child to two major sources of nutrition knowledge: classroom experiences of a formal or informal nature, and the school lunches served. Nutrition education should be an integral and progressive part of the school health-education curriculum. The child eager to learn is receptive to the presentation of facts, demonstrations, and activities that teach the cognitive, affective, and behavioral components of the nutritionally balanced eating habit. Because the child and his peers learn together, opportunities for support, understanding, and mutual reinforcement are maximized.

The school-age child is exposed to a series of experiences that can promote or detract from nutritional wellness. The breakfasts and lunches served in the nation's schools today have potential for promoting wellness but have much potential for improvement. Families need to be aware of this nutritional resource and of its strengths and weaknesses. In half of the nation's schools, children have the opportunity to obtain at least one meal prepared at school. It can be a hot or a cold meal, and for some children it is the only meal they will receive that day. The major questions to answer are (1) Is it a nutritious meal? and (2) Will the child eat it?

The mainstay of feeding at school is the school lunch program, established in 1946 and surrounded by political and social controversy ever since. About 13 million elementary students are fed each day, representing only half the number who actually have the opportunity to participate. While half of the cost is covered by state and federal governments, the other half is covered by parents. The guidelines for the menus provide

1. Eight ounces of fluid milk (may be skim, low-fat, or homogenized)
2. Two ounces of protein-rich canned or cooked meat, fish, or poultry, one egg, $\frac{1}{2}$ cup cooked dry peas or beans, 4 tbsp. peanut butter, or equivalent combinations of these foods
3. Two or more portions of vegetables and fruit to a total of $\frac{3}{4}$ cup
4. Bread or a bread substitute made with enriched flour [18]

Recognizing the need to furnish a nutritious morning meal to children, some schools, both elementary and secondary, are participating in a school breakfast program in conjunction with the U.S. Department of Agriculture [5]. According to the guidelines, breakfast must serve the following as often as possible:

1. Fruit or juice
2. Milk, bread, or cereal
3. Meat or a meat substitute

The purposes of these programs have been laudatory, but the implementation has in some instances compromised their achievements. For example, much of the federal contribution comes from surplus commodities, but because of changes in the availability of farm supplies, quality meals for the children are not necessarily assured. Also, as food and labor costs increase, more of the financial burden falls on the parents. Every increase in the price of lunches results in a decrease in the number of participating children. And while schools have programs to pay wholly or in part for school lunches, political and social controversies have frequently arisen. Unfortunately, the psychological health of some children has been threatened as well. Finally, nutritionally superior lunches are the exception. Studies show many school lunches deficient in complete proteins and vitamins A, B_1, B_6, C, and D. Parents and children alike need to be aware of various aspects of school lunch programs that affect their nutritional quality [5]. They need to be aware of the six food groups and of the distribution and preparation of menu items. Through parent–teacher groups, in cooperation with the school administration, nutritional quality can be improved.

Whether the child eats the food is another issue entirely. Variations in preparation techniques, storage time, and esthetic appeal can influence whether the child eats the lunch. Even very nutritious meals are worthless if children throw them away. Children can share with their parents information about lunches at school. Parents, listening carefully, can pick up cues as to the amounts and types of foods eaten. Children should be encouraged to try new foods and to eat foods even if they are not favorites. However, if the point is reached when more goes into the garbage than into the mouth, a brown bag lunch planned in accordance with the exchange list and prepared with the help of the child should be considered. The goal of a school lunch is for the child to receive and consume a nutritious meal. Whether the meal is prepared at home or at school is not important. What is important is that foods from most food groups be included that are palatable and acceptable to the child.

The nutritional status and eating habits of the school-age child follow him into the next stage of his development—adolescence. The self-responsibility behaviors and nutritional awareness developed in a school-age child are preparing him for upcoming roles as an adult.

Nutritional Wellness in the Adolescent

Adolescence is the bridge from childhood to adulthood. Is it a nutritionally shaky bridge? Much adverse publicity has been put forth about the eating habits and nutritional levels of adolescents, some deserved and some not. The report from the Health and Nutrition Survey on mean dietary intake suggests that adolescents' intake of most nutrients is adequate [22]. Other studies show that teenagers do have some sound nutrition knowledge. The goals of nutritional wellness for the adolescent are to build on past knowledge and behaviors and to add the knowledge and behavior that are necessary to meet the nutritional needs during this time period.

Nutritional needs are determined by the rate of physical growth and development. During early adolescence, there is an increase in growth rate, resulting in height and weight increases, changes in body configuration, and sexual development. During this period there is a greater difference between the growth rate of the girl and boy than at any other time. Girls experience the growth spurt usually between the ages of 10 and 12, and boys about 2 years later [24]. The nutritional intake must be adjusted to meet these varied demands. Adolescents need three balanced meals and snacks each day to meet these demands. Table 6-8 shows the breakdown of nutrients in the six food exchanges for use as a guide in planning for adolescents' nutritional needs.

Because of the highly individualized nature of the adolescent's growth spurt, the

Table 6-8. Recommended Food Exchanges for the Adolescent: Meat = 5–7, Bread = 5, Vegetable = as desired, Starchy Vegetable = 2, Fruit = 3, Milk = 4, Fat = 3–4.

Daily Meal Plan Exchanges

Breakfast	Lunch	Dinner	Evening Snack
1 Meat	3 Meats	3 Meats	1 Bread
1 Bread	1 Bread	1 Bread	1 Fat
1 Fat	1 Fat	1 Fat	1 Milk
1 Milk	1 Milk	1 Milk	1 Fruit
1 Fruit	1 Fruit	2 Starchy veg.	
Veg. as desired	Veg. as desired	Veg. as desired	

Note: Any exchanges not used for meals can be used for snacks. Portions or snacks may be adjusted to meet energy demands.

nurse needs to inform and reassure the parents about the nutritional implications [22].

1. More food is needed during the growth spurt.
2. Boys gain more lean body mass and therefore need more food than girls.
3. Girls experience the growth spurt at an earlier age than boys and thus need to increase their food intake sooner.
4. With the onset of menses, girls need to increase their intake of iron.
5. The increase in muscle mass and soft tissue growth necessitates additional iron [24].

Adolescents utilize values they had developed previously to influence eating practices, and also develop others. Food and friends become a valued duality. Adolescents enjoy food and the social pleasures of eating with friends. Group outings and fast food restaurants become more common. These valued social activities need not be curtailed because of limited nutritious food choices, since the missing foods can be consumed at home.

The environmental influence of family mealtimes may change during this time as activities expand and more meals are eaten away from home. The family as a group may need to plan together how to maintain family cohesiveness through shared meals. Each person may need to adapt daily activities to some extent to allow for family "together time." This process becomes difficult, as children grow, develop, and become more independent, but bonding should be maintained with some shared, though perhaps less frequent activities. If each person contributes something in the way of planning or preparation to the meal, the time together, though limited, is still enriching for all family members.

During adolescence, the teenager is exposed to more opportunities for group sports and physical activities. As his body matures, he develops the potential for skill development and perfection in a number of sports. The teenage athlete is becoming more commonplace, as organized sports are made available to both girls and boys. The teenager needs to be encouraged to participate as his skills and interests direct him, and to plan regular physical exercise as part of his daily routine. The balance of nutritional intake and energy expenditure that occurs as a result of regular exercise promotes nutritional wellness in an important part of the teenager's life.

Teenagers have acquired significant amounts of knowledge about nutrition through family experiences and the school health curriculum. It is time to put this knowledge to work for the benefit of the family and in preparation for their roles as independent adults. Teenagers can help plan menus, shopping lists, and the food budget, as well as participate in the preparation. They need a guided experience in translating nutrients into meals for everyone at a cost the family can afford. This is nutritional education at its best—translation into action. The parents in the well family will recognize that this truly is a wellness behavior in that the adolescent is learning positive skills for life as a well adult. Adolescents who can successfully plan and prepare meals have a sense of pride in their immediate accomplishments and in their skills for adult life.

Nutritional Wellness in the Young Adult

The years of young adulthood from 18 to 35 years of age are a period of continued development and excitement as one matures into the adult role. Many new facets are being incorporated into the adult life-style. Major events include leaving home for school, a job, and/or marriage; establishing a career; raising a family; and becoming an adult contributing member of a community.

During these years, physical growth and development have ceased. Nutrients consumed are therefore for maintenance and not growth. As age increases, the metabolic rate levels off and then decreases slowly, leading to a decrease in the number of calories required to meet the body's energy needs. Recommended intake of the six food groups for young adults is given in Table 6-9.

Values developed during earlier years change to accommodate the adult life-style and its responsibilities. The move away from home brings new challenges as the adult assumes sole responsibility for meal planning, preparation, and budgeting. If the adult has been involved in the various aspects of this process throughout earlier stages of development, the transition will be a relatively easy one. The adult who has learned to value good nutrition throughout his life will incorporate the necessary activities into his daily schedule. The adult who has not learned these behaviors and is faced with independent living plus a busy schedule will need to make a special effort to see that the necessary exchanges are being made. The nurse working with a young adult can help stimulate this awareness and suggest appropriate steps to take in establishing nutritious eating habits.

The environment of one's own home or apartment presents new considerations. The family unit during childhood had certain expectations during mealtimes

Table 6-9. Recommended Food Exchanges for the Young Adult: Meat = 7, Bread = 3–5, Vegetable = as desired, Starchy Vegetable = 1, Fruit = 3, Fat = 3–5.

Daily Meal Plan Exchanges		
Breakfast	Lunch	Dinner
1 Meat	3 Meats	3 Meats
1 Bread	1 Bread	1–2 Bread
Veg. as desired	Veg. as desired	Veg. as desired
1 Fruit	1 Fruit	1 Starchy veg.
½ Milk	1 Milk	1 Fruit
2 Fats	1 Fat	½ Milk
		1 Fat

Note: Any exchanges not used for meals can be used for planned snacks. Adjust the size of portions to meet energy demands and maintain appropriate weight.

and food selection that promoted a pleasurable eating experience and healthful digestion of food. Living alone may or may not present special problems, depending on the meaning attached by the young adult to the presence of others during meals. On the other hand, the young adult who lives with a spouse or roommates will find it necessary to adapt mealtime expectations to those of others.

Young adults living away from family have the opportunity to try foods and meal patterns that are different from those of past years. They can try to approximate their family's cooking techniques and try their own as well. The goal is to maintain a nutritionally balanced eating habit using the six exchanges within the context of a new environment, a changing life-style, and adult roles.

Exercise and activity have much to offer young adults. By exercising regularly, they are reinforcing a positive behavior developed earlier in life and contributing to a wellness life-style for later years. They are also increasing their opportunities for social interaction, which is important during this stage of development. Jogging, racquetball, skating, tennis, cycling, skiing, and dancing are excellent activities that have an important and popular social component. Clubs to promote these and other physical activities are springing up in many communities and are beneficial not only to the participants but to other community members who can see the fun and sociability of planned physical exercise.

NUTRITIONAL WELLNESS IN THE GROWING FAMILY

There are additional nutritional concerns for the growing family. Pregnancy places additional demands on the body, which require alterations in the woman's diet. Young parents should ask themselves if they have developed nutritional practices that are a good example for their growing family, and whether they want their children to develop their eating and nutritional habits. Examining values at this time of developing parenthood establishes the climate for nutritional education and practices as role-modeling parents. Parents can use this time during pregnancy to great benefit by evaluating current eating practices and by making changes necessary for total nutritional wellness. Not only will the parents benefit through a higher level of nutritional wellness, but they will also display the requisite behaviors from which the children will learn their nutritional wellness practices.

The 1970 report of the Committee on Maternal Nutrition confirmed that nutritional status prior to conception appeared to be an important factor in the progress and outcome of pregnancy. A woman who has a long history of well-balanced nutrition and thus is well nourished at the time of conception has an increased opportunity for the birth of a healthy term baby of normal birth weight.

Therefore, if a woman has been following a varied diet based on the previously described well-balanced nutritional plans for the earlier ages, she will be consuming all of the kinds of nutrients needed by the fetus for optimal growth and development. She will then be able to adapt her diet to meet the increased nutrient demands of the pregnancy. The RDA recommends an increase of 300 kilocalories daily above normal caloric requirements to meet the energy demands of pregnancy [22, 25]. This increased caloric intake should result in the recommended weight gain. An adequate caloric intake is necessary to promote optimal utilization of protein for growth of the fetus and prevention of depletion in the mother.

The basic considerations for alterations in the pregnant woman's diet should include the following:

1. Eating three meals a day at regular times, including breakfast, to avoid long intervals between meals. The fetus and the mother need a steady supply of nutrients, especially glucose. A snack at bedtime is recommended.
2. Increasing the intake of water and other liquids to 6 to 8 cups daily to provide an adequate supply for increasing blood volume and amniotic fluid.
3. Increasing servings from each food group to achieve the desired weight gain. At this time, it is preferable to have extra servings of protein in the diet.
4. Avoiding use of alcohol and caffeine during pregnancy as they may have harmful effects on the fetus. At the present time, safe levels of consumption are not known.

Table 6-10 summarizes the recommended food exchanges for the pregnant adult and should be used in conjunction with these guidelines.

Lactation increases caloric demand even more than does pregnancy. The breast-feeding mother must meet her usual nutrient requirements and also consume additional amounts to supplement those used up in milk production and in the breast milk itself. The Recommended Dietary Allowance for lactating mothers suggests an additional 500 kilocalories per day [22, 25]. Adding 500 kilocalories assumes that some maternal fat loss will occur. Therefore if the mother is thin, she should consume more than 500 kilocalories extra per day. The lactating mother should drink a liquid before nursing the baby. Table 6-11 summarizes the recommended food exchanges for the lactating mother.

Table 6-10. *Recommended Food Exchanges for the Pregnant Adult: Meat = 6–8, Bread = 4–5, Vegetable = as desired, Starchy Vegetable = 2, Fruit = 3–4, Milk = 3, Fat = 3–5.*

Daily Meal Plan Exchanges

Breakfast	Lunch	Dinner	Evening Snack
1 Meat	3 Meats	3 Meats	1 Meat
1 Bread	1 Bread	1 Bread	1 Bread
Veg. as desired	Veg. as desired	Veg. as desired	1 Fat
1 Fruit	1 Starchy veg.	1 Starchy veg.	
1 Milk	1 Fruit	1 Fruit	
1 Fat	1 Milk	1 Milk	
	1 Fat	1 Fat	

Note: Any exchanges not used for meals can be used for snacks.

In recent years, the federal government has taken an active role in promoting the well-being of the expectant mother. Comprehensive prenatal and infant services are provided throughout the country. A nutritional program was established recently to help growing families achieve nutritional wellness. The Women, Infants, and Children Supplemental Food Program (WIC) provides certain nutritious foods such as iron-fortified formulas, cereal, and juices for infants under 1 year; and milk, cheese, cereal, fruit or vegetable juice, and eggs for the pregnant and lactating mother, the infant, and her children aged 1 to 5. To participate in the WIC program, a woman must be receiving medical care during pregnancy from an

Table 6-11. *Recommended Food Exchanges for the Lactating Mother: Meat = 7–9, Bread = 5, Vegetable = as desired, Starchy Vegetable = 2–3, Fruit = 3–4, Milk = 4, Fat = 3–5.*

Daily Meal Plan Exchanges

Breakfast	Lunch	Dinner
1 Meat	3 Meats	3 Meats
1 Bread	1 Bread	1 Bread
Veg. as desired	Veg. as desired	Veg. as desired
1 Fruit	1 Starchy veg.	1 Starchy veg.
1 Milk	1 Fruit	1 Fruit
1 Fat	1 Milk	1 Milk
	1 Fat	1 Fat
Morning Snack	**Afternoon Snack**	**Evening Snack**
1 Meat	1 Bread	1 Meat
1 Bread	1 Fruit	1 Milk
Glass of water	Glass of water	1 Fat
		Veg. as desired

Note: Any exchanges not used for meals can be used for snacks.

approved health-care clinic and meet certain other guidelines. WIC nutritionists are often available to assist the mother in planning nutritious meals for the whole family, using WIC foods along with foods the family is already eating [21, 22].

During pregnancy and after the arrival of children, many women find they develop a habit of snacking when they are at home much of the day. The average housewife eats 18 times a day. This snacking is definitely not a positive habit to form as it increases calories without necessarily providing proper nutrients, leading possibly to obesity. The nurse should work with the mother to modify this behavior. The majority of women do not realize they are snacking that often, and sometimes just pointing out the behavior is sufficient to reduce it. Another source of the intake of "extra" food is the habit parents sometimes form of "cleaning" their children's plates at the end of a meal. Although as children the parents heard "clean your plate—there are children starving in China," this is a practice to avoid.

Nutritional Wellness in Middle Age

During the age span of 35 to 65 years, signs of aging become more visible. This is the time when many in this age group are combating the "middle-age" spread, and there is much preoccupation with the body. Because of this changing body image, adults experience a new surge of interest in exercise, eating patterns, and life-style changes that promote wellness in general. Adults have a choice as to the life-style they wish to maintain, and nurses can assist them by providing nutritional information and by being role models of good nutritional habits. Nurses alerting individuals to their poor habits is the first step in control. Middle-age adults should follow a meal plan based on the six food exchanges given in Table 6-12. They should be consumed as part of the individual's three meals daily or three meals plus daytime snacks daily.

One of the adult's major challenges is resisting foods that are not included as part of the six exchanges. Someone nearby always seems to be munching food—

Table 6-12. Recommended Food Exchanges for the Middle-Age Adult: Meat = 7, Bread = 3–5, Vegetable = as desired, Starchy Vegetable = 1, Fruit = 3, Milk = 2, Fat = 3–5.

Daily Meal Plan Exchanges

Breakfast	Lunch	Dinner
1 Meat	3 Meats	3 Meats
1 Bread	1 Bread	1–2 Bread
Veg. as desired	Veg. as desired	Veg. as desired
1 Fruit	1 Fruit	1 Starchy veg.
½ Milk	1 Milk	1 Fruit
2 Fats	1 Fat	½ Milk
		1 Fat

Note: Any exchanges not used for meals can be used for planned snacks. Adjust the size of portions to meet energy demands and maintain appropriate weight.

during coffee breaks or during lonely or dull moments. Many people consider food and eating with others socially as two of their main enjoyments in life.

The nurse's position can be a positive one while helping adults deal with these problems that can compromise nutritional wellness. Nurses can encourage individuals to serve well-balanced meals at social gatherings, to combine life-style needs with nutritious eating patterns, and to obtain their own unique exercise profile. This profile, developed with the help of a health professional, would include an evaluation of the adult's ability to handle a planned exercise program. These tests can be done by the adult's physician. Such tests determine the heart rate during exercise and indicate the point at which the person can exercise safely and still have a conditioning effect on the body systems. It is generally recommended that a healthy adult work out for a minimum of 30 minutes per day, at least 4 days a week, at the exercise heart rate. It is also suggested that the adult not miss 2 days in a row because this tends to destroy the benefits of the previous workout [11].

Some major benefits of a planned exercise program in addition to controlling weight are as follows [11]:

1. Development of a more efficient cardiovascular system, which may also reduce the risk of heart attacks
2. Lowering of the blood pressure
3. Reduction of physical and emotional stress and tension
4. Control of body fat
5. Daily feeling of psychological and physical well-being

More people are realizing that exercise can be their ace in the hole against obesity. A well-balanced diet and a high level of exercise may increase vitality and decrease common complaints such as constipation and heartburn during the middle years. Without regular exercise, weight may increase if caloric intake is not decreased. Many persons in the 60, 70, and 80-year age range are gaining a new lease on life with a carefully designed exercise program. The key to a good program is slow repetition that is consistent over time. There are no shortcuts. If the heart is to be strengthened and body fitness achieved, exercise should be done repeatedly and increased gradually.

Adults are increasingly taking stock of the impact of their past and current life-styles on future levels of wellness and illness, and they are realizing that they are not alone in this awareness because their ideas and concerns are shared by many others. Groups are forming, consisting of family members together or only adults, to participate in bicycle safety programs, evening exercise programs, and running events. Entire communities are becoming more involved in physical activities and sports, such as tennis, baseball, or basketball.

Because of major psychosocial crises during these middle years, it is important to consider the self-concepts of both men and women in relation to nutritional wellness. Aging in itself is not the real problem, but rather the defeatist and antagonistic attitudes that people have about aging. This can be a particularly trying time for the overweight or obese individual, who now begins to worry about life expectancy, feelings of inadequacy, and personal worth.

Menopause in women is not in itself a reason to gain weight. One reason for the common association of menopause and weight gain may be that older people need to eat less than they formerly ate in order to maintain weight. A woman who was brought up to believe that food is associated with love may particularly crave food when she psychologically feels unloved—a common feeling during menopause.

For many men, the most turbulent time of life is not adolescence, but middle age. The male adult may be haunted by a fear of failure even though he appears to be very successful. Thus far, science has not proved that a physical hormonal change occurs in men as it does in women. Men do begin a painful self-appraisal pattern during this time, however, looking at met and unmet goals. They too need to feel youthful and attractive to others, and food may help them meet these psychological needs.

One way a woman or man can increase self-esteem is to lose weight if overweight. Adults need to feel successful. Both sexes may feel more sexually attractive and more self-disciplined and confident to take on new tasks if they lose unwanted pounds. For a forward-moving person, change of life can mean anything the individual wants it to mean. It can mean an unlimited, productive life-style. The exciting element in this total picture is the individual's ability to reduce risks and promote wellness by simple wellness tasks such as eating a nutritious diet, exercising regularly, and relaxing.

Nutritional wellness in the adult workspace is an important element of nutritional wellness in the middle-age group. Adequate nutrition for the working individual is a challenge not easily met. Just as meals are planned at home, the foods eaten at work, whether they be "brown bagged" or eaten in a cafeteria, snack bar, or restaurant, must be considered as to how they fit into the overall daily meal plan.

With the increase of women in the work force, there is an accompanying increase in the total number of family members eating away from home. This changing pattern may reflect a lack of time and energy available for meal preparation at home. Several factors, however, influence positive experiences of eating in the work environment. Perhaps the greatest of these is *time*. It is important that there be midmorning and midafternoon breaks and a definite lunch period. During the breaks or lunch period, it is recommended that one leave the immediate work environment in order to relax and digest food. Instead of caffeinated coffee, it might be a welcome change to try herbal teas, cheeses, fruit juices, or a fresh fruit.

During the break, activity pace should also be changed. If one does sedentary work, then he can take a leisurely walk. If one works in a noisy environment or performs a more rigorous, physical job, a quiet place to sit and relax may be more beneficial.

The major goals of breaks are to provide fluid and nourishment for energy and a chance to relax while in the work environment. Utilizing breaks for these purposes are wellness behaviors.

Some questions the adult might ask about his workplace are the following:

1. If food is provided, does the food selection represent variety based on the recommended daily exchange list?
2. Are there adequate food-preparation facilities?
3. Are there facilities for storing bag lunches?
4. Are there clean, spacious, and well-lighted lounges or cafeterias in which to eat?
5. Are big-business lunches with rich foods, alcohol, and excess calories discouraged?

If the answer is "no" to one or more of these questions, the nurse can encourage action groups who work to improve nutritionally weak areas of the workplace. Whether the nurse is in the industrial setting, community, or home, it is imperative that she assist the family in assessing the work environment for its adequacy in meeting nutritional needs.

The middle years are an important time for nutritional education, both to promote wellness and to prevent or delay the onset of chronic disease. Cigarette smoking; overeating with excessive intake of sugar, salt, and fats; job stress; excessive intake of alcohol; and inadequate or inappropriate types of exercise are poor habits particularly common in the adult years. Neglect of proper nutrition is detrimental to the attainment of wellness, and people must recognize this fact. Attention to diet and exercise can make a vast difference in the present and in the future.

Nutritional Wellness for the Adult in Later Years

Perhaps more than any other life-style element, good nutrition is as critical at age 60 and over as in the younger years. There are several normal physiologic changes occurring in the elderly that should be considered in relation to their nutritional needs. These normal aspects of aging include a decreased sensitivity of the taste buds, decreased gastric secretions, and some changes in motor function and physical strength. All of these can affect not only what one eats but the manner in which one eats [16].

Just as during middle age, caloric intake should perhaps be decreased to compensate for declining body mass, metabolic rate, and physical activity. The present population of young people are highly motivated toward wellness activities such as well-balanced nutritional habits, exercise, and relaxation; this will result in a different type of elderly population in the future. Caloric requirements should cover the amount of energy needed to maintain the physiologic functions of the body as well as energy expended in physical activity. Some elderly people are more active than some teenagers; therefore, nutritional needs should be assessed based on individual energy expenditure.

Weight consciousness affects the elderly just as it does the young. But in this weight-conscious society of ours, there is good news for later years. Dr. R. N. Butler, Director of the National Institute on Aging, has noted that the overall mortality appears to be lowest among the elderly who are mildly overweight [3]. Therefore, there is no justification for undue anxiety as to the need for weight loss among older persons who are only moderately overweight. But there is justification for assisting the older well family in planning diets that promote vigor and well-being in later life.

The *best* guidelines for the individual call for adjusting food consumption to prevent becoming overweight or underweight. If the individual is aware of a decrease in activity levels, he can reduce food consumption accordingly. Nurses can assist older individuals in curtailing the consumption of foods that are poor sources of essential nutrients and in increasing those that are rich sources. Table 6-13 shows the recommended daily exchanges for the elderly.

Older people have had more time to establish values and beliefs about food practices. They may enjoy fresh garden foods much more than canned store-bought foods because of their taste as well as their association with enjoyable memories of working in the garden. They may like foods that they previously disliked because of normal physiologic changes, such as changes in taste-bud sensation.

Further, the quantity and quality of foods purchased can be influenced by changing financial status, availability of storage facilities for food, and the person's means of transportation to markets that provide varied and low-cost foods. The individual may have the misconception that a well-balanced diet is more costly. This belief is not necessarily true. The nurse can assist the elderly in choosing likable foods that are inexpensive yet meet the recommended exchange list requirements.

Table 6-13. Recommended Food Exchanges for the Adult in Later Years: Meat = 7, Bread = 3, Vegetable = as desired, Starchy Vegetable = 1, Fruit = 3, Milk = 2, Fat = 3.

Daily Meal Plan Exchanges

Breakfast	Lunch	Dinner
1 Meat	3 Meats	3 Meats
1 Bread	1 Bread	1 Bread
Veg. as desired	Veg. as desired	Veg. as desired
1 Fruit	1 Fruit	1 Fruit
½ Milk	1 Milk	½ Milk
1 Fat	1 Fat	1 Fat
		1 Starchy veg.

Note: Any exchanges not used for meals can be used for planned snacks. Adjust the size of portions to meet energy demands and to maintain appropriate weight.

For those who spend most of their money on other necessities, such as medicine and rent, and who actually have inadequate funds for food, public assistance and community programs such as the Food Stamp Program and senior nutrition programs should be considered. The federal Food Stamp Program has been modified so that a proxy can be sent to enroll in the program and pick up the stamps for the person who is unable to get to the stamp office. In some states, food stamps can be purchased by mail and can be used to pay for Meals on Wheels, a community program that provides meals to the elderly and other persons in their homes [12].

Instead of allowing the elderly person to become a member of the "tea and toast" crowd, the nurse can stimulate interest in nutritious foods by encouraging pleasurable meals and by suggesting a variety of colorful, likable, and easily chewed foods that fit into the recommended daily exchange list. The use of convenience foods and TV dinners can be a helpful suggestion, allowing the elderly to prepare their own meals and perhaps encouraging interest in learning about new foods and their preparation. Furthermore, smaller and more frequent meals may be more palatable.

Meals can be eaten with nearby friends and relatives to provide social stimulation and change of environment. Transportation should be considered for those who wish to attend group functions, such as the senior center trips, lunches, and dinners. Such events usually provide a warm, friendly atmosphere that increases the individual's self-esteem. Furthermore, out-of-town trips provide menu variety and put the individual in contact with others who are sampling different types of foods. This change of environment can stimulate new interest in different foods while providing a caring, relaxed atmosphere.

It is not unusual for the elderly to begin exercise programs in later life. Some elderly people are more active in their later years than before because of more leisure time and society's emphasis on prevention of illness and promotion of wellness behaviors. The elderly jog, swim, play tennis, play golf, and ride bicycles. They participate in senior citizen olympics and other group sports, such as baseball and basketball games, which promote sociability as well as activity. It is erroneous to assume that the next generation of elderly will be decreasing their physical activity. This population of the future realizes it cannot decrease activity, but must pursue exercise as the next best thing to an anti-aging pill.

The nurse's approach must be humane and realistic when encouraging the elderly person to modify lifetime eating habits. She must develop a diet plan *with*, not *for* the person. Informal one-to-one and small group discussions may be more acceptable to the elderly than the group lecture approach. Promises of improved appearance and freedom from illness based on a new diet plan may not be realistic with this age group. The older person's role in society is changing, and the reactions to life changes must be understood before nutritional counseling can be effective. Elderly people may not believe that nutrition is important at this stage of development, but they are usually concerned with good health. Nurses can therefore coordinate these two areas—health and nutrition—in order to promote optimal wellness for the elderly family member.

Issues and Questions in Nutritional Wellness

Nutritional issues and questions have surfaced because families are interested not only in what foods should be eaten to promote wellness, but also in the nature of their food and what is in it. Many people would like to live longer at an optimal level of wellness; they believe that proper nutrition can help them achieve this goal. Is our food safe to eat? How can I lose weight? If I change my eating habits, can I prevent disease? How can I encourage my family to eat more nutritious foods?

The changing nutritional scene is a demonstration of technologic advances in processing, storing, preserving, preparing, and transporting foods. Both advantages and disadvantages are associated with these efforts. Foods are cleaner, less perishable, and easier to prepare, but there is a question whether they taste as good. The development of new and unfamiliar ingredients in foods has caused nutrition-conscious people to question the nutritional value of some foods.

The consumer family is becoming a label-reading family. Nurses can help by reading labels with the family while pointing out some specific things to look for when reading labels. The family can now benefit from nutritional labels that state not only the ingredients but also the nutritional value of the food item. More foods are being nutritionally fortified with vitamins and minerals, and it is important to compare brands and similar products to determine the relative value of fortified foods and their cost.

Many of our food items are dated; it is essential that consumers know what these dates mean. The date on some items will let the consumer know how long it has been on the shelf. On other items, it is an expiration date after which one should not use the food. Those items marked to sell by a certain date are fresh and safe to buy even on that date but should be used immediately. The date marked on freshly cut meats, vegetables, or baked breads serves to inform the consumer when the food was prepared for sale. Consumers who have any questions about the method of dating and what it means should be encouraged to seek clarification from the grocer or directly from the company. The labeling changes and additions, which have resulted because of consumer interest, are providing the American people with better food, better nutrition, and the knowledge with which to make informed decisions about what to purchase.

NUTRITIONAL WELLNESS QUESTIONS

As the number of informed "label readers" increases, more questions are being asked and should be asked about the safety of food. The nurse should help the family obtain information to address their concerns about the safety of food additives, excessive vitamin intake, sugar and salt substitutes, and drug and pesticide contamination of foods. It is within the role of the nurse to assist families in seeking the most current and accurate data available. To aid the nurse in assisting the family, the following questions and answers highlight some of the current nutrition issues.

Are natural vitamins better than synthetic vitamins? There has been much discussion as to the superiority of natural vitamins—those extracted from plants or animals—over synthetic vitamins. The chemical structure of the two is almost the same. Natural vitamins are more expensive and seem to have no definitive advantages. However, the position taken by most nutritionists is that a well-balanced diet should be the source of vitamins for each family member. The Recommended Dietary Allowances (RDA) are the levels of intake of essential nutrients considered by the National Food and Nutrition Board to be adequate to meet the known nutritional needs for most healthy persons.

Can one take too many vitamins? A multistrength type of vitamin taken daily probably is not toxic to adults, but excessive amounts could be hazardous to children. If vitamin supplements are left within reach of children, poisoning can occur. It is important that the nurse help the family to recognize the potential hazard for children. About 4000 cases of vitamin poisoning are reported each year; more than 75 percent of the cases involve children [22].

There are vast differences in what is considered toxic doses of various vitamins for adults. Very large doses of certain vitamins can induce undesirable signs and symptoms, such as nausea and intestinal distress. Excessive intake of vitamin C, for example, can cause the development of scurvylike symptoms after the cessation of prolonged intake, the destruction of the vitamin B_{12} content of a meal, and an increased incidence of reproductive failure [17].

Does vitamin C cure the common cold? Extravagant claims have been made regarding the therapeutic effects of vitamin C. Although much controversy still exists over the effects of massive doses of vitamin C, the Department of Drugs of the American Medical Association has stated that a review of studies reveals little convincing evidence to support claims of cures for the common cold. The use of vitamin C in massive doses has not demonstrated a net beneficial impact on health and may contribute to some harmful side effects. The daily allowance of 75 mg, as recommended by the National Research Council, appears to be reasonable [17].

Is vitamin E a miracle drug? Vitamin E has been claimed to promote physical endurance, enhance sexual potency, prevent heart attacks, slow the aging process, and relieve many other ailments—even cancer. These health claims, however, remain unsubstantiated. According to the National Food and Nutrition Board, such claims have been inadequately documented. There seems to be no evidence to validate the advantages of adding vitamin E to the diet in dosages greater than the RDA—15 IUs daily for adult men and women [17].

Should a baby be fed blenderized table foods or processed baby foods? This question can be answered by the parents in terms of convenience and expense. Table foods are probably more inexpensive, but the already pureed, processed baby foods are more convenient. The parents must ensure that food, blenderized or processed, is safe and nutritious for the baby. In recent years, consumer concerns have encouraged the baby food industry to reduce the amount of sodium, sugar, and food additives in baby foods.

Is it okay to feed a baby skim milk? Fomon believes that skim milk is unsatisfactory as a food for infants [10]. Skim milk does not supply enough kilocalories; therefore, energy deficits are supplied from body stores of fat. Many doctors recommend that the infant remain on formula milk for 1 year.

If a person is at risk for the leading diseases and health problems, is there a prudent diet that would contribute to prevention? Yes, four principles are recommended for a prudent diet. It is suggested that all adults consider the following points as the family members develop their nutritional plan [4]:

1. Avoid excessive intake of calories.
2. Increase dietary fiber intake.
3. Reduce total fat intake to approximately 30 percent of energy intake.
4. Take a high proportion of fat in the polyunsaturated form.

Is there a relationship between a diet high in fat and colon cancer? Data are accumulating that warrant serious consideration of this relationship. High-fat diets supply large levels of sterols and bile acids to the large bowel, where they may be changed by bacterial action into carcinogenic substances. Colon cancer has been related to diets particularly high in animal fat, especially beef, and may be a result either of carcinogens in the meat or of a synthesis of harmful metabolites from fats present in the high-protein foods. Societies in which there is less colon cancer eat less sugar, fat, and protein. They tend to eat more high-fiber, high-bulk foods [4].

Should adults increase the fiber content of their diets? Dr. D. P. Burkitt has been a pioneer in studying the incidence of colon cancer in westernized societies in contrast with some African countries that have a low incidence of colon cancer. He believes that the colon cancer prevalent in westernized societies is directly related to the lack of roughage in the diet. The African's intestinal activity is increased in quantity and frequency. It is believed that the rapid transit of feces through the intestines precludes opportunities for contamination by carcinogens. It must be noted, however, that equally direct associations have been noted between the incidence of colon cancer and the intake of sucrose, protein, and dietary fats in the two societies [4].

It has also been proposed that the western low-fiber diet is related to obesity and diabetes. If a large amount of fiber is added to the diet, there appears to be a slower rate of nutrient absorption through the colon, as well as a decrease in gastrointestinal hormones. Because of these factors there is less need for insulin. Furthermore, many believe that the bulk is more filling and the obese individual may desire less food if dietary fiber is ingested regularly.

Bran and other fiber supplements may also have value in relieving and preventing constipation, diverticular disease, and hemorrhoids because they encourage the formation of softer stools. It is suggested, however, that fiber be ingested along with large amounts of water to prevent esophageal or colon obstruction [4].

Is a high intake of sugar hazardous to health? The excessive intake of sugar has been associated with a variety of illnesses, particularly obesity and dental caries. There continues to be controversy regarding sugar's relationship to coronary disease, hypertension, elevation of serum triglycerides, and diabetes [1, 4, 23].

Are presweetened cereals harmful to a child's health? The sale and advertisement of presweetened cereals has been a highly controversial issue. These cereals can contain sugar in proportions as high as 68 percent of total solids. Most cereal, however, is eaten with milk, which tends to have a protective effect with high-sugar foods. Actually, there is such widespread use of sugar in the United States that the effects of sweetened cereal intake would be too small to detect. The main objection to the use of presweetened cereals seems to be their generally low nutrient value in relation to the number of calories and the fact that a high-sugar diet tends to encourage children to expect sweetness as a natural part of their diet [4].

Is saccharin a safe alternative to sugar? As of 1978, the National Academy of Sciences survey of the subject indicated that saccharin is definitely a carcinogen in humans, although its potency is low in comparison to other carcinogens. Most relevant studies have been performed with rats as subjects; however, studies in humans have thus far shown conflicting data.

Does an excess consumption of salt cause hypertension? A real issue is whether a total population should reduce its consumption of salt in order to reduce the risk of the one fifth who will develop hypertension. There is no evidence that adding salt to the diet of normotensive persons will induce hypertension. However, the U.S. Dietary Goals have proposed reducing salt intake to 5 gm per day as a blanket approach to protecting the general population [4]. Beginning a low-salt diet early in life may inhibit the development of hypertension in persons at risk [3]. The current opinion is that once hypertension has developed, sodium restriction is important in lowering the blood pressure [6]. Furthermore, sodium restriction seems to potentiate drugs in the control of hypertension.

What effect does food faddism have on nutritional status? Faddism is described as the pursuit of an interest followed widely but for a brief time with zeal and enthusiasm [20]. These deviant food behaviors are usually of great concern to health professionals. It is possible that foods consumed by health food faddists were at one time a normal part of man's diet. An adequate intake of nutrients is possible with some fad diets, but often these diets lack essential nutrients and result in signs and symptoms. Extreme faddism may result in clinical signs of malnutrition, such as bleeding gums, loss of weight, and hyperpigmentation. On the other hand, an excessive intake of some foods or vitamins can result in vitamin toxicity.

Certain diets are believed to have special values. It is usually thought that these virtues include special nutritional value or medicinal properties. One example would be the natural or organic food phenomenon. Foods grown without the use of added chemicals or pesticides are often referred to as *organic*. The greatest problem with this diet seems to be the limited variety of foods in certain parts of the country and its greater expense.

Is a vegetarian diet safe? Vegetarians who avoid all animal foods have been found to have a lower caloric intake than normal; this results in shorter stature and lighter weight than that of persons eating regular diets. Protein appears to be inadequate and serum vitamin B_{12} levels lower [8, 9]. Vegetarianism, however, is relatively safe if the diet is supplemented with dairy products. Populations who have under necessity experienced food shortages and have eaten vegetarian diets with dairy products have been found to have reductions in mortality and morbidity from diseases [20].

Are food additives safe? Some food additives such as ascorbic acid and other vitamins are safe, natural, and essential for our nutritional well-being. Others, however, are questionable. It is reasonable to mistrust new additives and to insist on stronger legislative controls on additives. Many additives only improve the appearance of food. Modern refrigeration and quick turnover of food on the shelves with less overstocking can reduce the need for some additives.

What about low and reduced-calorie foods? There has been so much confusion about low and reduced-calorie foods that the Food and Drug Administration issued the following rules, effective July 1980. Any food that is labeled or advertised as "low calorie" must contain no more than 40 calories per serving, and any product labeled "reduced calorie" must have at least one third fewer calories than any product to which it is being compared. The exception to the reduced calorie rule is bread. A one-third reduction would result in a bread unappealing to the eye or taste. Therefore, the designation "reduced calorie" can be used on breads if calorie content is 25 percent lower than that of regular bread.

Various issues and commonly asked questions have been reviewed. In order for the consumer family to be knowledgeable about the topics discussed, the following list of agencies is provided to be consulted for further information. These agencies are actively involved with nutritional research, financial support, and education for students and the public [7, 19, 22].

INTERNATIONAL NUTRITION AGENCIES

Food and Agricultural Organization (FAO)—aim is to improve the nutrition of the people of all countries; aids in establishing home economics programs in colleges. Headquarters: Rome, Italy.

World Health Organization (WHO)—concerned with the improvement of sanitary conditions and nutrition; coordinating authority for international health work. Headquarters: Geneva, Switzerland.

United Nation's Children's Fund (FAO, WHO, and UNICEF are divisions of the United Nations)—provides food for undernourished children internationally. Division of WHO—Headquarters: Geneva, Switzerland.

Agency for International Development (AID)—administers the Food for Freedom program, which uses agricultural surpluses to feed the world's needy people. Headquarters: Department of State, Washington, D.C. 20012.

UNITED STATES GOVERNMENT NUTRITION AGENCIES

Department of Health and Human Services (DHHS)—formerly the Department of Health, Education and Welfare, DHHS coordinates federal programs for children and families across the nation. Address: Office of Child Development, Box 1182, Washington, D.C. 20013.

Department of Agriculture (USDA)—USDA administers the Food and Nutrition Service, which in turn administers the USDA's various food-assistance programs, such as the Food Stamp Program, National School Lunch Program, and the WIC program. Address: Washington, D.C. 20250.

Food and Drug Administration (FDA)—protects consumers by enforcing laws and regulations to prevent distribution of adulterated or misbranded foods. Address: 5600 Fishers Lane, Rockville, MD 20852.

National Institutes of Health (NIH)—provides nutritional information and is actively involved in nutritional research. Address: Office of Information, Room 2310, Bldg. 31, 9000 Rockville Pike, Bethesda, MD 20014.

Public Health Service (USPHS)—Division of DHHS; works to improve human health. Address: 5600 Fishers Lane, Rockville, MD 20852.

Consumer Information Center—free catalog on sources of nutrition and related materials can be ordered. Address: Pueblo, CO 81009.

Nutrition Foundation—provides educational information on nutrition. Address: Office of Education and Public Affairs, 888 17th Street, N.W., Suite 300, Washington, D.C. 20036.

Administration on Aging—provides information on food stamps, homemakers, and home health aides. Address: Washington, D.C. 20201.

PRIVATE AND LOCAL CONSUMER NUTRITION GROUPS

American Dietetic Association—provides nutritional information to the public. Address: 430 N. Michigan Ave., Chicago, IL 60611.

Society for Nutrition Education—provides nutritional information to the public. Address: 2140 Shattuck Ave., Suite 1110, Berkeley, CA 94704.

Local groups and agencies, such as the county extension agency, which provides information about foods and their preparation.

References

1. Ahrens, R. A. Sucrose, hypertension and heart disease: an historical perspective. *Am. J. Clin. Nutr.* 27:403, 1974.
2. Alfin-Slater, R. B., and Jelliffe, D. B. Nutritional requirements. *Pediatr. Clin. North Am.* 24:4, 1977.
3. American Academy of Pediatrics. Salt intake and eating patterns of infants and children in relation to blood pressure. *Pediatrics* 53:115, 1974.
4. Arlin, M. Controversies in nutrition. *Nurs. Clin. North Am.* 14:199, 1979.

5. Cornacchia, J. H., and Staton, W. M. *Health in Elementary Schools*. St. Louis: Mosby, 1979.

6. Dahl, L. K. Salt and hypertension. *Am. J. Clin. Nutr.* 25:231, 1972.

7. Dept. of Health, Education and Welfare. *Guide to Consumer Services,* Pub. No. (OS) 76-512. Washington, D.C.: U.S. Government Printing Office, 1976.

8. Ellis, F. R., and Montegriffo, V. M. F. Vegetarians: clinical findings and investigations. *Am. J. Clin. Nutr.* 23:249, 1970.

9. Ellis, F. R., and Mumford, P. The nutritional status of vegans and vegetarians. *Proc. Nutr. Soc.* 26:205, 1967.

10. Fomon, S. J. *Infant Nutrition* (2nd ed.). Philadelphia: Saunders, 1974.

11. Hunt, H. How much exercise do we need? *Blue-Print for Health—Help Yourself!* Blue Cross Association, 1978.

12. Krause, M. V., and Mahan, L. K. *Food, Nutrition and Diet Therapy*. Philadelphia: Saunders, 1979.

13. Lewis, C. M. *Nutrition—The Basics of Nutrition, Family Nutrition*. Philadelphia: Davis, 1977.

14. Lewis, C. M. *Nutrition—Weight Control*. Philadelphia: Davis, 1976.

15. National Research Council, National Academy of Sciences. *Recommended Dietary Allowances* (8th ed.), 1974.

16. Nizel, A. Role of nutrition in the oral health of the aging patient. *Dent. Clin. North Am.* 20:569, 1976.

17. Owen, A. L., Lanna, G., Owen, G. Counseling patients about diet and nutrition supplements. *Nurs. Clin. North Am.* 14:247, 1979.

18. Pipes, P. L. *Nutrition in Infancy and Childhood*. St. Louis: Mosby, 1977.

19. Robinson, C. H., and Lawler, M. R. *Normal and Therapeutic Nutrition*. New York: MacMillan, 1977.

20. Robson, J. R. K. Food faddism. *Pediatr. Clin. North Am.* 24:189, 1977.

21. Ross Laboratories. *What is WIC?* Columbus, Ohio: Ross Laboratories, 1977.

22. Suitor, C. W., and Hunter, M. F. *Nutrition—Principles and Application in Health Promotion*. Philadelphia: Lippincott, 1980.

23. Trowell, H. C. Dietary fiber hypothesis of the etiology of diabetes mellitus. *Diabetes* 24:762, 1975.

24. Whaley, L. F., and Wong, D. L. *Nursing Care of Infants and Children*. St. Louis: Mosby, 1979.

25. Worthington, B. S., Vermeersch, J., Williams, S. R. *Nutrition in Pregnancy and Lactation*. St. Louis: Mosby, 1977.

Assessment Tool

The nurse should indicate for each item whether the family or family member accomplishes the item according to criteria indicated in the columns. If an item or section does not apply, the points represented by that item or section should be so indicated by marking the "not applicable" column. In scoring at the end of each section, the category "total points possible" means the total number of points that could be attained if every item applied. The "total not applicable" category shows the total points for items or sections that do not apply to the family at this time; this number should be subtracted from the "total points possible" to obtain the "total applicable" score. When comparing "total applicable" with the "total points attained," the nurse and the family can see the numerical difference in what should or could be achieved and what does exist at the present time. Scores in each section should be transferred to the summary section at the end of the chapter's assessment tool.

	Usually (2 pts)	Some-times (1 pt)	Never (0 pt)	Not appli-cable
I. Family Promotes Nutritional Wellness by				
A. Formulating a daily mealtime plan	——	——	——	——
B. Identifying six food-exchange categories	——	——	——	——
C. Identifying three examples from each of the six food exchanges	——	——	——	——
D. Encouraging each family member to eat three meals a day or the number appropriate for age*				
1. Mother	——	——	——	——
2. Father	——	——	——	——
3. Child	——	——	——	——
4. Child	——	——	——	——
5. Other	——	——	——	——
E. Serving meals at approximately the same time each day	——	——	——	——
F. Drinking water/fluid with each meal	——	——	——	——
G. Drinking water/fluid between meals	——	——	——	——
H. Sharing one meal a day	——	——	——	——
I. Providing a relaxed mealtime	——	——	——	——
J. Providing an unhurried mealtime atmosphere	——	——	——	——
K. Providing a bright, well-lighted, ventilated room	——	——	——	——
L. Valuing mealtime as an event, not just a habit	——	——	——	——
M. Providing fresh fruits and vegetables whenever available	——	——	——	——
N. Establishing guidelines about mealtime atmosphere	——	——	——	——
O. Identifying cultural influences on eating habits	——	——	——	——
P. Understanding meaning and significance of food to life-style	——	——	——	——
Q. Obtaining sufficient financial resources for nutritional wellness	——	——	——	——
R. Participating in daily exercise*				
1. Mother	——	——	——	——
2. Father	——	——	——	——
3. Child	——	——	——	——

*If there are greater or fewer than five members in the family, add or subtract them for this item and adjust the "total points possible" accordingly in the summary.

	Usually (2 pts)	Some-times (1 pt)	Never (0 pt)	Not appli-cable
4. Child	___	___	___	___
5. Other				
S. Planning family exercise activities	___	___	___	___
T. Feeling good about self*				
1. Mother	___	___	___	___
2. Father	___	___	___	___
3. Child	___	___	___	___
4. Child	___	___	___	___
5. Other				
U. Describing self using positive terms*				
1. Mother	___	___	___	___
2. Father	___	___	___	___
3. Child	___	___	___	___
4. Child	___	___	___	___
5. Other	___	___	___	___
V. Remaining within 10 percent of desired weight*	___	___	___	___
1. Mother	___	___	___	___
2. Father	___	___	___	___
3. Child	___	___	___	___
4. Child	___	___	___	___
5. Other	___	___	___	___
W. Valuing nutritional wellness	___	___	___	___

Total points possible   _84_

Total not applicable   ___

Total applicable   ___

Total points attained   ___

II. Practicing Nutritional Wellness
During Developmental Stages
   A. *Infant*

	Usually (2 pts)	Some-times (1 pt)	Never (0 pt)	Not appli-cable
1. Feeding breast milk or formula	___	___	___	___
2. Holding baby close during feedings	___	___	___	___
3. Feeding promptly	___	___	___	___
4. Following recommended feeding intervals	___	___	___	___
5. Adding iron supplements by age 4 to 5 months	___	___	___	___
6. Feeding appropriate sources of iron	___	___	___	___
7. Introducing solid foods in conjunction with developmental cues	___	___	___	___
8. Offering a variety of food textures and colors	___	___	___	___

*If there are greater or fewer than five members in the family, add or subtract them for this item and adjust the "total points possible" accordingly in the summary.

	Usually (2 pts)	Sometimes (1 pt)	Never (0 pt)	Not applicable
9. Allowing tactile experiences with food	——	——	——	——
10. Avoiding possible allergens	——	——	——	——
11. Introducing new foods one at a time	——	——	——	——
12. Allowing child to determine quantities of food	——	——	——	——
13. Allowing child to self-feed according to developmental cues	——	——	——	——
14. Providing foods according to recommended food exchange	——	——	——	——

Total points possible ___28___
Total not applicable _____
Total applicable _____
Total points attained _____

B. *Toddler*

	Usually (2 pts)	Sometimes (1 pt)	Never (0 pt)	Not applicable
1. Gauging food-intake expectations according to child's growth rate	——	——	——	——
2. Encouraging use of child's favorite dishes and utensils	——	——	——	——
3. Offering easily chewed foods	——	——	——	——
4. Allowing food choices within recommended food exchange	——	——	——	——
5. Allowing child mobility during mealtime	——	——	——	——
6. Encouraging self-feeding	——	——	——	——
7. Allowing child to explore food with hands and eyes	——	——	——	——
8. Supervising all mealtimes	——	——	——	——
9. Avoiding extremely hot or cold foods	——	——	——	——
10. Keeping hazardous or poisonous substances out of reach	——	——	——	——
11. Meeting nutritional needs of child in a relaxed manner	——	——	——	——
12. Providing foods according to recommended food exchanges	——	——	——	——

Total points possible ___24___
Total not applicable _____
Total applicable _____
Total points attained _____

C. *Preschool*

	Usually (2 pts)	Sometimes (1 pt)	Never (0 pt)	Not applicable
1. Recognizing child's eagerness to learn	——	——	——	——
2. Teaching food practices by				
a. Eating wholesome foods	——	——	——	——
b. Avoiding eating in front of television set	——	——	——	——

	Usually (2 pts)	Some-times (1 pt)	Never (0 pt)	Not appli-cable
c. Avoiding use of foods as bribes	___	___	___	___
d. Encouraging a relaxed attitude at mealtime	___	___	___	___
3. Teaching child about nutrition				
a. Pointing out nutritious foods in books and magazines	___	___	___	___
b. Role playing appropriate eating behaviors	___	___	___	___
c. Playing games that teach about nutrition	___	___	___	___
d. Screening food advertisements on TV	___	___	___	___
e. Allowing child to help select nutritious foods at the store	___	___	___	___
4. Inquiring about food attitudes and practices in the school programs	___	___	___	___
5. Encouraging nutritional education in the school	___	___	___	___
6. Recognizing changes in growth rate and corresponding changes in food intake	___			
7. Recognizing normal decrease in milk intake	___	___	___	___
8. Offering foods that have been periodically refused	___	___	___	___
9. Offering easily chewed meals and meat substitutes	___	___	___	___
10. Offering finger foods	___	___	___	___
11. Offering simple, mild-tasting foods at room temperature	___	___	___	___
12. Offering complementary foods	___	___	___	___
13. Offering foods according to recommended food exchanges	___	___	___	___
14. Encouraging self-feeding	___	___	___	___
15. Ignoring negative mealtime behaviors	___	___	___	___
16. Praising positive mealtime behaviors	___	___	___	___
17. Allowing choice in choosing reward system	___	___	___	___
18. Encouraging physical activity and exercise	___	___	___	___
19. Providing toys that provide physical exercise	___	___	___	___
20. Encouraging participation in family exercise activities	___	___	___	___

Total points possible   *54*

Total not applicable   ___

Total applicable   ___

Total points attained   ___

	Usually (2 pts)	Some- times (1 pt)	Never (0 pt)	Not appli- cable
D. *School Age*				
1. Recognizing the impact of teacher, peers, and parents in the development of self-concept	___	___	___	___
2. Recognizing slower pattern of growth and changes in food intake	___	___	___	___
3. Providing foods according to the recommended food exchanges	___	___	___	___
4. Recognizing influences on the development of values by				
a. Eating with friends	___	___	___	___
b. Eating outside the home	___	___	___	___
c. Exposure to junk foods	___	___	___	___
d. Reemphasizing importance of nutritious foods	___	___	___	___
e. Encouraging child to select foods for family meals and school lunches	___	___	___	___
f. Screening food advertisements on TV	___	___	___	___
g. Helping the child develop a consumer awareness in relation to TV advertising	___	___	___	___
5. Assuring some time for family members to get meals together	___	___	___	___
6. Encouraging physical activity at home and school	___	___	___	___
7. Providing and encouraging nutritious snacks	___	___	___	___
8. Avoiding concentrated sugar in food and drink	___	___	___	___
9. Praising child when he selects nutritious snacks	___	___	___	___
10. Serving nutritious snacks to visitors	___	___	___	___
11. Encouraging nutrition education in school health curriculum	___	___	___	___
12. Encouraging activities in school that teach nutrition	___	___	___	___
13. Working through school organizations to assure nutritious school lunches	___	___	___	___
14. Monitoring whether child eats lunches at school	___	___	___	___
15. Involving child in preparation and planning of brown bag lunch utilizing the food exchange list	___	___	___	___

Total points possible   *42*

Total not applicable   ___

Total applicable   ___

Total points attained   ___

	Usually (2 pts)	Sometimes (1 pt)	Never (0 pt)	Not applicable

E. *Adolescence*

1. Adapting nutritional patterns to changing growth rate
2. Providing foods according to the recommended food exchanges
3. Understanding the nutritional implications of the growth spurt
4. Understanding the social importance of friends and food
5. Supplementing fast food meals with nutrients at home
6. Providing family mealtimes
7. Participating in sports and physical activities daily
8. Assisting in meal planning, meal preparation, and budgeting

Total points possible   _16_
Total not applicable
Total applicable
Total points attained

F. *Young Adult*

1. Adapting food intake to maintenance levels
2. Eating foods according to the recommended food exchanges
3. Adapting food patterns to changing life events by
   a. Menu planning
   b. Food preparation
   c. Budgeting
   d. Shopping
4. Exercising regularly

Total points possible   _14_
Total not applicable
Total applicable
Total points attained

G. The *Pregnant Woman*

1. Assessing food patterns in terms of future role modeling
2. Modifying food practices as necessary to achieve desired model
3. Eating foods during pregnancy according to the recommended food exchanges
4. Increasing intake by 300 kcal per day during pregnancy

	Usually (2 pts)	Some-times (1 pt)	Never (0 pt)	Not appli-cable
5. Eating three meals a day plus bedtime snack during pregnancy	——	——	——	——
6. Increasing fluid intake during pregnancy	——	——	——	——
7. Avoiding alcohol and caffeine	——	——	——	——
8. Eating foods during lactation according to the recommended food exchanges	——	——	——	——
9. Increasing intake by 500 kcal per day during lactation	——	——	——	——
10. Drinking liquid prior to nursing	——	——	——	——

Total points possible   _20_
Total not applicable   ——
Total applicable   ——
Total points attained   ——

H. *Middle-Age Adult*

	Usually (2 pts)	Some-times (1 pt)	Never (0 pt)	Not appli-cable
1. Realizing impact of decreasing metabolic rate on nutritional wellness	——	——	——	——
2. Following a meal plan based on the recommended food exchanges	——	——	——	——
3. Balancing nutrients and calories to prevent obesity	——	——	——	——
4. Eating nourishing foods at social events	——	——	——	——
5. Adapting eating patterns to life-style	——	——	——	——
6. Obtaining exercise profile	——	——	——	——
7. Exercising a minimum of 30 minutes per day, 4 days a week at the exercise heart rate	——	——	——	——
8. Realizing benefits of a planned exercise program	——	——	——	——
9. Supporting communitywide sports activities	——	——	——	——
10. Understanding impact of psychosocial crises on nutritional wellness	——	——	——	——
11. Modifying life-style to achieve or maintain optimal weight	——	——	——	——
12. Meeting nutritional needs in the workplace through				
a. Nutritious snacks	——	——	——	——
b. Lunch breaks	——	——	——	——
c. Nutritious lunch foods	——	——	——	——
d. Changing activity levels during breaks	——	——	——	——
e. Promotion of availability of nutritious foods	——	——	——	——

	Usually (2 pts)	Some-times (1 pt)	Never (0 pt)	Not appli-cable
f. Promotion of safe storage of bag lunches	——	——	——	——
g. Promotion of pleasant eating spaces	——	——	——	——

Total points possible   _36_
Total not applicable   ——
Total applicable   ——
Total points attained   ——

I. *Elderly*

	Usually (2 pts)	Some-times (1 pt)	Never (0 pt)	Not appli-cable
1. Realizing physiological changes that affect nutrition	——	——	——	——
2. Adapting caloric intake to compensate for changes in metabolic rate and physical activity	——	——	——	——
3. Eating foods according to recommended food exchanges	——	——	——	——
4. Understanding how values influence food choices	——	——	——	——
5. Planning nutritious meals consistent with income levels	——	——	——	——
6. Using community resources as necessary or desired to improve nutrition	——	——	——	——
7. Participating in planned and regular exercise programs	——	——	——	——

Total points possible   _14_
Total not applicable   ——
Total applicable   ——
Total points attained   ——

III. Nutritional Issues, Agencies, and Resources

A. Family expresses knowledge about the following issues:

	Yes (2 pts)	No (1 pt)	Not appli-cable
1. Food labeling	——	——	——
2. Food dating	——	——	——
3. Natural versus synthetic vitamins	——	——	——
4. Excess vitamin intake	——	——	——
5. Vitamin C as a cure for colds	——	——	——

	Yes (2 pts)	No (1 pt)	Not applicable
6. Vitamin E as a cure-all	——	——	——
7. Processed baby foods	——	——	——
8. Use of skim milk for infants	——	——	——
9. Prevention of specific diseases	——	——	——
10. Relationship between colon cancer and high-fat diet	——	——	——
11. Use of fiber in the diet	——	——	——
12. Use of sugar	——	——	——
13. Use of presweetened cereals	——	——	——
14. Use and safety of saccharin	——	——	——
15. Role of salt intake in hypertension	——	——	——
16. Effects of food faddism	——	——	——
17. Safety of vegetarian diets	——	——	——
18. Safety of food additives	——	——	——

Total points possible   *36*

Total not applicable   ——

Total applicable   ——

Total points attained   ——

B. Family is aware of function and purposes of agencies and resources involved in nutrition research, financial support, and education

1. International
   a. Food and Agricultural Organization
   b. World Health Organization
   c. U.N. Children's Fund
   d. Agency for International Development
2. Federal
   a. Department of Health and Human Services
   b. Department of Agriculture
   c. Food and Drug Administration
   d. National Institutes of Health
   e. Public Health Service
   f. Consumer Information Center
   g. Nutrition Foundation
   h. Administration on Aging
3. Private and local
   a. American Dietetic Association
   b. Society for Nutrition Education
   c. Local community groups and agencies

Total points possible   *30*

Total not applicable   ——

Total applicable   ——

Total points attained   ——

Assessment Tool Summary

	Subtotal points possible	Subtotal not applicable	Subtotal applicable	Subtotal points attained
I. Promotion of Nutritional Wellness	84	_____	_____	_____
II. Practicing Nutritional Wellness During Developmental Stages				
A. Infant	28	_____	_____	_____
B. Toddler	24	_____	_____	_____
C. Preschool	54	_____	_____	_____
D. School Age	42	_____	_____	_____
E. Adolescence	16	_____	_____	_____
F. Young Adult	14	_____	_____	_____
G. The Pregnant Woman	20	_____	_____	_____
H. Middle-Age Adult	36	_____	_____	_____
I. Elderly	14	_____	_____	_____
III. Nutritional Issues, Agencies, and Resources				
A. Nutritional Issues	36	_____	_____	_____
B. Agencies and Resources	30	_____	_____	_____

Total points possible   398

Total not applicable   _____

Total applicable   _____

Total points attained   _____

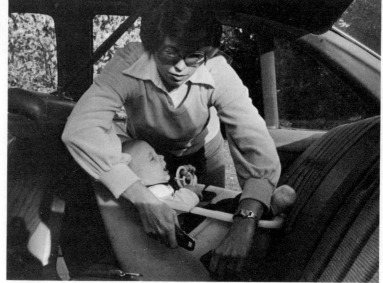

SEVEN

Safety Wellness in the Family's Environments

This chapter focuses on wellness factors in several of the family's environments: the home, the community, the school, and the workplace. These environments and the wellness factors within their structures influence the overall wellness of the family. Wellness demands attention from all family members, no matter where they find themselves throughout the day.

The primary environment is the immediate home. A significant portion of each person's life is spent in the home, and this locus provides a setting in which safety wellness can be promoted or diminished. Within the home, accidents are the major threat to safety wellness. Each family member faces certain threats from accidents related to his developmental level, and in turn, safety wellness through accident prevention can be promoted in specific ways because of developmental stage. In addition, the home environment exposes family members to certain agents that, if present or used improperly, can cause accidents in and around the home. Wellness promotion through accident prevention becomes a function of awareness and proper use of agents in the environment by the family member as a consumer. The threat to safety wellness can be seen by reviewing some statistical data.

Accidents and Their Relation to Wellness in the Home

Accidents are like many other events faced by families in that they have causes. By knowing the causes, accidents can be controlled or prevented, and unhealthy effects minimized. Brownfain has observed the following [4]:

If we label all of life's unpleasant surprises as accidents, then we come to perceive ourselves as the playthings of fate and we cultivate a philosophy of carelessness and irresponsibility. On the other hand, if we look for causes and hold ourselves accountable for the mishaps in our lives, we become people of resource and confidence, increasingly able to control the direction of events.

Increasing the family's awareness of the chief accident problems, providing factual information, and suggesting ways for the family to improve its level of safety wellness are the goals for the nurse and are the purposes of this chapter.

Accidents are the greatest single cause of death and injury among children under the age of 19. In 1974 accidents, poisonings, and violence accounted for 37 percent of the deaths among children in this age group. A total of 758,504 hospital days were a direct result of these accidents [21]. Mechanical suffocation is the most frequent type of accident in infants under 1 year of age [26]. Accidental poisoning is one of the major causes of death in children from 1 to 5 years of age. The highest incidence of poisoning occurs in those in the 2-year-old group, with the second highest incidence in 1-year-old children. There are over 500 toxic substances in the average home, and the majority of all poisonings (about 34%) occur in the kitchen. More than 700 species of plants are known to have caused death or illness. For example, the ingestion of one leaf of a poinsettia plant can kill a child [26].

According to the National Safety Council's 1978 facts handbook, a total of 104,000 deaths from accidents occurred in 1977 [19]. This figure includes all reported deaths from violence, excluding homicides and suicides. The following list shows the types of accidents and corresponding number of deaths reported:

TYPE OF ACCIDENTS	NUMBER OF DEATHS
1. Motor vehicles	49,500
2. Falls	14,000
3. Drownings	7100
4. Fires	6600
5. Poisonings by solids and liquids	3900
6. Suffocation from ingestion or inhalation of objects or foods	3000
7. Firearms	2000
8. Poison gases or vapors	1600
9. Miscellaneous	16,300

Most accidental deaths in the 5-to-24 age group are caused by motor vehicles. In many of the vehicle accidents, the victim was either walking or riding a bicycle. Next in order of occurrence are drownings, poisonings, and firearms accidents [19].

Motor vehicle accidents remain the number one killer in the middle-age category of 25 to 44 years, followed by poisonings, drownings, falls, and fires. After accidents, cancer and heart disease are the second and third leading causes of death for this age group. Accidents drop to the fourth leading cause of death in the 45-to-64 age range and sixth in the 65-to-74 range. The major types of accidents in the latter age category are motor vehicle accidents in which the elderly person is a pedestrian. Falls rank second as causes of accidental injury. In the age group 75 years and over, falls are the major types of accidents experienced [19].

Accidents: A Function of Developmental Stage

Each accident has a specific cause, and the type of accident a person suffers is closely related to his stage of growth and development. For example, poisoning is more frequent in the 1-to-5 age group, and most of these poisonings occur in children 1 to 2 years of age. Poisoning, foreign body aspiration, and burns are more frequently seen in preschool-age children as a result of their developmental explorations with hands and mouth. Children who are older and less protected are more often involved in falls, drownings, and motor vehicle accidents.

Potential accident situations can be foreseen by parents who have knowledge of their own child's typical patterns of growth and development. Children are naturally curious, impulsive, and impatient. The young child needs to touch and feel.

Adult supervision will enable the child to learn within the safety limits for his level of growth and development.

Physical, developmental, emotional, and social development contribute to accidents. Exceptional physical strength seems to be a characteristic among many accident-prone children, possibly because they are more active and therefore are exposed to more accident hazards. Studies show that many accidents occur in the late afternoon hours, suggesting a possible role played by increase in fatigue and relaxation of supervision. It is the dinner hour, when children as well as parents are often hungry and tired. Children are less careful and parents are less watchful at this time of the day. Sex, like age, is another factor that contributes to childhood accidents. Boys, at all ages, have more accidents than girls. This tendency increases as the child gets older [26]. This risk factor should be carefully considered by the nurse and family in helping children learn safe behaviors.

Most studies of the emotional and personality factors associated with accidents have concentrated on accident-prone children—for example, children who seek out unusual substances such as paint, kerosene, or bleach. These children seem to have difficulty adjusting to their environment, to be undergoing emotional stress, and to have poor family relationships. Accident-prone children often appear to be aggressive, impulsive, and easily frustrated. Acceptance by the peer group is important for maintaining status among playmates, and this factor may lead to more hazardous situations.

In most studies in which socioeconomic status of the family was considered, a higher frequency of accidents was found among the lower socioeconomic groups. The relationship between socioeconomic factors and accidents seems to reflect the existence of actual hazards in the physical environment. These hazards include such factors as poor quality of the physical structure or overcrowding, and the social-emotional environment such as family educational level and group values [22]. Another emotional factor to consider is the bonding within the family. Children in more closely knit families have fewer accidents than those from families where there is discord [26].

SAFETY WELLNESS DURING INFANCY

Nurses and parents must consider the interests and resulting hazards toward which the child's activities may lead. The protection and education needed by each sex and age group may then be adapted to the prevention of accidents to which they are most liable. Each contact with a parent is an opportunity for the nurse to educate about potential hazards; thus wellness of the child and parents can be promoted.

The importance of parental role modeling can be observed as early as infancy. It is possible to teach an infant accident prevention by having him become accustomed to safety measures being provided for him and by seeing that he observes the actions of cautious parents. Infants need to see, touch, taste, and smell the elements of their surroundings in order to grow and develop properly. An understanding of how infants grow and develop can assist parents in helping the infant experience these sensory events in a safe manner.

Parents who promote wellness learn the developmental stages and the potential safety hazards in advance of the development of each new skill, such as rolling over and creeping. One of the most important factors in accident prevention in this and other age groups is parents' recognition of the child's changing capabilities. A surprisingly large number of babies fall from furniture specifically designed for infants. One of the most common accidents of this type is falling from the crib with the side rail down.

Babies begin to turn over, sit up, and reach for objects during their first year. As babies gradually acquire these skills, parents should be alert so as to keep all hazardous items out of reach. Infants put everything into their mouths. Articles frequently aspirated are beads, coins, peanuts, and safety pins left at the bedside or in the crib. Only toys appropriate for the infant should be present in his environment.

Safety factors must be kept in mind while bathing the infant. A baby should never be left alone. The baby should never be given a can of baby powder to play with because he may inhale the powder if he shakes the can. Some professionals discourage the use of powders completely. The baby should be held securely to promote safety as well as to alleviate fear of the bath. Grids on the bottom of the tub may prevent the baby from slipping from the parent's arms into the water.

The side rails of the crib should always be raised and secure when an adult is not present. The bars on the crib should be close enough to one another so that the baby's head, legs, and arms cannot become caught between them. Federal regulations specify requirements for safe spacing, but some older and possibly unsafe cribs may be acquired secondhand. The crib should not be placed near a stove or radiator or venetian blind cord because the baby could be burned by a stove or could become entangled in the blind cord.

A firm mattress should be used, one that fits the crib smoothly and snugly. Only mattress covers designed specifically for the mattress should be used. Plastic bags and pillows should never be used because they are very pliable and can easily cause suffocation.

When the infant starts to crawl, guardrails at the top and bottom of stairs will help prevent falls as long as they are securely attached to the walls. It is sometimes impossible to attach a gate securely, and the weight of a child pulling up can cause it to break away. In such cases, the child would be safer with no gate and with parents who are *always* alert and watchful. During this time, electrical outlets should be covered with safety caps to prevent children from inserting fingers or other objects into the outlet, resulting in burns or death.

Safety in cars is an important consideration for infants. Their small bodies offer practically no protection against impact during an auto crash. Infants cannot ride safely in the parents' arms because the force of a crash makes it impossible for the parent to maintain hold of the infant. The child is safer if placed in an approved infant car seat that is positioned in the backseat of the car [26]. General Motors makes such an infant car seat that meets federal safety standards.

Any car seat or restraint system is ineffective if improperly or inconsistently used. Efforts are being made to educate the public about the importance to infants of car safety. One successful approach has been one-to-one instruction and counseling by the family pediatrician or obstetrician [16]. Nurses can be very effective in this approach as part of the prenatal teaching team. The infant's first ride home from the hospital should be in an approved car seat so that the baby immediately begins experiencing safe riding practices. Once an infant or child accepts a safe car seat, he will not only be protected from injury in the event of a crash, but he will also be less distracting to the driver.

Promoting safety wellness is the responsibility of the infant's parents. Some key points nurses should emphasize in assuring a safe environment follow. As these activities are achieved, the infant maximizes his potential for wellness by beginning life in a well environment.

PARENTS SHOULD
1. Develop a positive relationship with one another to promote an optimal level of bonding.
2. Provide appropriate safety role models for the infant.
3. Understand the changing developmental needs of the infant.
4. Provide a safe physical environment for the child.
5. Assume total responsibility for safety wellness for the infant.

SAFETY WELLNESS FOR THE TODDLER
Responsibility for accident prevention for the toddler lies with the child's parents. However, it is also the responsibility of all members of the health team who teach parents the care of children to help parents understand risks to their children in relation to the child's age, and to help them learn behaviors that promote safety wellness. The nurse's knowledge about children not only helps her explain potential hazards but also enables her to predict the occurrence of particular accidents at certain ages. For example, if the 3-year-old child is in the kitchen while the parent is cooking, the nurse can share her knowledge that while children at this age enjoy mimicking their parents' activities, they do not yet have good motor coordination and are not able to make accurate judgments as to which skills are within their abilities. The nurse can conclude that the 3-year-old child is a prime potential accident victim if he tries to cook like his mother. Further, when the child is in the high chair, he should always be tended by an adult or older child.

Likewise, the child aged 2 to 3 is a prime potential victim of poisoning. He is more likely than children of other age groups to ingest nonfood substances within his reach. Obviously, potential poisons should be kept out of the range of access for the inquisitive toddler and preferably be locked up. All poisonous or toxic substances should be labeled with warning stickers such as "Mr. Yuk," and the child can be taught a beginning awareness of which substances are forbidden. When a baby begins to crawl and then to walk, his realm of activity naturally begins to expand, and he is more able to leave a confined, protected environment. Therefore, the role of the protector, the parent, must likewise expand. Just imagine how these tiny explorers might react to a brightly colored box of soap detergent or drain cleaner. Show the baby brightly colored pills, and he may see a new version of the beads he enjoys playing with.

Potentially hazardous items are found in most homes. Therefore, parents must review their methods of storing and using these products. A majority of accidental poisonings involving children occur between the ages of 1 and 3, and a majority of these accidents occur in or near the home. Accidents are the principal cause of death among toddlers and account for many handicaps and disfiguring scars.

Special attention should be paid to storage areas below the counter tops. The parent must assume that it will not be long before the child will be able to open doors, drawers, and containers and to climb. Powders and liquids should be stored in their original containers. Any poisonous substance should be kept out of the kitchen or any place where it might be mistaken for food. Unwanted poisons or medicines should be flushed down the toilet or buried underground.

The toddler moves quickly but has little appreciation of impending danger. Because of his desire for intrusive behavior, he is prone to poking into or pulling down on light cords, plugs, and tablecloths. Covers for electrical outlets should be used throughout the house. Small appliances should be kept out of the child's reach. Guards should be placed in front of fireplaces, radiators, and wall heaters. The child should not be alone in the tub, wading pool, or around any open bodies of water. He can learn to enjoy and appreciate water safely. Even shallow water is dangerous. Play areas should be fenced and supervised at all times by adults. The toddler should never be left to play alone, even for an instant. As with the infant, only toys appropriate for his age should be present in the environment.

If visiting outside the home, the parent should assess safety hazards in the new environment. Hazardous objects should be removed before the child enters the environment. A different situation provides new challenges and opportunities for exploration.

Parents need to have outside social contacts, which means they also have the responsibility of choosing appropriate baby-sitters. A mature, responsible individual with a clear understanding of the developmental needs of the child should be chosen. Parents should leave emergency telephone numbers with the sitter, and the sitter should be experienced in emergency first-aid measures. The sitter should closely supervise the child just as the parents would if they were in the home environment.

Ensuring the child's safety in the car is also essential. Vehicle fatalities dominate the motor accident mortality of all pediatric age groups after the age of 1 year. Such fatalities account for more than one third of all accidental deaths among preschool boys and for two fifths among preschool girls. Children over the age of 3 years are often involved in pedestrian accidents; whereas, children under 3 years of age are more often inside the car in which restraints have been improperly used [26]. Young children are much more vulnerable in a car crash than adults because of their smaller size, incomplete body development, and different body proportions. Because of these differences, children under age 4 need a type of seat restraint other than the lap seat belt and shoulder belt that can protect adults from injuries [27]. According to the Insurance Institute for Highway Safety, the use of specially designed child seat restraints for all children weighing less than 40 pounds can reduce the injury rate for these children. Children's car seats manufactured before April 1971 do not meet the safety standards and should not be used. The parent should carefully examine the labels of car restraint systems and purchase only those that meet federal specifications and that are appropriate for the size of the child. The American Academy of Pediatrics' Committee on Accident Prevention has issued recommendations for the proper use of safety devices for children traveling in cars. They have emphatically stated that the child's size and weight determine the appropriate type of auto safety restraint for him [12]. Approved devices are available for infants and toddlers.

Standard seat belts may be used for children who weigh more than 40 pounds [18]. The combination lap-and-shoulder harness is even more helpful because it protects the child from jackknifing forward and being ejected from the seat. It further helps the child to become accustomed to restraints while traveling in a car. Early development of this habit will promote its use throughout all stages of life.

Establishing simple safety rules of behavior in the automobile are also very important. Parents should not allow children to ride in the front seat. They should say "no" to all roughhousing and stop the car temporarily if the situation gets out of control. Lollipops on sticks or toys with sharp edges should not be allowed in the car, nor should heads and arms be allowed to dangle out of the windows. Doors should be locked before starting the car. Children should be taught to keep fingers away from the car doors and to keep their hands off the controls of the car even when the car engine is not running.

The National Safety Council reports that more than 300 children are fatally injured each year in vehicle accidents on home property. The majority of these fatalities involves cars backing out of driveways, and the highest incidence of these accidents happens to children between the ages of 13 months and 9 years [12]. Parents should always check the driveway and underneath the car carefully before backing out. Only after getting a complete picture through the rear-view mirror of the scene behind the car should parents back out slowly, all the while checking for children running behind the car. Furthermore, parents can educate children about moving cars and parked cars. They should help the children develop a sense of awareness about hazards in their environment.

The primary means of preventing accidents in the toddler age group is to make the house and car as accident proof as possible, to provide careful supervision of the child's play, and to provide consistent guidance so the child can learn to promote his own safety within his environment. The child must learn to respond to the command "no," but it should not be overused. Often a firm statement will suffice. Verbal reinforcements and added privileges are often as meaningful as "don'ts" and "no's."

Understanding their own child will help parents maintain control of the situation. Children grow and mature by imitating their parents, and toddlers are especially receptive to learning situations. For this reason, parents can use actual situations to teach the child to handle as well as to anticipate the unexpected. Simple instructions at the child's own level of understanding are the most effective.

Parental worries about safety and accidents should be put into perspective. Parents must realize that some minor injuries are bound to happen during childhood and should use the occasion of these injuries to help the child understand the extent to which he caused the accident. Blaming inanimate objects gives the child a distorted sense of the world; compensating minor accidents with cookies or gifts only reinforces the child's perception of his own innocence. A careful, patient explanation should teach the child about the relationship between cause and effect and about his responsibility to be alert to dangers. The major parental responsibilities in promoting safety for the toddler include the following:

PARENTS SHOULD

1. Understand how changing developmental stages affect safety wellness.
2. Provide appropriate parent substitutes if unable to be home with the child.
3. Provide for the child's safety in an automobile.
4. With close supervision, begin educating the child about environmental safety hazards.
5. Provide a hazard-free environment that still allows exploration.
6. Provide appropriate role models that enhance safety wellness.

SAFETY WELLNESS FOR THE PRESCHOOL CHILD

Preschoolers are active and inquisitive. Their self-control begins to increase, but their sense of judgment and understanding are still immature. Their increase in initiative and their desire to imitate adults often put them in hazardous situations. Always seeking new experiences, they may play with matches, turn on hot water faucets, or close themselves into old cabinets and refrigerators. They are likely to explore manholes, culverts, and electrical sockets. They enjoy taking things apart, putting them together, and experimenting with them. Therefore, dangerous items such as knives, matches, electrical equipment, and lighters should be kept out of reach. Parents should see that outdoor play equipment, hammocks, and swings are secure with seasonal inspections to repair bolts or paint rusty edges. They should make sure that the child has mastered playing with such equipment before leaving him alone with them. All toys should be appropriate for the child's age, and he should be taught to play with them safely. Rusty nails, damaged furniture, and gardening equipment should be discarded. The yard should be cleared of rubbish. Lawnmowers, tools, shears, and rakes should be locked in a separate cabinet or shed. Potential poisons such as insecticides and paints should be kept out of reach and preferably kept under lock and key.

Preschoolers are fascinated by animals; therefore, they should be taught caution and respect for pets but should stay away from strange animals. If a child is bitten by an animal, it is important to catch the animal so that it can be tested for rabies. The wound should be washed with soap and water, and the police as well as the physician should be notified.

Since preschoolers may be going out on their own for the first time, they must be carefully taught about crossing the street and interpreting traffic signals. Children should be aware of the boundaries and limitations that have been set for them by adults. The child should be taught his full name, address, and telephone number, and that the police officer is his friend and can be sought out if help is needed. He also can be taught how to call for help in other emergencies by dialing the operator.

Preschoolers are capable of learning basic water safety and swim strokes. However, children also need a healthy respect for the water so that they understand the dangers as well as the recreational aspects. Encourage children to wait 20 minutes after eating before playing in the water. Make sure there is adult supervision at all times. Adults in charge should be capable of giving mouth-to-mouth resuscitation if the need arises. Safety can be learned by doing safe things. Parents can encourage creative play and games dealing with water safety. Water safety is important in the home as well as outside the home. The child should be attended to at all times while in the bathtub, and water temperature should always be checked carefully before placing the child in the water.

As with the younger child, the preschooler should always use an approved restraint system while riding in a car. Safety rules should be made and enforced by the parents. Safe riding should become a habit. The major concepts to guide parents in promoting the preschooler's safety include the following:

PARENTS SHOULD
1. Provide a hazard-free environment that allows the child to grow and develop within his environment.
2. Guide the child in the development of motor skills in the use of safe play equipment.
3. Help the child develop a beginning sense of judgment and understanding of a safe environment.

SAFETY WELLNESS FOR THE SCHOOL-AGE CHILD
As the child grows and goes to school, he is no longer under the watchful eye of his parents. He needs to become more independent and more responsible for his own safety. Understanding *why* precautions are necessary is as important as

understanding the consequences of not taking precautions. Childproofing the environment at this age is good, but it does not replace teaching the child about his own responsibility for promoting safety in his environment.

By knowing where the gravest dangers lurk, adults can do much to prevent tragic accidents. The main cause of death and injury to children between 5 and 14 years of age is the automobile. Most accident victims are struck by cars. Children must learn to be cautious of automobiles when they are playing. Many other victims are involved in collisions while riding in cars; again, parents must establish and enforce safe riding by wearing seat belts. Drownings, fires, and firearms also present a threat, especially for children who may find and handle guns at home [19]. Children can be taught both caution and safety. If the child wishes to learn how to handle guns, he should be taught by a qualified person.

Many school-age children find themselves in the high-risk situation of riding school buses. Statistics compiled by the National Safety Council indicate that of the approximately 180 people killed in school bus accidents in 1977, 95 were pupils and 80 others were drivers [19]. Children in school bus accidents are often thrown against unpadded sides of the bus, are not wearing seat belts, or are thrown against sharp objects, such as fire extinguishers. Children should be encouraged to sit in their seats and to maintain a reasonable level of noise.

Bicycles have recently been listed by the Consumer Product Safety Commission as the products with the greatest risk for the consumer [26]. With the increase in bicycle riding in this country, there has been a proportionate increase in motor vehicle accidents involving cyclists. In New York state alone, 9493 bicycle injuries were reported in 1973 and 9799 in 1974. These statistics represent a 15 percent increase in just 1 year [20]. Lack of knowledge seems to be a greater problem than defiance of the law. Cyclists are often seen ignoring lights and riding on the wrong side of the road.

Parents, the school curriculum, and community agencies can be instrumental in increasing children's knowledge of bicycle safety. They can point out unsafe practices and explain safer ones. The child can practice safe cycling under the guidance of an adult. Positive behaviors should be praised and encouraged. Children should be taught to anticipate and react appropriately to hazardous situations in the roadway. Parents should be aware of bicycle safety resources in their community and encourage their child to participate.

Before parents purchase a bicycle for a child, they should consider the area in which the child will be riding the bicycle, the age of the child and the size of the bicycle in relation to the age, and the safety instruction that will be given to the child. The following is a set of safety rules for bicycle riders:

1. Follow traffic rules and regulations. Bicycle riders are subject to the same regulations as motorists.
2. Make a bicycle equipment safety check periodically. Make sure all parts are working properly.
3. Put reflectors and lights on the bicycle.

4. Make sure that the bicycle and its hand brakes are the correct size for the rider.
5. Do not carry other passengers.
6. Ride in single file if riding in a group.

Drownings are common during the school-age years mostly because of lack of supervision but possibly also because of an increase in the number of private and home pools. These drownings might be prevented if communities made a concentrated effort to provide better adult supervision at recreational pools, to provide pool areas with adequate fencing and locks, and to provide swimming lessons and instruction in safety practices to the children. All children should learn how to swim and should learn basic water safety as early as possible in life and no later than school age. The family who has a pool should establish basic rules of conduct and safety, abide by them, and enforce them when guests use the pool. Members of the family should be certified in cardiopulmonary resuscitation (CPR) and be able to rescue a troubled swimmer from the water.

The school age is an appropriate time for the child to learn how to handle encounters with strangers if he has not already. Children should be taught not to speak to or accept rides with strangers, and to inform their parents if anyone tries to lure them into a car.

School-age children are interested in making things and have developed sufficient hand-and-eye coordination to use more complicated and potentially dangerous materials. They should be instructed in the proper use of and storage of equipment, such as sewing machines, tools, kitchen utensils, and appliances, and should be closely supervised until skills are well developed.

As school-age children become more involved in sports and outdoor play, they must learn the skills necessary for the sport, proper use of equipment, and rules of play. All three areas contribute to safety in sports and self-responsibility not only for physical wellness but for safety in the physical environment. This is an important area in which the child can develop a sense of safety consciousness, as schools and communities encourage physical development of the body. Concepts for the parents and child in the development of safety wellness in the school-age child include the following:

PARENTS SHOULD
1. Encourage children to assume greater responsibility for their safety.
2. Encourage children to identify safe factors in their environment and to modify unsafe factors as necessary.
3. Encourage participation in community safety programs.

CHILDREN SHOULD
1. Observe safety rules and precautions in home, school, and play activities.
2. Develop consciousness of causes and effects of accidents.
3. Participate in community activities that teach safety.

SAFETY WELLNESS DURING ADOLESCENCE

Adolescents become progressively more independent than school-age children as they move toward adulthood. This increased mobility includes the use of cars, motorcycles, and exposure to drugs and alcohol. While adolescents may be more physically independent and mobile in their environment, they lack emotional maturity. This lack of emotional maturity is further complicated by the many stresses faced by today's adolescents. Pressures from parents and teachers to achieve in school, select their life's work, and develop a sense of identity as adults provide much stress for the teenager. Pressure from peers to try new experiences and to conform to the actions of the crowd can minimize the adolescent's awareness of personal actions and safety.

Accidents with motor vehicles continue to be a major cause of death and injury in this age group. If a teenager obtains a driver's license, he must be taught proper use and maintenance of the automobile. Seat belts should be worn at all times by the teenage driver as well as his passengers. The teenager should be aware of traffic regulations, observe the posted speed limit, and demonstrate the ability and willingness to follow all the rules as conditions for use of the family car. Formal driver-education courses are offered in the schools and should be taken by each teenager who wants to learn to drive. The shared responsibility of parent and child in the development of safety wellness in the adolescent includes the following:

PARENTS SHOULD

1. Understand the adolescent's need for increased independence.
2. Educate the child in the proper use of automobiles.
3. Provide freedom within limits to participate in age-related activities, such as sports and use of the automobile.

ADOLESCENTS SHOULD

1. Assume responsibility for their own actions.
2. Learn to use automobiles responsibly.

The younger generation's involvement with drugs also increases their potential for harming themselves while driving a car. Perception and judgment can be impaired as a result of use of drugs, especially alcohol. Many adolescents experience alcohol in the company of family or friends. Because it is a drug so widely used, the adolescent should be taught by his family how to use it responsibly. In the safety of the home, he should learn his response to and tolerance for alcohol. He should develop the sense of responsibility not to drive when his judgment is impaired and not to ride with anyone whose state of mind is impaired. He should be firm enough in his convictions and sense of self to overcome any coercion from peers.

SAFETY WELLNESS FOR THE ADULT

During the adult stage of development, the family member is usually autonomous and accepts responsibility for his own actions that may relate to safety in the home and work environment. Indeed, accidents remain a leading cause of death in the 25 to 44 age group. A large proportion of these accidents occur in the work environment. In 1977, the National Safety Council reported 13,000 work-related deaths, with 1800 occurring in manufacturing industries and 11,200 occurring in nonmanufacturing industries [19]. Programs to prevent, identify, and correct hazards should be active in every work setting, along with awareness and involvement of workers in activities that maximize safety.

Because many adults drive automobiles, auto accidents account for many injuries and accidental deaths in this age group. The adult who wishes to minimize his risk of being involved or injured in a motor vehicle accident should

1. Consider safety features when buying a car.
2. Be patient with other drivers on the road.
3. Buckle his seat belt.
4. Avoid being in a hurry when driving.
5. Drive within the designated speed limits.
6. Avoid driving in bad weather whenever possible.

Automobile safety is an ongoing effort that requires an attitude of prevention and a sense of personal responsibility for the well-being of oneself, others in the car, and others on the road.

In the home, adults must maintain a sense of safety awareness in order to prevent accidents throughout life. Being aware of hazards and taking a positive approach to reducing them will help maintain positive interactions within and around the home. Full understanding of the safety-wellness concept will enable the adult family member to make good decisions in a variety of situations throughout life without relying on rote recall of specific safety rules. Important safety concepts for the adult include the following:

ADULT FAMILY MEMBERS

1. Are aware of safety hazards in the home and work environments
2. Recognize safety factors in use of the automobile
3. Incorporate safety-wellness thinking into all areas of living

SAFETY WELLNESS FOR THE ELDERLY

Certain threats to safety wellness are faced by the elderly because of physical changes in their bodies. Some major reasons for falls among the aged are decreased vision, dizziness, disturbances of equilibrium, and proprioceptive problems. The healthy nerve cells that control walking steadiness seem to diminish in the elderly; in fact, there is a generalized diminished functioning of the nervous, circulatory, and musculoskeletal systems, which predisposes the elderly to falls and other accidents.

With this decrease in balance and judgment, the elderly person may jaywalk or step out in front of an approaching car. The elderly person may not make it across the road before the light changes. To combat this problem, some communities with a large number of elderly persons have reset traffic signals to allow more time for safe crossing.

Whenever the nurse encounters the elderly client, she should provide education to the client in methods of compensating for his physical shortcomings. In the home setting, scatter rugs should be avoided as they can get tangled in feet, canes, and walkers. All living spaces should be well lighted. The top and bottom steps should be marked with light carpet or light-colored paint in order to distinguish them more clearly. Handrails should be securely fastened. Bathtubs can be made safer by installing handrails and nonskid treads. Avoidance of clutter may be more important in this stage of development as the older adult may experience a loss of physical agility and reaction time. The older person should know what community resources are available, including emergency services, which he can contact if he has an accident at home.

The older person should be taught safe use of medications to avoid accidental poisonings. All medications should be labeled and taken only according to directions. The nurse should encourage the older citizen to know the name of each medication he is taking and to be aware of potential side effects.

Even though the elderly person may change physically or mentally, and despite necessary alterations in his environment, he can still maintain the attitude that safety is important. Indeed, safety wellness can be maintained throughout this stage of the life cycle with awareness, acceptance, and adaptation.

OLDER FAMILY MEMBERS SHOULD

1. Be aware of physical and mental changes that may affect their safety.
2. Make necessary changes in home environment as physical and mental changes occur.
3. Maintain an attitude of safety wellness.

Safety wellness can be accomplished by viewing separately each developmental stage and its characteristics that require special considerations. The well family works with each family member to make the home environment safe within the context of each stage of development. This lifelong attention to safety wellness as families grow and develop will result in persons who experience living in a home environment that is not only free from hazards but that promotes a more productive life. Each child not only grows up in this enriched environment, but he also learns the skills necessary to accept responsibility for safety wellness for the next generation.

Accidents: A Function of Agent Factors

A variety of agents with potentially dangerous properties may be found in or around the home. The following substances are the most common poisoning agents in the home setting [13].

DRUGS
Aspirin
Acetaminophen
Tranquilizers
Barbiturates
Cough medicines
Antibiotics
Laxatives
Rubbing alcohol
Boric acid
Iron medications
Vitamins
Nose and throat sprays
Steroids
Oil of wintergreen
Antihistamines
Oral contraceptives

EXTERNAL PREPARATIONS
Baby powder
Deodorizers
Water softeners
Lead paint
Cosmetics

CLEANING AGENTS
Cleansers
Soaps
Lye
Polishes
Bleaches
Disinfectants
Acids
Toilet bowl cleaners
Drain cleaners

PETROLEUM PRODUCTS
Gasoline
Kerosene
Turpentine

Family members should go through the home thoroughly to identify these and other potential poisons, making sure they are labeled and stored properly, and discarding all out-of-date medications.

ASPIRIN AND OTHER MEDICATIONS

For many years, aspirin has been the leading cause of accidental poisoning and poisoning deaths among children. Salicylates remain the most frequently ingested poison among children, with household products and plants taking second and third places [26]. According to the National Clearing House for Poison Control, however, there has been a sharp decline in salicylate poisoning since 1963. At that time aspirin was no longer the leading cause but actually was exceeded by other substances in accidental ingestions of childhood [11].

A growing source of concern is a similar drug on the market—acetaminophen. Its increased usage has been accompanied by a rapid increase in the incidence of overdoses. American experience has demonstrated a doubling of acetaminophen overdose cases between 1973 and 1975 and a drop in salicylate overdose cases of approximately 25 percent [17].

One reason salicylate and acetaminophen overdoses are so frequent is their ready availability in the home. Aspirin for children is often orange flavored, so that it appears to be an innocuous candy rather than a potent drug. Since putting objects into the mouth is a normal activity of young children in the age group of 18 to 30 months, they appear to be most at risk with these medications as well as with other hazardous substances.

Some events that have played a part in lowering the incidence of these accidental poisonings involving children are the following [11]:

1. In 1950, a restriction on the number of flavored children's aspirins to 50 1¼-grain tablets per container
2. In 1967, a further reduction to 36 1¼-grain tablets per container
3. In 1969, introduction by two major manufacturers of a protective bottle cap
4. In 1972, mandatory safety packaging of both children's and adult's aspirin preparations

Assuming a 2-year impact period, the decrease in baby aspirin ingestions attributable to safety packaging was estimated to be in the range of 48 to 56 percent, while the impact of adult aspirin safety packaging estimates for a 3-year period was 43 percent fewer aspirin ingestions by children [7].

The child-resistant containers for these substances must be sufficiently difficult that they cannot be opened by 80 percent of children under 5 years of age, but they must allow access to at least 90 percent of adults, who should be able to open and properly close the packaging conveniently. There is an exception in the case of a few people such as the old or handicapped, whom the law allows to obtain prescription medicines in ordinary packaging without safety features on request of the physician or consumer. Conventional packaging should be restricted to households without children [8].

Aspirin is such a commonly ingested drug that we frequently forget what a potential danger it can be. Other drugs have equal danger potential. Adults often take drugs in front of children and call them "candy." Because children are imitators, medicines should be taken out of sight of children and should be referred to as medicine, not candy. Otherwise, a child may at a later time seek out the "candy" and consume large quantities of it. All medicines should be stored out of reach in their original containers and preferably in a locked cabinet. All medicines left over at the end of an illness should be flushed down the toilet.

One of the most impressive clinical manifestations of salicylate intoxication is hyperventilation. Parents should check the child for rapid and difficult breathing and fast heartbeat. Parents should contact their physician or the local poison control center if these symptoms are noted. Immediate care involves removal of the salicylates from the stomach, fluid therapy, and observation of the child for

Table 7-1. Oral Pediatric Dosages of Acetaminophen (Tylenol)

Age	Dosage Drops	Elixir	Frequency
3 months–1 year	0.6 ml *or*	2.5 ml	As often as
1–3 years	0.6–1.2 ml *or*	2.5–5 ml	every 6
3–6 years	1.2 ml *or*	5.0 ml	hours
Over 6 years	—	10.0 ml	

Source: Hoole, Greenberg, and Pickard [15].

from 12 to 24 hours. The poison control center telephone number should be displayed prominently near the telephone along with other emergency numbers.

Families should be cautioned to take medication as directed. The old theory that "if one helps, then two has to help more," is a fallacy. Parents may give a double dose or may give pills more frequently than directed in hopes of hastening the healing process. Strict adherence to dosage directions will obviate overdoses of aspirin and acetaminophen, and the principle applies to all family members taking any medication. Tables 7-1 and 7-2 indicate acceptable oral dosages of acetaminophen and aspirin for children [15].

LEAD POISONING

While lead poisoning is classified as a preventable disease, thousands of children in the United States are victims of lead poisoning each year. Lead ingestion is particularly common in the 18 to 30-month age group because of the tendency toward mouthing. Pica is the term used in describing this indiscriminate and habitual appetite for nonfood substances. Some common sources of lead are dirt, clay, ashes, chips of lead-based paint, and laundry starch. A few chips of lead-based paint the size of a thumbnail can contain 100 mg or more of lead, which is 200 times the daily level of ingestion usually considered safe (0.5 mg) [26].

Parental characteristics may play a role in ingestion of lead by a child. As many as 50 percent of mothers whose children have pica also demonstrate the behavior [6]. Imitation may account for this behavior and increased oral activity may be

Table 7-2. Oral Pediatric Dosage of Aspirin

Body Weight	No. of 81-mg (1¼ grain) Tablets	Frequency
7–11 kg (14–24 lb.)	1	As often as
11–16 kg (24–35 lb.)	2	every 4
16–23 kg (35–50 lb.)	3	hours
Over 23 kg (over 50 lb.)	4	

Source: Hoole, Greenberg, and Pickard [15].

related to relief of anxiety. Bottle-feeding after 18 months is more common in children who suffer lead poisoning. Gratifications obtained by sucking the bottle may be transferred to chewing wooden windowsills. The most common maternal pattern seen is dependence. Mothers who feel a sense of despair may be unable to stimulate the child toward constructive activity [26]. The nurse should be alert for these high-risk factors.

Availability of lead in the home environment also contributes to lead poisoning. Since 1940 the use of lead-based paint has been restricted to exterior surfaces. This does not, however, provide assurance that the child will not find sources of lead paint on old toys and furniture and other items that have been more recently painted with exterior paint. Families who purchase toys and household items secondhand should be alert for the possibility that the paint on the item contains lead. If there is any doubt at all about lead content in the paint, the item should be scraped and repainted with a lead-free paint. If uncertain whether paint on the walls or woodwork of the home contains lead, the family can contact their local health department for help in analyzing paint chips. If the paint does contain lead, the surface should be scraped and repainted with a lead-free paint.

Airborne lead from leaded gasolines has increased the amount of lead in our environment, and lead from auto exhausts contributes to the lead content of soil and dust. Individuals living near busy highways are quite likely at greater risk for lead poisoning. Since there is no way for these individuals to reduce the amount of lead they inhale, they need to know if and when a health problem is developing.

Unfortunately, there are no specific signs and symptoms of lead poisoning in the early stages, although some irritability and vomiting may occur. In the later stages of lead poisoning, convulsions and coma may result. Treatment must begin before lead encephalopathy occurs. If the parents have any question about lead poisoning, particularly if their child has pica, the nurse should encourage them to take the child to a physician for a blood test before symptoms and permanent damage can occur. If the child has already ingested lead, the nurse can prepare the family and the child for multiple injections of medication such as calcium disodium edetate (EDTA) and British antilewisite (BAL) to counteract the lead poisoning [26].

The nurse's role in lead poisoning involves identification of signs and symptoms of lead poisoning, assistance in screening procedures, and identification and education of the high-risk groups. Furthermore, the nurse can participate in community, state, and federal efforts that attempt to provide better housing for everyone. The nurse should encourage a decrease in exposure to lead from all known sources. The reduction of environmental exposure to lead must be a constant goal. The family must be encouraged to remove the old paint and cover the walls with lead-free paint. If the house or apartment is rented, the landlord is responsible. The nurse should also consider becoming involved in community action programs to abolish this hazard from a family's environment. Lead poisoning is preventable, and prevention occurs at the community level as well as the family level.

LYE AND DRAIN CLEANERS

The ingestion of caustic agents such as lye and drain cleaners poses a serious problem for children. These substances should not be present in or around the home. If one of these products is needed in the home, the family should use only what is needed and then dispose of the remainder. These extremely caustic substances should not be present because they could seriously harm the family's or a visitor's children. If ingested these substances cause caustic burns to the mouth, throat, and esophagus. The healing process often leaves scars and strictures requiring periodic dilatation of the esophagus. This type of poisoning results in long-term care and severe pain for the child. Should a child ingest one of these products, the local poison control center should be contacted immediately. First-aid treatment usually calls for giving olive oil or butter orally to soothe the membranes. The child should *not* vomit. If an acid is swallowed, give milk or water to dilute it. If an alkali has been swallowed, give milk or fruit juice or water. A child under 5 years of age should be given 1 to 2 cups of fluids; if over 5 years of age up to 1 quart should be given [25].

PETROLEUM PRODUCTS

Kerosene, gasoline, motor oil, paint thinners, lighter fluid, and wax removers are common items around the home that should be identified, labeled, stored safely, and kept out of reach of young children. If one of these substances is ingested, vomiting should *not* be induced. If the child regurgitates the substance, he may suffer additional irritation to the mouth, throat, and esophagus, as well as aspiration pneumonia. As with any poisoning, the local poison control center should be contacted for specific instructions. Mineral oil is sometimes given to dilute the poison and soothe the burns [25].

Locked storage should be provided for highly toxic substances and the storage area should be away from foods. Substances should be kept in original containers and labeled properly. The teenager or adult must be cautioned against siphoning gasoline. Gasoline is a poison and can cause aspiration pneumonia. With the increased prices of gasoline and the possibility of gasoline shortages, siphoning becomes more popular, thereby increasing risks.

CARBON MONOXIDE POISONING

Both the home and the automobile should be considered possible sources of exposure to the poisonous agent, carbon monoxide. Carbon monoxide has been called a "silent killer" because it is odorless, tasteless, and colorless. The most common cause of carbon monoxide poisoning in the home is the unvented gas heater. Charcoal grills should not be used indoors for the same reason—lack of adequate ventilation. If there is no vent to dispel the carbon monoxide, it will displace the oxygen in the room. All home heating systems should be checked periodically for operating efficiency, and all space heaters should be vented to the outside. If gas is used in the kitchen, the kitchen should be well ventilated and pilot lights checked often, since they frequently go out, allowing fumes to invade the kitchen. Every older child and adult should know the cutoff location for gas, electricity, and water. If a problem with gas is suspected, the utility company should be contacted immediately. Drivers of automobiles should be aware that carbon monoxide can seep through the floor of a car. The family who is stuck in a snowdrift or a traffic jam, or who needs warmth when camping should not keep the car engine running for extended periods of time without opening the windows.

Symptoms of carbon monoxide poisoning include dizziness, nausea, and vomiting. A person suffering from carbon monoxide poisoning or any other inhaled gaseous poison should be provided with fresh air, and the physician should be notified at once. Cardiopulmonary resuscitation should be administered if breathing has stopped, but the rescuer should not inhale the breath of the victim.

PLANT POISONING

Another group of agents to which members of the family are exposed is plants. With the growing interest in household and outdoor plants, there is a greater chance of accidental plant poisoning. Although plant poisoning fatalities are rare, most of the deaths and illnesses are experienced by children and could have been prevented by proper identification of the plant and watchfulness of the parents. Table 7-3 lists the more common poisonous plants [14, 23]. Poisoning from ingestion or touching of plants may be difficult to recognize. Symptoms may not appear for several days or even weeks after exposure. Some plants produce symptoms immediately, while other plants such as the yew can cause death suddenly without any warning signs.

The toxic effects of plants vary considerably. It is important to note that only certain parts of plants may be toxic. For example, rhubarb stems are edible, but the leaves are toxic. The toxicity may vary with the age and size of the victim, the age

Table 7-3. Poisonous Plants

Amaryllis	Holly	Oleander
Azalea	Iris	Poinsettia
Baneberry	Jack-in-the-pulpit	Poison hemlock
Belladonna	Jerusalem cherry	Poison ivy
Bittersweet	Jimsonweed	Pokeweed
Bloodroot	Lily of the valley	Potato leaves
Castor-bean plant	Marijuana	Rhododendron
Climbing nightshade	Mistletoe	Rhubarb leaves
Daffodil	Morning glory	Tomato leaves
Dieffenbachia	Mountain laurel	Wisteria
Foxglove	Mushrooms	Yew

Source: U.S. Department of Health, Education and Welfare, Bureau of Product Safety [23].

of the plant, and the amount eaten or inhaled. A poisonous plant can cause a variety of symptoms, ranging from gastritis or skin rash to paralysis of the respiratory system, resulting in death. The poison hemlock is an example of a plant that paralyzes the respiratory nerves. All parts of this plant are toxic when green. Hemlock was the chief ingredient of the cup of poison administered to Socrates, and throughout the ages has been used for poisoning. The victim of such poisoning should be encouraged to vomit and helped to maintain respirations. Vomiting should never be induced if the victim is unconscious.

The best way to prevent accidental poisoning from plants is to keep plants away from children who are not old enough to understand the meaning of poisons. Older children should be taught to recognize harmful plants. Poisonous plants should be identified by parents so that proper information can be given to the physician in case of poisoning. If the name of the plant that has been ingested is not known, a sample of it can be taken to the physician or poison control center. The parent should explain the amount and part of plant that was ingested, the time since ingestion, age of the victim, and symptoms observed.

HOUSEHOLD EQUIPMENT

Electrical and mechanical equipment constitutes another group of agents that can contribute to accidents in and around the home. Children must be kept away from dangerous equipment. Garden equipment and tools such as lawn mowers and shears should be kept in restricted areas. Adults who use the equipment should know how to do so correctly and also how to maintain the item properly.

Electrical appliances should be disconnected after using, and hands should not be wet when touching them. Appliances such as hair dryers should be used with caution in the bathroom, and cords should never come in contact with water. Only Underwriters' Laboratory approved appliances should be used, indicating that certain safety standards such as mechanical and electrical construction, nontoxicity of paints, materials, and substances, and ability to withstand abuse have been met.

Two of the main causes of accidents with electricity are carelessness and lack of knowledge. Family members should read instruction booklets before using any appliance and should know how to operate them properly. Electrical appliances should never be used around standing water. Repair of electrical equipment should be done at home only if the person is knowledgeable and understands safety precautions. Otherwise, the appliance should be taken to a quality repair shop. Any appliance that is not working properly should not be used. Equipment should be disconnected before cleaning or repairing and when not in use. Cords from appliances should not be stretched across work cabinets or across the range in the kitchen. All electrical cords in the house should be checked periodically and replaced if they show signs of wear.

Children need to be taught respect for electricity at the earliest possible age. As they become older, they should be taught how to use appliances safely and how to inspect cords for wear. Safety lessons throughout childhood should help the child grow into a safety-conscious adult.

A particularly hazardous piece of electrical equipment is an unused refrigerator or freezer and should never be accessible to any child. Children love to hide and to play games, and they may become locked in these airtight containers. The door should either be locked or removed completely. The best way to prevent an accidental suffocation is to remove the door and have the appliance hauled away.

TOYS

Toys are a common agent factor to which all children are exposed from birth through childhood. Many toys appear to be harmless, yet they can hurt and kill. Children strangle on balloons, choke on rattles, inhale noxious fumes from model-kit glue, and burn themselves with alcohol lamps from chemistry sets. The eyes of stuffed animals are potential hazards if they pull off easily. Some have been found to be made of poisonous jequirity beans.

The developmental age of the child dictates certain precautions. For example, tiny objects should not be within an infant's reach. Ideal toys for the infant are brightly colored ones with smooth surfaces. They should be too large to enter the infant's mouth and should have no loose parts. If a toy can be dismantled by a parent, it should not be given to an infant. Toys that produce heat, require electricity, or contain chemicals should be purchased only for older children. Bicycles and other riding toys should fit the size of the child. Bicycles should have skid-resistant surfaces on pedals and reflectors on the front, rear, and sides. Table 7-4 lists toys and play equipment appropriate for various developmental stages.

Fortunately, there are several guides available to help parents select safe toys for children. The *Good Housekeeping* Seal of Approval indicates that the magazine permits manufacturers who advertise in *Good Housekeeping* to put this seal on toys that it investigates and accepts for performance and safety. Technically, the seal guarantees only that a refund can be obtained if a toy is found to be defective. Actually, the testers check representative samples for poor construction, toxicity of paints, sharp and pointed edges, and loose parts. They also test for electrical hazards, although all toys must have the Underwriters' Laboratory Seal of Approval label before being submitted. *Good Housekeeping* testers once turned down a clay-type molding substance claimed by the manufacturer to be harmless and edible. It was harmless when fresh from the box, but after a short period of play on the floor it was probably not germfree as claimed.

Several agencies deal with monitoring and assuring safety of toys. The Underwriters' Laboratory sets standards for electrical toys, and toys that meet the standards are given a seal of approval. No electrical toy should be purchased without this seal. *Consumer Reports* is an independent, nonadvertising magazine that maintains its own testing laboratories and reports to the public. Periodically, reports on toys or other playthings and their safety features and hazards are published in *Consumer Reports*. The American Academy of Pediatrics' Accident

Table 7-4. Safe Toys for Developmental Stage

Developmental Stage	Recommended Toys
Birth–1 year	Brightly colored objects Mobiles hung out of reach Plastic cups Unbreakable rattles Plastic squeeze toys Stuffed animals
1–3 years	Large smooth blocks Spinning tops Pull toys Stuffed animals Push toys Building blocks Nontoxic finger paints Playdoh or modeling clay Rocking horses Small riding toys
3–6 years	Nontoxic paints and coloring books Jump ropes Blackboards Puzzles Kiddie cars and tricycles Phonograph Small table-and-chairs set Dollhouse and furniture
6–8 years	Games and puzzles Ice skates and roller skates Sleds Toy musical instruments Puppets Baseballs and footballs Carpenter bench and tools Bicycles Gym sets
8 years and up	Electric trains Chemistry sets Games Tools Microscopes Modeling kits Hobby and craft kits Bicycles

Prevention Committee acts as a toy safety clearinghouse. It reports on hazardous toys and calls them to the attention of the manufacturer directly or through the National Safety Council. The Consumer Product Safety Commission has authority to ban unsafe toys from the marketplace. It attempts to enforce regulations that forbid the sale of toys capable of causing harm to children.

The ultimate responsibility for keeping unsafe toys from children rests with the parents. Parents must be conscious of toy safety when purchasing toys and advising friends and relatives who wish to purchase toys for the child. Each toy should be examined carefully before purchasing or giving it to the child. Parents who have further questions about toy safety may write to the Consumer Product Safety Commission, 7315 Wisconsin Avenue, Suite 701 E, Bethesda, MD 20207, or call 800-638-2666.

If parents believe a product is unsafe, they can submit a formal petition to the commission, or write or call in a complaint. The complaint or petition should explain how the product is defective and whether it caused an injury. A recommendation can be included as to whether the product should be regulated or banned. Once the commission investigates and finds a product unsafe, it requires the manufacturer to notify purchasers and repair or replace the product. If the manufacturer refuses to act, the commission can initiate legal action.

Accidents: Functions of an Unstable Environment

A safe assumption is that every household will undergo certain changes as the family alters its life-style. Many accidents occur when a family moves from apartment to apartment or from home to home. But even common events such as the birth of a child, the finishing of a basement, or the installation of an automatic dishwasher can alter the environment. Peak activity periods during the day such as mealtimes can cause instability in the home. Each of these events creates a situation that may threaten safety wellness of the family.

The well family also must gear itself for the unexpected. Imagine a 3-year-old helping mother to prepare dinner in the kitchen. The doorbell rings and the mother goes to answer it. While she is at the door chatting with a visitor, the 3-year-old is attracted to cleaning products in the cabinet left open beneath the sink. An "unexpected" or accidental poisoning could occur.

Imagine a family of four who has just moved into a new home. Dad is arranging furniture while mother tends to the newborn infant. The 3-year-old, who has been left to play by himself for awhile, finds father's gardening supplies, which include fertilizers and other chemicals. Again, an "unexpected" and accidental poisoning could occur.

Unfamiliar places such as stores, vacation spots, movies, sports events, and someone else's home can provide opportunities for accidents simply because they are unfamiliar. It is impossible to control all surroundings; however, one can set rules and limits for the child. Parents might have a "look, but don't touch" rule in public places. While on vacation, parents might take a walk around the environment, noting off-limits areas and establishing safety rules. If the family is in the same vacation spot as the previous year, they should remember that each child is now a year older and will see the place with new eyes. Although last year a child may have paid no attention to a potential hazard, this year it may become a real one.

Holidays present a different environment for the family. Often new or greater numbers of people are in the home and greater fatigue develops due to preparations. Both factors can mean less careful supervision of young children.

At no season of the year does the word *home* take on more meaning than at Christmastime. However, tragedy may result due to carelessness with holiday decorations and plants. Safeguards in relation to the use of the Christmas tree are as follows:

1. Buy a fresh tree shortly before Christmas so that it will be less flammable.
2. Anchor the tree firmly so that it will not fall.
3. Place the tree away from all sources of heat.
4. Request that guests not smoke near the tree.
5. Remove the tree shortly after the holidays.

Other activities that promote safety at holiday time include purchasing only Underwriters' Laboratory approved lights for the tree, purchasing flameproof decorations, and removing Christmas wrappings as soon as possible to prevent a fire hazard.

An Agent Factor: Nature of the Home Environment

The home itself presents many agent factors through its nature and individual characteristics. Locations of most home accidents are as follows [2]: kitchens, 41 percent; bathrooms, 21 percent; bedrooms, 12 percent; other places, 26 percent. The inside and outside of a home should be kept in good repair. Accomplishing this goal is a great responsibility and involves never-ending tasks. Boards become loose, concrete steps crack, and numerous other problems develop over the years of living. Whether the family owns or rents, these repairs must be made as soon as possible to prevent accidents as well as larger repair bills. Some communities have housing codes to assure quality construction of new homes and to protect the occupants of rented properties. These standards should be met and upheld.

Obvious fire hazards should be avoided, such as clutter in closets, basements, and attics. The amount of flammable liquids present such as gasoline and charcoal lighter fluid should be kept to a minimum, stored in proper and labeled containers, and never used around anything that may produce a spark.

The electrical supply to the home should be adequate to cover the appliances in the home. A competent electrician should be consulted if major appliances are to be added to the home or if lights dim when an appliance is turned on. Electrical circuits should not be overloaded. In case electrical service is interrupted, such as during a storm, flashlights should be stored throughout the house to prevent accidents.

At least one smoke detector should be present in every household; larger or multilevel homes should have more than one. A smoke detector sounds its warning before smoke has accumulated to deadly levels, providing time to extinguish the fire or to escape. They are available in battery-operated or electric models. The family should make sure that the detector chosen has been tested by a nationally recognized testing service such as the Underwriters' Laboratory. Batteries should be monitored and replaced periodically, with replacement batteries kept on hand.

Fireplaces are another home feature that may increase the chance of fire in the home and, thus, burns to children. Before starting the fire, all paper items should be removed from the general vicinity. A screen should enclose the front of the fireplace in order to confine live embers and sparks and to prevent children from playing in the fire. Chimneys should be cleaned periodically.

Each family should have a fire escape plan and conduct fire drills periodically. Fire ladders can be used for upper-floor rooms. The local fire department can be consulted about development of an adequate escape plan for the home. Agents for extinguishing fires should be present throughout the house. Salt and baking soda can be kept in a can in the kitchen to extinguish grease fires. Approved fire extinguishers should be kept in the home and garage areas. Emergency numbers should be posted near the phone so that the fire department can be contacted immediately.

An Agent Factor: Nature of the School Environment

The school community system is a microcosm of the larger community, the system from which the students, faculty, and staff come. Each individual brings to the school community certain levels of physical, social, and psychological health. Within the school environment, these levels of health change and develop, partly through the influence of the environment.

Two major dimensions comprise the school environment: the physical and psychosocial worlds of the school. The *physical world* is defined by the school building and its facilities and surroundings. The *psychosocial world* comprises the affective climate among the persons in the system—students, teachers, staff, and parents. These domains build a school environment that can promote wellness, illness, or some state in between. The physical and psychosocial environments

embrace all efforts to provide at school physical, emotional, and social conditions which are beneficial to the health and safety of pupils. It includes the provision of a safe and healthful school day, and the establishment of interpersonal relationships favorable to mental health [9].

We will focus only on the physical environment in this chapter.

School buildings have much potential for impact on physical and mental wellness. While many school buildings are far from new, the primary goal is to maintain an environment free from hazards, both actual and potential. Buildings must be kept in good repair and potential problems averted through quick detection and maintenance. Delaying snow removal on school property can cost dearly in terms of auto or bus accidents and falls. Faculty, staff, and students can develop a safety consciousness, which includes anticipation of potential hazards. School buildings should at the very least meet state and local regulations for fire and other safety measures.

Maintenance and repair of school buildings can affect levels of psychological wellness by promoting a sense of pride and belonging in its inhabitants. When young children are taught how to help take care of their school facility and to be alert for hazards and other deficits, a sense of community pride through sharing responsibility is fostered. Older students can learn the benefits of sharing the responsibility for school building maintenance and safety in terms of monetary benefits. Dollars not spent to repair the results of vandalism are dollars that can be spent on instruction and other activities to benefit the students.

Facilities within the school building should be provided with the goal of maximizing wellness. Light, ventilation, and temperature control should promote physical wellness. Classrooms should be large enough to allow comfortable movement within the room. Areas and programs should be available for physical exercise and recreation of students and staff. The school as a workplace should anticipate and respond to the needs of staff as well as students.

Concern has been expressed recently about school bus safety. Each day over 300,000 school buses transport over 20 million children to and from school. For some the ride is short. For others it may be 1 hour or longer. The school is responsible for every child while he is on the bus. A recent report of the National Transportation Safety Board reported that 90 percent of the school buses in the United States are unsafe. Tough requirements have been proposed at the federal level to improve the safety of school buses, but adoption of these requirements is uncertain due to lobbying efforts and general bureaucratic inertia. Proposed national standards include [9]

1. Seating systems that include proper padding, firm anchoring to the floor, approved passenger seat belts, and higher seat backs
2. Improved emergency exits
3. Interior protection for passengers
4. Greater floor strength
5. Greater crash resistance of bodies and frames
6. Safer vehicle operating systems
7. Improved safety glass for windshields and passenger windows

Schools can do much to ensure safety for all students who ride school buses. Bus drivers who are physically and mentally well should be selected. Drivers should be trained in safe operation of the bus, first aid, and management of unruly student behavior. Frequent and rigorous inspections of buses should be conducted and defects corrected immediately. Bus routes should be planned to avoid overcrowding.

Schools should be built or renovated with as many fire-retardant materials as possible. A sprinkler system should be present in larger facilities, and fire extinguishers and fire alarms should be clearly evident throughout the school. School personnel should be trained periodically in the operation of alarms and extinguishers. The primary means of fire control is prevention. All personnel and students should be knowledgeable about preventing fires. Fire drills should be held frequently and regularly so that all persons can leave the building quickly and calmly.

RESPONSIBILITY FOR THE SCHOOL ENVIRONMENT

The school is an important and integral part of the community and therefore the responsibility for its well-being is shared. Although the board of education makes policy, and the school personnel carry it out on a day-to-day basis, the families and other citizens in the community share in the outcomes of decisions made by school staff. Schools clearly reflect the values of the communities that they serve, and demands made by the community will ultimately be heeded. Members of the community, through its families, have access to school operation through local parent-teacher organizations. Active involvement over time is necessary to identify and develop the political structure necessary for relevant and effective decision making. When families have an awareness of factors in the school environment and a working knowledge of the political system, environmental factors can be altered if necessary, to promote maximum wellness in the school environment.

An Agent Factor: Nature of the Work Environment

Each adult in the family spends considerable time in a work environment. For adults who are not employed outside the home, the work environment is the home. Issues concerned with factors to promote wellness in the home have been addressed earlier. In the many offices, factories, and other places where one can work, many of the safety factors relevant in the home are still important.

The physical environment can promote wellness through adequate lighting, heat, physical structure, and psychological milieu, or it can threaten wellness through outright hazards. Many workers suffer needless injuries from accidents and other insults yearly, which can be due to unsafe working conditions or work practices. Many others begin developing chronic diseases due to exposure to hazards present in the work environment. Chemicals and radiation are factors in some work environments, and these are implicated in the development of certain diseases in later years.

Each workplace should have ongoing programs to identify and reduce hazards, protect workers, and encourage awareness of safety and health protection in the workplace. If a workplace does not have such programs, workers should seek their development. The extensiveness of such programs will vary according to the number and type of employees and the nature of the workplace, but every setting in which workers are employed should have some means by which workers are informed, protected, and helped to become both aware and vigilant regarding prevention of exposure to accidents and other threats to wellness.

Health promotion is another wellness concept that can and should be addressed in the work environment. All persons are deeply affected by their life-styles with regard to the occurrence in later life of heart disease, obesity, hypertension, dental disease, and mental illness. Workplaces are logical centers for development of educational self-care programs focused on primary prevention and wellness promotion. Screening programs for various health problems are present in some work settings, but few have taken the important steps toward primary prevention through health-promotion activities. Some concepts that could easily and appropriately be addressed in the work setting are

1. Nutritional wellness promotion through education about balanced, high-fiber, low-salt diets
2. Cardiovascular wellness promotion through exercise and cardiovascular fitness
3. Mental wellness promotion through anticipating life events in later years, responsible use of alcohol and other drugs, stress reduction, and relaxation

Programs such as these can have significant impact on the individual worker, the family, and the entire community.

Community Environmental Safety Factors

A well family may conscientiously render their home safe and free from most potential hazards, taking into account the developmental stage of each family member and the various agent factors within the home. But safety wellness can be threatened by other sources. The broader community in which the family lives can produce unsafe living conditions through automobile noise, water, air, and pesticide pollution.

Community air pollution is defined as the presence in the surrounding air of substances put there by human activities in concentrations sufficient to compromise any aspect of health. These man-made pollutants come from industrial exhausts, incineration, home heating, dust from roads, debris, engine enhaust, and chemical crop spraying. Air pollution can take the form of solid particulates, liquids, or gases in the air [1]. Each community experiences air pollution problems unique to its own setting in terms of causes and community approaches to solutions. The well family should be aware of sources of pollution and community efforts to control them. As individual polluters, family members should be especially knowledgeable about the role of automobiles in contaminating the air.

Automobiles are a major source of external pollution. Automotive pollution contains highly toxic nitrogen oxides, ozone, hydrocarbons, and carbon monoxide. Through the Clean Air Act of 1970, Congress mandated that carbon monoxide be reduced to 10 percent of the 1970 levels by 1975 and nitrogen oxides to 10 percent of 1971 levels by 1976. These standards were not met, but they did influence progress in cleaning up the air. Stricter legislation reducing gasoline consumption levels has also reduced pollution from autos. The target set by the 1975 Energy Policy and Conservation Act for 1978-model cars to average 18 miles per gallon (mpg) was reached in 1977. The 1979-model cars should average 19 mpg, and the 1980 autos, 20 mpg. The efficiency standards are to reach an average of 27.5 mpg by 1985 [13]. The family should reduce pollution from autos by minimizing driving trips and using alternate means of transportation such as buses, bicycles, walking, and car pooling. Keeping the family car in good working condition and tuned up, and driving at moderate speeds also help to reduce the amount of pollution from this source.

Noise pollution is another fact of life in our modern society. Extremely loud noise, particularly over a long period of time, can cause loss of hearing as well as neurologic, cardiovascular, and endocrine system damage [13]. Many feel that excessive noise in the home environment can cause undue stress, which may result in violent acts by individuals. Noise often combines with other factors such as weather, individual moods, and the degree of loudness and intensity to cause varying degrees of stress.

The U.S. government has taken steps to reduce noise levels by such legislation as the Federal Noise Control Act of 1972 and the Model Noise Control Ordinance of 1975. Standards have been set for acceptable levels of noise in terms of decibels [13]. In order for legislation to work, the consumer can reduce noise by the following methods [13]:

Check noise levels of appliances before purchasing.
Buy only necessary appliances.
Place pads under vibrating machinery.
Close doors when operating machinery.
Lower loudness adjustment of telephone and doorbell.
Enforce city ordinances related to external community noises.
Organize the neighborhood for reducing local noise.
Encourage discussion in schools about need to reduce noise levels, such as low-
    ering the volume of musical instruments with amplifiers.
Enjoy silence and walks in quiet places.
Substitute quiet places for noisy places, occasionally.

Family members can assume individual responsibilities for lowering the volume of radios, TVs, stereos, and voices. Alleviation of noise pollution requires responsibility and vigilance from government and individuals. Much day-to-day household noise can be dealt with effectively within the home.

A mandate for clean water has been issued through recent legislation. "The nation's water will be clean enough for swimming, other recreational uses, and the propagation of fish, shellfish and wildlife by July 1, 1983, and there will be no more discharges of pollutants whatsoever by 1985" [13].

That statement was issued by the 1972 Water Pollution Control Act. Was it a little ambitious? Federal water standards have existed since they were developed by the Public Health Service in 1914 [13], and yet citizens continue to be plagued by bacteria, viruses, and other pollutants in their drinking water. Industrial emissions and consumer household discharges of soaps and cleaning fluids into the water supply make water pollution an important safety concern. As of 1975, carcinogens have been found in 32 percent of the 80 U.S. cities surveyed by the Environmental Protection Agency (EPA) [24]. Nitrate fertilizer use has increased on both the household and agricultural levels. These may also contaminate water supplies from runoff from fields and lawns.

Some strategies that the well family can utilize to improve the environment are as follows [13]:

1. Organize citizens' groups for the improvement of drinking water.
2. Find out about the local water supply.
   Is it downstream from operations that use pesticides and pollutants?
   Do manufacturers have permits to discharge pollutants into water of streams?
   Does the water supply come from city supplies or wells?
   Is the treatment plant approved by the EPA?
   What are the credentials of the treatment staff?
3. Use cold water for drinking. Hot water may contain more metals and pipe impurities.
4. Conserve water by fixing leaks in pipes.
5. Make sure water pipes are not lined with lead or asbestos.
6. Be cautious of bottled water. Some is contaminated with bacteria or heavy metals.
7. Do not buy water filters and purifiers. They may ultimately turn into breeding grounds for bacteria. Boil water if it needs purification.

The public has become increasingly aware of problems associated with the use of pesticides and other chemicals. Are we poisoning ourselves? This possibility is an issue among scientists, farmers, and environmentalists as well as consumers. The public seems to be trapped in a dilemma of wanting more and better foods to feed the growing population and being unable to provide enough affordable food that is safe for human ingestion. Billions of gallons of pesticides are sprayed on U.S. crops and forests annually. Pesticides alleviate disease and hunger, but they may also be factors in cancer, skin disease, birth defects, sterility, and miscarriages. The EPA estimates that although 40,000 people were treated for pesticide poisoning in 1978, most cases go unreported or are misdiagnosed [3].

What can be done to control the use of pesticides? Much research is being done to curtail or improve their use. Eradication may be unrealistic, but alternative methods may be helpful. Integrated pest management (IPM) is one method that combines beneficial insects, special plant breeds, restrained spraying, and "commonsense" farming [3]. For example, farmers can spray early to allow beneficial insects time to recover and catch July bollworms on cotton. Texas A&M University has an IPM program in which fields are swept with nets weekly. Their catch is reported to Bugnet, a computer that alerts the farmer when insect numbers reach damaging levels. Only then is the crop sprayed. Dropping sterilized males by air to divert female weevils from other, fertile partners is another experiment now in progress. Even viruses are used to attack such insects as the pink bollworm and gypsy moth [3].

Many people are not satisfied with what is now considered legally safe. Safety regulations governing exposure limits for farmworkers, chemical workers, and consumers are more effective than in the past, but are they effective enough? Many people believe they are not and that workers and the general public are exposed to unreasonable and unnecessary risks. Even though inspectors are hired to check produce for pesticide residues that exceed state and federal safety limits, some problems continue to exist. For example, in California five inspectors gather about 7000 fruit and vegetable samples annually; about 1 percent has been found to contain more pesticide than the law allows [3]. Although everyone continues to be exposed to chemicals in the environment, it is often difficult to ascertain the degree of poisoning. Many of the symptoms, such as nausea, headaches, and diarrhea, closely resemble those of other illnesses.

What positive actions can the well family take to promote wellness? The consumer can encourage adequate safety testing on both imported and domestically grown foods. Furthermore, the consumer can carefully wash raw foods before eating them. Rain may wash some insecticides off food, but it can also wash them down deeper into the leaves. Thus, consumers must remember to scrub all parts well. Public action citizens' groups can be organized to encourage the banning of pesticides that have been proved hazardous to humans. These groups can also promote the balanced use of pesticides. Families should control their use of pesticides in the yard and garden and should encourage their neighbors to do so as well.

The family must be well informed on these important wellness issues and be aware of where their own community leaders stand. They need to know what sources of pollution and threats to safety exist in their community and what is being done to ameliorate unhealthful conditions. They need to know what community groups are involved and what they are doing. They need to become involved themselves in the community's efforts to deal with its environmental problems.

Further, many consumer service agencies and resources exist that promote safety, accident prevention, and improvement of the community environment. Some of these agencies provide services directly to individual families, while others work with community groups or governmental bodies. The well family should be aware of what each agency can do to enhance safety wellness in their lives [10].

FEDERAL AGENCIES

Department of Agriculture (USDA)—directed by law to acquire and disseminate useful information on agricultural subjects. Address: Washington, D.C. 20250.

Extension Service: in cooperation with state and county governments, conducts continuing education programs for youth and adults in agricultural production, home and family life subjects.

Department of Commerce—fosters, serves, and promotes the nation's economic development and technologic advancement. Address: Washington, D.C. 20234.

National Bureau of Standards: provides consumer product information for better purchase decisions.

Department of Health and Human Services (DHHS)—formerly the Department of Health, Education and Welfare: concerned with the nation's human needs.

    a. *Consumer Education:* provides support to states, local education agencies, institutions of higher learning, and nonprofit organizations for the initiation or expansion of consumer education services. Address: Office of Education, Washington, D.C. 20202.

    b. *Office of Consumer Affairs:* coordinates federal activities in the consumer field and seeks ways to aid and protect the consumer. Address: Office of Consumer Affairs, Washington, D.C. 20201.

    c. *Food and Drug Administration (FDA):* protects consumers by enforcing laws and regulations to prevent distribution of adulterated or misbranded foods, drugs, medical devices, cosmetics, and veterinary products. Address: 5600 Fishers Lane, Rockville, MD 20852.

    d. *Social Security Administration:* provides monthly benefits to insured persons and their dependents in the event of retirement, disability, or death, and provides health insurance (Medicare) to persons 65 and over (also to some under 65 who are handicapped). Address: 6401 Security Blvd., Baltimore, MD 21235. Also, see local telephone directories.

    e. *U.S. Public Health Service (USPHS):* sets national standards for health; provides for education and research. Includes Alcohol, Drug Abuse, and Mental Health Administrations. Address: 5600 Fishers Lane, Rockville, MD 20852. Also, Center for Disease Control, 1600 Clifton Road, N.E., Atlanta, GA 30333.

Department of Interior, National Park Service—maintains a network of 300 natural, historic, and recreational areas for public campsites. Address: Washington, D.C. 20240.

Department of Labor, Occupational Safety and Health Administration (OSHA): sets and enforces job safety and health standards for workers, trains employers and employees in proper occupational safety and health practices. Address: Washington, D.C. 20210.

Department of Transportation, National Highway Traffic Safety Administration: works to reduce highway deaths, injuries, and property losses. Address: Washington, D.C. 20590.

Consumer Product Safety Commission—an independent regulatory agency to protect the consumer against unreasonable risks associated with consumer products, to assist consumers in evaluating the comparative safety of consumer products, to develop uniform safety standards for consumer products. This agency invites consumers to participate in the standards-setting procedures. Consumers are encouraged to assist in surveys to identify safe products. Address: Washington, D.C. 20207.

Environmental Protection Agency (EPA): works to abate and control pollution systematically, by proper integration of a variety of research, monitoring, standard-setting, and enforcement activities. Address: Washington, D.C. 20460.

U.S. Postal Service: provides mail service; protects customers from dangerous articles, contraband, fraud, and pornography. Address: Washington, D.C. 20260.

Consumer Information Center: provides helpful consumer catalogs. Address: Pueblo, CO 81009.

Federal Trade Commission (FTC): promotes free and fair competition in the American marketplace by enforcing antitrust laws and other statutes. Acts to curb deceptive advertising. Address: Washington, D.C. 20580 (guide to federal consumer services).

PRIVATE AGENCIES

Consumer's Union of United States, Inc.: nonprofit organization to provide product information to consumers. Publishes monthly magazine, *Consumer Reports*, and other publications. Address: Mt. Vernon, NY.

Good Housekeeping Institute—provides consumers with product information. Allows use of *Good Housekeeping* Seal of Approval on approved products.

A special group of resources that cut across governmental and private sponsorship are the poison control centers. The concept of the poison control center was initiated and developed in 1953 as a pilot project in Chicago by the Illinois Chapter of the Academy of Pediatrics. At present, there are nearly 600 centers in the United States. The National Clearinghouse for Poison Control Centers was established by the Public Health Service in 1956, in order to coordinate the activities of the various poison control centers. Autonomous organizations have since been developed by local hospitals in cooperation with health departments. Most are located in hospitals [5]. They furnish information on poisons and the proper emergency procedures to professionals and the general public. Some furnish warning stickers such as "Mr. Yuk" for parents' use in labeling hazardous household products. The nurse should be aware of the local center in her community and advise every family to include its phone number on their list of emergency numbers.

This chapter has examined safety wellness from several perspectives of the family's environments. The home as the primary environment was addressed as a common site for accidents, which are the greatest threat to safety wellness in any environment. Accidents in and around the home were discussed in relation to two primary causes: the developmental stage of the family member and the nature of a particular agent. We reviewed the responsibility of each family member in promoting safety wellness for himself and the family. The elements in concept development that promote an attitude of safety consciousness were identified. The family's community and other environments outside the home were discussed in order to point out safety-wellness factors and the family's responsibility in effecting them. The nurse who works with the well family can be the catalyst in the development of a family who is truly interested in promoting the most wellness-enhancing environments possible through constant vigilance and responsible decision making.

References

1. Anderson, C. L., Morton, R. F., and Green, L. W. *Community Health* (3rd ed.). St. Louis: Mosby, 1978.
2. Arena, J. M. *Poisoning—Toxicology, Symptoms, Treatments.* Springfield, Ill.: Thomas, 1974.
3. Boraiko, A. The pesticide dilemma. *National Geographic* 157:145, 1980.
4. Brownfain, J. J. When is an accident not an accident? *J. Am. Soc. Safety Eng.* 20:6, 1962.
5. Brunner, L., and Suddarth, D., et al. *Lippincott Manual of Nursing Practice.* Philadelphia: Lippincott, 1974.
6. Chisalm, J., and Kaplan, E. Lead poisoning in childhood—comprehensive management and prevention. *J. Pediatr.* 73:942, 1968.
7. Clark, A., and Walton, W. W. Effect of safety packaging on aspirin ingestion by children. *Pediatrics* 63:687, 1979.
8. Consumer Product Safety Commission. *Poison Prevention Packaging.* Washington, D.C., 1978.
9. Cornacchia, J. H., and Staton, W. M. *Health in Elementary Schools* (5th ed.). St. Louis: Mosby, 1979.
10. Dept. of Health, Education and Welfare. *Guide to Federal Consumer Services.* Pub. No. (OS) 76-512. Washington, D.C.: U.S. Government Printing Office, 1976.
11. Done, A. K. Aspirin overdose: Incidence, diagnosis, and management. *Pediatrics* 62:890, 1978.
12. Fontana, V. J. *A Parent's Guide to Child Safety* (1st ed.). New York: Crowell, 1973.
13. Fritsch, A. J. *The Household Pollutants Guide.* Garden City, N.Y.: Anchor Press, 1978.
14. Geigy Agricultural Chemicals. *Plants That Poison.* Ardsley, N.Y.: Ciba-Geigy Corp.
15. Hoole, A., Greenberg, R. A., and Pickard, C. G. *Patient Care Guidelines for Family Nurse Practitioners.* Boston: Little, Brown, 1976.
16. Kanthor, H. A. Car safety for infants: Effectiveness of prenatal counseling. *Pediatrics* 58:320, 1976.
17. Kumack, B. N., and Peterson, R. G. Acetaminophen overdose: Incidence, diagnosis, and management in 416 patients. *Pediatrics* 62:898, 1978.
18. National Highway Traffic Safety Administration. *What to Buy in Child Restraint Systems.* Washington, D.C.: U.S. Government Printing Office, 1971.
19. National Safety Council. *Accident Facts, 1978 Edition.* Chicago, 1978.
20. New York State. *Accident Facts Reports.* Albany, N.Y.: Department of Motor Vehicles, 1974.
21. Post, S., and Langford, A. J. A very present danger. *Can. Nurse* 75:42, 1979.
22. Ross Laboratories. *Public Health Currents.* 12:4, July–August, 1972.

23. U.S. Dept. of Health, Education and Welfare, Bureau of Product Safety. *Typical Poisonous Plants.* Washington, D.C.: U.S. Government Printing Office, 1973.

24. U.S. Government, Environmental Protection Agency. *A Drop to Drink—A Report on the Quality of Our Drinking Water.* June 1976.

25. West Virginia University Cooperative Extension Service. *First Aid for Poisoning,* Pub. No. 225. Morgantown, W.Va.

26. Whaley, L., and Wong, D. L. *Nursing Care of Infants and Children.* St. Louis: Mosby, 1979.

27. Williams, A. F., and Zada, P. Injuries to children in automobiles in relation to seating location and restraint use. *Accid. Anal. Prev.* 9:69, 1977.

Assessment Tool

The nurse should indicate for each item whether the family or family member accomplishes the item according to criteria indicated in the columns. If an item or section does not apply, the points represented by that item or section should be so indicated by marking the "not applicable" column. In scoring at the end of each section, the category "total points possible" means the total number of points that could be attained if every item applied. The "total not applicable" category shows the total points for items or sections that do not apply to the family at this time; this number should be subtracted from the "total points possible" to obtain the "total applicable" score. When comparing "total applicable" with the "total points attained," the nurse and the family can see the numerical difference in what should or could be achieved and what does exist at the present time. Scores in each section should be transferred to the summary section at the end of the chapter's assessment tool.

	Usually (2 pts)	Sometimes (1 pt)	Never (0 pt)	Not applicable
I. Accidents: A Function of Developmental Stage				
A. Parents express knowledge of relationship of developmental characteristics to accidents according to				
1. Physical strength	___	___	___	___
2. Sex of child	___	___	___	___
3. Personality factors	___	___	___	___
4. Family bonding	___	___	___	___
Total points possible				*8*
Total not applicable				___
Total applicable				___
Total points attained				___
B. Parents promote safety wellness during *infancy* through				
1. Role modeling	___	___	___	___
2. Comprehension of developmental patterns	___	___	___	___

	Usually (2 pts)	Some-times (1 pt)	Never (0 pt)	Not appli-cable
3. Anticipating potential safety hazards prior to child's changing capabilities	——	——	——	——
4. Keeping hazardous items out of reach	——	——	——	——
5. Close supervision around water (bath, pool)	——	——	——	——
6. Using crib with properly spaced bars	——	——	——	——
7. Using crib with firm mattress	——	——	——	——
8. Utilizing snug-fitting mattress covers, not thin plastic bags	——	——	——	——
9. Avoiding use of pillows in crib	——	——	——	——
10. Careful supervision around stairways	——	——	——	——
11. Covering electrical outlets	——	——	——	——
12. Using federally approved car restraints and seats	——	——	——	——
13. Using car restraint system consistently	——	——	——	——

Total points possible ___26___
Total not applicable ———
Total applicable ———
Total points attained ———

C. Parents promote safety wellness for the *toddler* through

1. Recognizing the child's increasing physical abilities and scope of activity	——	——	——	——
2. Recognizing child's potential for poisoning	——	——	——	——
3. Labeling poisonous substances	——	——	——	——
4. Storing poisonous substances safely	——	——	——	——
5. Covering electrical sockets	——	——	——	——
6. Constant supervision around water	——	——	——	——
7. Teaching water safety near pool	——	——	——	——
8. Supervising all play activities	——	——	——	——
9. Anticipating safety hazards in new environments	——	——	——	——
10. Selecting responsible and knowl-edgeable baby-sitters	——	——	——	——
11. Using federally approved car re-straints and seats consistently	——	——	——	——
12. Establishing safety rules for riding in car	——	——	——	——

	Usually (2 pts)	Some-times (1 pt)	Never (0 pt)	Not appli-cable
13. Checking driveway before backing car out	____	____	____	____
14. Educating child about safety hazards	____	____	____	____
15. Explaining causes and effects of accidents	____	____	____	____
Total points possible				30
Total not applicable				____
Total applicable				____
Total points attained				____

D. Parents promote safety wellness for the *preschooler* through

	Usually (2 pts)	Some-times (1 pt)	Never (0 pt)	Not appli-cable
1. Recognizing increased initiative and desire to imitate adults	____	____	____	____
2. Recognizing potential hazards inside and outside the home	____	____	____	____
3. Supervising the child's mastery of play equipment	____	____	____	____
4. Careful supervision around lawn and garden equipment	____	____	____	____
5. Properly storing toxic substances	____	____	____	____
6. Educating the child to be cautious around animals	____	____	____	____
7. Teaching the child to interpret traffic signals correctly	____	____	____	____
8. Teaching careful street crossing	____	____	____	____
9. Teaching boundaries and limitations in his environment	____	____	____	____
10. Teaching child his name, address, and phone number	____	____	____	____
11. Teaching child how to seek help in emergencies—for example, police officer, fire fighter	____	____	____	____
12. Teaching basic water safety	____	____	____	____
13. Teaching safe play activities in the water	____	____	____	____
14. Constant supervision during the bath	____	____	____	____
15. Using federally approved car restraints and seats consistently	____	____	____	____
16. Establishing safety rules for riding in the car	____	____	____	____
17. Selecting responsible and knowledgeable baby-sitters	____	____	____	____
Total points possible				34
Total not applicable				____
Total applicable				____
Total points attained				____

	Usually (2 pts)	Sometimes (1 pt)	Never (0 pt)	Not applicable
E. Parents promote safety wellness for the *school-age child* through				
1. Encouraging the child to assume responsibility for own actions by				
a. Teaching why precautions are necessary	___	___	___	___
b. Teaching the consequences of not taking precautions	___	___	___	___
2. Encouraging the child to exercise caution around automobiles and school buses as a passenger or a pedestrian, including				
a. Using seat belts consistently	___	___	___	___
b. Obeying traffic signals	___	___	___	___
c. Keeping body parts inside car at all times	___	___	___	___
d. Maintaining reasonable level of noise	___	___	___	___
3. Teaching the child bicycle safety rules such as				
a. Using caution while riding on the street	___	___	___	___
b. Obeying traffic signals	___	___	___	___
c. Riding on the right side of the road	___	___	___	___
d. Anticipating potential hazards in the roadway	___	___	___	___
e. Being aware of and/or participating in community programs that teach bicycle safety	___	___	___	___
4. Considering age and size of child when purchasing a bicycle	___	___	___	___
5. Teaching bicycle safety while child learns how to ride bicycle	___	___	___	___
6. Encouraging the child to learn how to swim	___	___	___	___
7. Encouraging adequate supervision in private or community pools	___	___	___	___
8. Establishing rules for use of family pool	___	___	___	___
9. Encouraging CPR training and proper techniques of water rescue	___	___	___	___
10. Teaching child to be cautious of strangers	___	___	___	___
11. Teaching proper use of equipment around home, such as tools and appliances	___	___	___	___

	Usually (2 pts)	Some-times (1 pt)	Never (0 pt)	Not appli-cable
12. Teaching proper use of skills, sports equipment, rules of play	____	____	____	____
Total points possible				_40_
Total not applicable				____
Total applicable				____
Total points attained				____

F. Parents promote safety wellness for the *adolescent* through

1. Encouraging self-responsibility for safety within his environment	____	____	____	____
2. Allowing adolescent's use of automobile only after demonstration of skills and responsible attitude in its use	____	____	____	____
3. Encouraging formal driver-education instruction	____	____	____	____
4. Encouraging responsible use of alcohol	____	____	____	____
Total points possible				_8_
Total not applicable				____
Total applicable				____
Total points attained				____

G. The *adolescent* promotes safety wellness by

1. Observing traffic safety rules and regulations	____	____	____	____
2. Demonstrating skill in simple automobile maintenance	____	____	____	____
3. Driving only when mentally sound	____	____	____	____
Total points possible				_6_
Total not applicable				____
Total applicable				____
Total points attained				____

H. The *adult* promotes safety wellness by

1. Being aware of safety hazards in the work environment	____	____	____	____
2. Maintaining safe driving practices by				
a. Considering safety features when purchasing a car	____	____	____	____
b. Exhibiting patience with other drivers on the road	____	____	____	____
c. Using seat belts consistently	____	____	____	____
d. Avoiding driving when rushed	____	____	____	____

	Usually (2 pts)	Some-times (1 pt)	Never (0 pt)	Not appli-cable
e. Avoiding driving in inclement weather whenever possible	——	——	——	

Total points possible   _12_
Total not applicable   ——
Total applicable   ——
Total points attained   ——

I. *Elderly family members* promote safety wellness by

	Usually	Some-times	Never	Not appli-cable
1. Being aware of changes in physical and mental status	——	——	——	——
2. Making changes in environment to compensate for physical and mental changes	——	——	——	——
3. Being aware of community resources to contact in case of accidents	——	——	——	——
4. Using medications safely through a. Proper labeling	——	——	——	——
b. Knowing the name and side effects of each	——	——	——	

Total points possible   _10_
Total not applicable   ——
Total applicable   ——
Total points attained   ——

II. Accidents: A Function of Agent Factors

A. The family promotes safety wellness with potentially hazardous substances by

	Usually	Some-times	Never	Not appli-cable
1. Identifying potential poisons in the home	——	——	——	——
2. Labeling potentially dangerous substances	——	——	——	——
3. Storing potential poisons in a safe place a. Drugs	——	——	——	——
b. Petroleum products	——	——	——	——
c. Cleaning agents	——	——	——	——
d. External preparations	——	——	——	——
4. Notifying local poison control center if any family member ingests a potentially hazardous substance	——	——	——	——
5. Exercising extreme caution in use of medications, especially around children by a. Avoiding ingestion of medicine in front of children	——	——	——	——

	Usually (2 pts)	Some-times (1 pt)	Never (0 pt)	Not appli-cable
b. Using child-resistant medicine containers	___	___	___	___
c. Storing medicines in original containers	___	___	___	___
d. Storing out of reach of child	___	___	___	___
e. Knowing side effects of household medicines, particularly aspirin and acetaminophen	___	___	___	___
f. Taking medication only as directed	___	___	___	___
6. Identifying common sources of lead in the home	___	___	___	___
7. Knowing signs and symptoms of lead poisoning	___	___	___	___
8. Identifying pica in child	___	___	___	___
9. Discarding lye and drain cleaner containers immediately after use	___	___	___	___
10. Knowing first-aid measures to take if child ingests lye or drain cleaners	___	___	___	___
11. Identifying petroleum products in and around the home	___	___	___	___
12. Labeling petroleum products	___	___	___	___
13. Storing petroleum products in a safe place	___	___	___	___
14. Knowing first-aid measures to take if child ingests a petroleum product	___	___	___	___
15. Avoiding siphoning gasoline	___	___	___	___
16. Avoiding use of unvented space heaters	___	___	___	___
17. Avoiding use of charcoal grills inside home	___	___	___	___
18. Checking home heating system periodically for operating efficiency	___	___	___	___
19. Checking pilot lights of furnaces and gas stoves	___	___	___	___
20. Avoiding idling automobile engines with windows closed	___	___	___	___
21. Knowing signs and symptoms of carbon monoxide poisoning	___	___	___	___
22. Knowing first-aid measures for carbon monoxide poisoning	___	___	___	___
23. Identifying poisonous plants in and around the home	___	___	___	___
24. Knowing signs and symptoms of plant poisoning	___	___	___	___

	Usually (2 pts)	Some-times (1 pt)	Never (0 pt)	Not appli-cable
25. Knowing first-aid measures for plant poisoning	____	____	____	____

Total points possible   *66*
Total not applicable   ____
Total applicable   ____
Total points attained   ____

B. The family promotes safety wellness with household equipment by

	Usually	Some-times	Never	Not appli-cable
1. Keeping children away from dangerous equipment in and around the home	____	____	____	____
2. Disconnecting electrical appliances after use	____	____	____	____
3. Using only Underwriters' Laboratory approved appliances	____	____	____	____
4. Properly disposing of an unused refrigerator or freezer	____	____	____	____
5. Ensuring a well-ventilated kitchen	____	____	____	____
6. Knowing utility source shutoffs	____	____	____	____

Total points possible   *12*
Total not applicable   ____
Total applicable   ____
Total points attained   ____

C. The family promotes safety wellness with toys by

	Usually	Some-times	Never	Not appli-cable
1. Identifying potentially dangerous toys	____	____	____	____
2. Selecting only toys appropriate for developmental stage of child	____	____	____	____
3. Being aware of agencies that identify and monitor toy safety				
a. Good Housekeeping Institute	____	____	____	____
b. Consumer's Union reports	____	____	____	____
c. Underwriters' Laboratory	____	____	____	____
d. American Academy of Pediatrics	____	____	____	____
e. Consumer Product Safety Commission	____	____	____	____
4. Parents assuming full responsibility for child's exposure to safe toys	____	____	____	____
5. Parents knowing process for reporting an unsafe toy	____	____	____	____

Total points possible   *18*
Total not applicable   ____
Total applicable   ____
Total points attained   ____

	Usually (2 pts)	Some- times (1 pt)	Never (0 pt)	Not appli- cable
III. Accidents: Functions of An Un- stable Environment				
A. Family is aware of life events that threaten safety wellness, such as				
1. Moving to new home	____	____	____	____
2. Birth of a child	____	____	____	____
3. Home repairs	____	____	____	____
4. Peak activity periods, such as meal- time	____	____	____	____
5. Unexpected events	____	____	____	____
6. Visitors in the home	____	____	____	____
7. Vacations	____	____	____	____
8. Holidays	____	____	____	____

Total points possible   *16*
Total not applicable   ____
Total applicable   ____
Total points attained   ____

	Usually (2 pts)	Some- times (1 pt)	Never (0 pt)	Not appli- cable
IV. An Agent Factor: Nature of the Home Environment				
A. The family promotes safety wellness by				
1. Properly maintaining inside and out- side of the home	____	____	____	____
2. Avoiding fire hazards by				
a. Minimizing clutter	____	____	____	____
b. Using caution with flammable substances	____	____	____	____
c. Checking for faulty electrical wiring	____	____	____	____
d. Ensuring adequate wiring for elec- trical usage	____	____	____	____
e. Providing at least one smoke de- tector for home	____	____	____	____
f. Providing a screen for fireplace	____	____	____	____
g. Keeping children away from fire in fireplace	____	____	____	____
h. Cleaning fireplace chimney pe- riodically	____	____	____	____
i. Keeping flammable materials from vicinity of fireplace	____	____	____	____
j. Conducting fire drills in home	____	____	____	____
k. Providing appropriate fire extin- guishers throughout the house	____	____	____	____
l. Keeping emergency fire depart- ment numbers posted near tele- phone	____	____	____	____

Total points possible   *26*
Total not applicable   ____
Total applicable   ____
Total points attained   ____

	Usually (2 pts)	Some-times (1 pt)	Never (0 pt)	Not appli-cable
V. An Agent Factor: Nature of the School Environment				
A. The family promotes safety wellness by				
1. Encouraging a school environment that promotes physical and psychological safety wellness by communicating appropriately with school and community personnel regarding				
a. Structure in good repair inside and outside	——	——	——	——
b. Prompt removal of ice and snow in immediate vicinity of school	——	——	——	——
c. Adherence to local, state, and federal regulations for fire and other safety control measures	——	——	——	——
d. Sufficient lighting, ventilation, and temperature control	——	——	——	——
e. Adequate space within classrooms	——	——	——	——
f. Provision of special areas for physical exercise and recreation	——	——	——	——
g. School bus safety	——	——	——	——
2. Teaching the child responsibility for maintaining safety standards in school environment	——	——	——	——
3. Teaching the child to be alert to hazards and other deficits	——	——	——	——
4. Teaching the child to share responsibility for the school environment	——	——	——	——
5. Assuming ongoing responsibility for promoting and maintaining safety and wellness in the school environment	——	——	——	——

Total points possible *22*
Total not applicable ——
Total applicable ——
Total points attained ——

	Usually (2 pts)	Some-times (1 pt)	Never (0 pt)	Not appli-cable
VI. An Agent Factor: Nature of the Work Environment				
A. The family promotes safety wellness by				
1. Encouraging a work environment that promotes physical and psychological safety wellness through awareness of				
a. Adequate lighting	——	——	——	——
b. Proper maintenance of physical environment both inside and outside	——	——	——	——

	Usually (2 pts)	Some- times (1 pt)	Never (0 pt)	Not appli- cable
c. Adequate heat	___	___	___	___
d. Adequate ventilation	___	___	___	___
e. Awareness of accident hazards in- cluding				
(1) Unsafe work practices	___	___	___	___
(2) Toxic chemicals	___	___	___	___
(3) Unsafe physical structure				
2. Promoting programs to monitor and reduce hazards that protect workers and encourage safety awareness	___	___	___	___
3. Encouraging health promotion and self-care activities that contribute to a wellness life-style by				
a. Nutritional wellness	___	___	___	___
b. Cardiovascular wellness	___	___	___	___
c. Mental wellness	___	___	___	___
d. Responsible use of drugs	___	___	___	___
e. Stress management	___	___	___	___

Total points possible   _26_
Total not applicable   ___
Total applicable   ___
Total points attained   ___

VII. Community Environmental Safety
Factors
   A. The family promotes environmental
      wellness by

	Usually	Some- times	Never	Not appli- cable
1. Being aware of sources of air pollu- tion within the community	___	___	___	___
2. Knowing about community efforts to control air pollution	___	___	___	___
3. Minimizing use of automobile	___	___	___	___
4. Utilizing alternate means of transpor- tation whenever possible	___	___	___	___
5. Being aware of sources of excessive noise in the community	___	___	___	___
6. Participating in community efforts to reduce excessive noise	___	___	___	___
7. Identifying sources of excessive noise in the home	___	___	___	___
8. Alleviating sources of excessive noise in the home	___	___	___	___
9. Knowing quality of local water supply	___	___	___	___
10. Knowing sources of water pollutants in the community	___	___	___	___
11. Conserving water when possible	___	___	___	___
12. Avoiding asbestos-lined or lead water pipes	___	___	___	___

	Usually (2 pts)	Some-times (1 pt)	Never (0 pt)	Not appli-cable
13. Avoiding use of water filters and purifiers	——	——	——	——
14. Using bottled water cautiously	——	——	——	——
15. Encouraging proper testing techniques for pesticides on domestic and imported foods	——	——	——	——
16. Washing raw foods before eating	——	——	——	——
17. Supporting citizens' action groups to ban pesticides that have been proved harmful to the human body	——	——	——	——
18. Promoting the balanced use of pesticides	——	——	——	——
19. Avoiding or controlling use of pesticides in garden and yard	——	——	——	——
20. Knowing name and function of agencies that promote wellness in the environment				
a. Department of Agriculture	——	——	——	——
(1) Extension Service	——	——	——	——
b. Department of Commerce	——	——	——	——
(1) National Bureau of Standards	——	——	——	——
c. Department of Health and Human Services	——	——	——	——
(1) Consumer Education	——	——	——	——
(2) Office of Consumer Affairs	——	——	——	——
(3) Food and Drug Administration	——	——	——	——
(4) Social Security Administration	——	——	——	——
(5) U.S. Public Health Service	——	——	——	——
d. Department of Interior				
(1) National Park Service	——	——	——	——
e. Department of Labor				
(1) Occupational Safety and Health Administration	——	——	——	——
f. Department of Transportation				
(1) National Highway Traffic Safety Administration	——	——	——	——
g. Consumer Product Safety Commission	——	——	——	——
h. Environmental Protection Agency	——	——	——	——
i. U.S. Postal Service	——	——	——	——
j. Consumer Information Center	——	——	——	——
k. Federal Trade Commission	——	——	——	——
l. Consumer's Union of United States, Inc.	——	——	——	——

	Usually (2 pts)	Some-times (1 pt)	Never (0 pt)	Not appli-cable
m. Good Housekeeping Institute	___	___	___	___
n. Poison Control Centers	___	___	___	___

Total points possible   _86_

Total not applicable   ___

Total applicable   ___

Total points attained   ___

Assessment Tool Summary

	Subtotal points possible	Subtotal not appli-cable	Subtotal appli-cable	Subtotal points attained
I. Accidents: A Function of Developmental Stage				
A. Parents' knowledge of relationship of developmental characteristics to accidents	8	___	___	___
B. Parents' promotion of safety during infancy	26	___	___	___
C. Parents' promotion of safety during toddlerhood	30	___	___	___
D. Parents' promotion of safety during the preschool years	34	___	___	___
E. Parents' promotion of safety during the school-age period	40	___	___	___
F. Parents' promotion of safety during adolescence	8	___	___	___
G. Adolescent's promotion of safety for self	6	___	___	___
H. Promotion of safety during the adult years	12	___	___	___
I. Promotion of safety during old age	10	___	___	___
II. Accidents: A Function of Agent Factors				
A. Potentially hazardous substances	66	___	___	___
B. Household equipment	12	___	___	___
C. Toys	18	___	___	___
III. Accidents: Functions of an Unstable Environment	16	___	___	___
IV. An Agent Factor: Nature of the Home Environment	26	___	___	___
V. An Agent Factor: Nature of the School Environment	22	___	___	___
VI. An Agent Factor: Nature of the Work Environment	26	___	___	___
VII. Community Environmental Safety Factors	86	___	___	___

Total points possible   _446_

Total not applicable   ___

Total applicable   ___

Total points attained   ___

Index